Milan
& the Italian Lakes

View from the Duomo/Photocreo/Fotolia

mustsees **Milan & the Italian Lakes**

Editorial Director	Cynthia Clayton Ochterbeck
Production Manager	Natasha G. George
Texts, Photo Editing and Layout	Buysschaert&Malerba, Milan
	Zino Malerba (photo editing and layout)
	Aaron Maines (principal writer), Giacomo Serra (editor),
	Timothy Stroud (translations)
Cartography	Cartographie Michelin Paris
Interior Design	Chris Bell, cbdesign
Cover Design	Chris Bell, cbdesign, Natasha G. George
Contact Us	Michelin Travel and Lifestyle North America
	One Parkway South
	Greenville, SC 29615, USA
	travel.lifestyle@us.michelin.com
	www.michelintravel.com
	Michelin Travel Partner
	Hannay House
	39 Clarendon Road
	Watford, Herts WD17 1JA, UK
	www.ViaMichelin.com
	travelpubsales@uk.michelin.com
Special Sales	For information regarding bulk sales, customized editions and premium sales, please contact us at:
	travel.lifestyle@us.michelin.com
	www.michelintravel.com

Michelin Travel Partner

Société par actions simplifiées au capital de 11 288 880 EUR
27 cours de l'Île Seguin - 92100 Boulogne Billancourt (France)
R.C.S. Nanterre 433 677 721

© Michelin Travel Partner
ISBN 978-2-067197-54-1
Printed: November 2014
Printed and bound in Italy

MIX
Paper from
responsible sources
FSC® C015829
www.fsc.org

Note to the reader:
While every effort is made to ensure that all information printed in this guide is correct
and up-to-date, Michelin Travel Partner accepts no liability for any direct, indirect or
consequential losses howsoever caused so far as such can be excluded by law. Admission
prices listed for sights in this guide are for a single adult, unless otherwise specified.

Welcome to Milan

Porta Nuova

Francesca Malerba

TABLE OF CONTENTS

TABLE OF CONTENTS

5

★★★ATTRACTIONS

Unmissable attractions awarded three stars in this guide include:

Duomo area p 30

G. Glinsk/Fotolia.com

Castello Sforzesco p 37

EricRed/Fotolia.com

Basilica di Sant'Ambrogio p 54

Lorenzo Galluzzi/Fotolia.com

Isola Bella, Lake Maggiore p 83

Bergfee/Fotolia.com

Lake Garda p 95

Frank/Fotolia

Balbianello, Lake Como p 92

Roberto Zocchi/Fotolia.com

Bellagio, Lake Como p 91

Luigi Giordano/Fotolia.com

★★★ATTRACTIONS

Unmissable sights in and around Milan

For more than 75 years people have used the Michelin stars to take the guesswork out of travel. Our star-rating system helps you make the best decision on where to go, what to do, and what to see.

★★★	Unmissable
★★	Worth a trip
★	Worth a detour
No star	Recommended

Milan

The Lakes

★★★Three Star

★★Two Star

★One Star

STAR ATTRACTIONS

ACTIVITIES

From elegant city life to lakeside lounging, visitors to Milan and the lakes will find they're never short of things to do. We recommend every activity in this guide, but our top picks are highlighted with the Michelin Man logo.

Milan

Events

On foot

On water

Milan from above

Kids

MUST KNOW

Teatro alla Scala

© E. Grund/age fotostock

© Eurasia Press/Photononstop

Isola San Giulio, Lake Orta

🏛 Bars / Cafés

🏛 Milanese Life

The Lakes

🏛 Events

🏛 On foot

🏛 On water

🏛 Panoramic views

🏛 Kids

ACTIVITIES

CALENDAR OF EVENTS

Milan and the Lakes play host to some important and colorful annual events. Please note that dates may change from year to year. *For more detailed information and other events, contact tourist offices in Milan (see p14; www.turismo.milano.it and www.visitamilano.it).*

6 January

Corteo dei Magi (Parade of the Magi) – On the day of Epiphany, a costume parade winds through the streets from the Duomo to Sant'Eustorgio.

February

Capodanno cinese (Chinese New Year) – Shows, concerts and costume parades in Via Paolo Scarpi, heart of Milan's Chinatown.

February/March

Carnevale Ambrosiano – Italy's longest carnival holds a parade on the Saturday following Ash Wednesday.

April

Marathon Stramilano – Tens of thousands of runners take to the streets on the 15 km course. www.stramilano.it.

Design Week – *FuoriSalone, held during the weeklong Salone del Mobile.* This unmissable event turns galleries, museums, stores and other institutions into jam-packed meeting places. The press publishes the programme (*see Must Do*). www.fuorisalone.it.

May

Orticola – This colorful flower and plant show is held in the gardens of Via Palestro. It is an important event for experts and a pleasure for those with green fingers. www.orticola.org.

Cortili Aperti – For one Sunday the loveliest courtyards of the palazzi of Milan are open to the public. For all information: Associazione Dimore Storiche – Sezione Lombardia, Via San Paolo 10, 02 76 31 86 34, www.adsi.it.

December: Prima della Scala

Erica Zane/Michelin

MUST KNOW

Careno/Fotolia.com

June: *Festa di San Giovanni, Lake Como*

May/June

Giro d'Italia – The traditional arrival of the most important Italian cycling race in Milan.

June

Festa dei Navigli – *1st Sun.* Fêtes, parades and concerts by night throughout the Navigli.

Festa di San Giovanni – *24 June, Lake Como, Isola Comacina.* A magnificent firework display starting at 10pm. 1200 launch places will send more than 1 tonne of fireworks over the lake. During the day, lamps call *Lumaghitt* will float on the lake surface.

June-July

Milanesiana (Literature Music Cinema) – In June and July theaters and other cultural spaces are the gathering places for the Milanese and representatives of international culture and art. www.provincia.milano.it.

August

Settimane musicali, *Stresa and the Borromeo Islands* – Symphonic music in Stresa and other places on and around Lake Maggiore. www.stresafestival.eu.

September

MiTo Settembre Musica – This eclectic festival, held in both Milan and Turin, fills three weeks with jazz, world music, classical music and the avant-garde. www.mitosettembremusica.it.

Centomiglia del Garda – *Lake Garda.* The oldest sailing-boat race in Italy, which not long ago celebrated its 60th anniversary. The lake will be filled with up to 300 boats, creating a wonderful spectacle. www.centomiglia.it.

December

Prima della Scala – *7 Dec, St Ambrogio's Day, patron saint of Milan.* A gala evening for the opening of the Milan theater season. www.teatroallascala.org.

Fiera degli "Oh bej, oh bej!" – *7-10 Dec, Castello Sforzesco.* The name is dialect for "Beautiful things." Christmas market with the sale of handcrafts, secondhand goods and regional specialities.

13

PRACTICAL INFORMATION

WHEN TO GO

The best periods to visit Milan are from March to May and September to October. The city's humid atmosphere makes it feel hotter in summer and colder in winter than the mercury indicates. In recent years, the city has suffered increasingly frequent heatwaves arriving from North Africa in July, August and even June. In winter, the worst risks are biting cold, icy roads and rain, especially when they last for several days. The area around Milan is also notorious for heavy fog, which causes delays and flight cancellations, and can seriously inhibit visibility while driving. Springtime averages 16-17° C, rising to 22° C in May. In summer, highs of 25-30° C are normal but in particularly hot years, like 2010 and 2012, a high of 35° C and a sultry atmosphere can be common. In autumn, temperatures remain similar to September, between 21° and 26° C, but quickly drop in early November. Winter can be severe, with temperatures possibly falling to a low of -4° C and a maximum of 4-6° C.

Leaving weather considerations aside, Milan's most enjoyable week may occur during the Salone del Mobile (*see p102*), while other people prefer August, when most of the city's residents leave Milan for summer holidays, leaving those who remain behind feel like they have the city all to themselves.

KNOW BEFORE YOU GO
Useful Websites

www.turismo.milano.it and **www.visitamilano.it** – Attractions, events, tourist offers in Milan, the city and surrounding areas, apps for smartphones.

www.comune.milano.it – The Milan City Council site for local news, which can also be interesting to visitors.

www.atm-mi.it/en/ – Public transportation (network map, timetables, travel tickets and cards, apps for smartphones).

www.bikemi.com – Milan's bike-sharing scheme.

www.car2go.com, www.e-vai. com, Enjoy, EqSharing, GuidaMi – Milan's car-sharing scheme.

info.openwifimilano.it – Milan's free wifi network.

Guided Tours

If you have only a morning free, **City Tour** will give you a bus tour of Castello Sforzesco, Leonardo da Vinci's *Last Supper*, the museum in La Scala, and Milan's Duomo, with commentary provided in English by a qualified guide. City Tour promises up to 50 tickets a day to see the *Last Supper*, so there is no need to book in advance. The panoramic tour buses run by 🚌 **City Sightseeing** offer two 90-minute trips to the city's major attractions with a recorded commentary in eight languages. Departure and arrival in Piazza Castello / Foro Bonaparte 76 (on the corner via Cusani) (€25, ages 5–15 €10; 02 86 71 31; www.city-sightseeing.it).

MUST KNOW

Visitor Information

Italian National Tourist Board
www.enit.it.
Italian National Tourist Website
www.italia.it.
* **UK** – 1, Princes Street, London
W1B 2AY. 020 7408 1254.
* **USA** – **New York:** 630, Fifth
Avenue - Suite 1965. 212 2455618.
Los Angeles: 10850 Wilshire Blvd. -
Suite 725. 310 820 1898.
Chicago: 500 N. Michigan Avenue
Suite 506. 312 644 0996.
* **Canada** – 110 Yonge Street,
Suite 503, Toronto M5C 1T4.
416 925 4882.

Tourist Offices in Milan

The following offices will
answer all your questions and
provide you with a free map of
the city:
Piazza Castello (*on the corner
of Via Beltrami; open Mon–Fri
9am–6pm, Sat 9am–1pm and
2–6pm, Sun and public holidays
9am–1.30pm and 2–5pm; 02 77
40 43 43; iat.info@provincia.
milano.it*);
Centrale Railway Station
(*Departure zone, near platform
21; open Mon–Fri 9am–5pm, Sun
and public holidays 9am–12.30pm;
02 77 40 43 18/9, iat.info@
provincia.milano.it*);
Malpensa Airport (*Meeting Milan
Welcome Desk, ground floor –
Arrivals B (public area); Mon–Sun
8am–8pm; 02 58 58 00 80*).

International Visitors

Italian Embassies abroad

UK – London,
www.amblondra.esteri.it.
USA – Washington, DC,
www.ambwashingtondc.esteri.it.
Canada – Ottowa,
www.ambottawa.esteri.it.

Italian Consulates Abroad

* **UK** – **London**,
www.conslondra.esteri.it.
Edinburgh,
www.consedimburgo.esteri.it.
* **USA** – **New York**,
www.consnewyork.esteri.it.
* **Canada** – **Montreal, Toronto**,
www.constoronto.esteri.it.

Foreign Embassies and Consulates in Italy

* **Australia** – **Consulate:** Via
Borgogna 2, Milan. 02 77 67 42 00.
Embassy: Via Antonio Bosio 5,
Rome. 06 85 27 21.
www.italy.embassy.gov.au.
www.italy.embassy.gov.au.
* **Canada** – **Consulate:** Piazza
Cavour 3, Milan. 02 62 69 42 38.
Embassy: Via Salaria 243,
Rome. 06 85 44 41.
www.canadainternational.gc.ca.
* **Ireland** – Honorary consulate in
Milan: Piazza S. Pietro in Gessate 2,
Milan. 02 55 18 75 69.
Embassy: Via Giacomo Medici 1,
Rome. 06 69 79 121.
www.ambasciata-irlanda.it
* **UK** – **Consulate**: Via XX
Settembre 80/a, Rome. 06 42 20
24 31. **British General Consulate**:
Via S. Paolo 7, Milan. 06 42 20 24 31.
British Embassy: Via XX Settembre
80/a, Rome. 06 42 20 00 01.
www.gov.uk
* **USA** – Consular agent at Marco
Polo Airport. **Consulate:** Via
Principe Amedeo 2/10, Milan.
02 29 03 51. **Embassy:** Via Veneto
121, Rome. 06 46 741.
www.usembassy.it.

Entry Requirements

In Italy (and also in Switzerland
for those interested in Lake
Lugano and the Swiss part of Lake
Maggiore), no visas are required

for stays of less than 90 days for citizens of Australia, New Zealand, Canada and the US. Travelers must be in possession of a valid national passport. Citizens of European Union countries need only a national identity card (or passport if you are from the UK). In the event of loss or theft, report the incident to your embassy or consulate and to the local police.

Customs Regulations

For regulations on imports, exports and duty-free allowances, US citizens should consult **www.hmrc. gov.uk**. British citizens can visit **www.hmce.gov.uk** (enter "Travel" option).

Health

US visitors should verify whether their insurance covers overseas health care and emergencies. If not, it's wise to purchase optional cover. British subjects should obtain a **European Health Insurance Card (EHIC)**, available from central post offices, before leaving home. However, cover is minimal; separate travel and medical insurance is highly recommended.

Accessibility

For information of access to buildings in the city, information can be obtained from Tourist Offices (*see p15*) or by email to **Sportello Disabilità Regione Lombardia** (*Mon–Thu 9am– 6.30pm, Fri 9am–3pm; 02 67 65 47 40; sportello_disabili@regione. lombardia.it*).
To find out more about traveling on the ATM public transport network (subways, trams and bus lines), call the number *02 48 60 76 07* (Mon–

Sun 7.30am–7.30pm) or visit the website **www.atm-mi.it**.
All Milan buses and the new tram coaches are fitted with a ramp for entry and exit. Many metro (subway) stations have moving staircases, stair lifts and elevators (but it is always best to telephone first to be sure they are in operation).
Information and the assistance-request service for traveling on the Italian State railways are available at the number *199 30 30 60* (Mon– Sun 6.45am–9.30pm; from landline or a mobile phone) or free number 800 90 60 60 (from landlines only). You can also consult the site **www.trenitalia.com.** To request assistance (at least two days in advance) on the Trenord railway network, call *02 72 49 44 94* (*www.trenord.it*).
Tourism for All UK (formerly Holiday Care), 0845 124 9971. www.tourismforall.org.uk.
Disability Rights UK, 12 City Forum, 250 City Road, London EC1V 8AF. 020 7250 3222. www.radar.org.uk.
Society for Accessible Travel & Hospitality – www.sath.org.

GETTING THERE
By Air

Milan is served by three airports: **Malpensa** (*www.sea-aeroportimilano.it*), approximately 50km/32 mi northwest of Milan, has Terminals 1 and 2 and is served by all the major airlines, including American Airlines, Delta, United Airlines, Aer Lingus, British Airways, easyJet, and Flybe.
Linate (*www.sea-aeroporti milano.it*) is the nearest to Milan, just 7km/4.5 mi east of the city center, and is frequented by the

major European companies, including Aer Lingus, British Airways, KLM and easyJet.

Orio al Serio (*www.sacbo.it*), 45km/30mi northeast of Milan (5km/3mi southeast of Bergamo), is used by low-cost airlines, notably Ryanair.

Airport Transfers

By Bus: Malpensa airport has connections to Centrale railway station every 20 minutes, with a single stop at FieraMilanoCity (Viale Teodorico), operated by the companies **Stie** (*€10; www.stie.it*), **Malpensa Shuttle** (*€10; www. malpensashuttle.it*) and **Malpensa Bus Express** (*€10; ecomm. autostradale.it*). On the days the Rho-Pero convention complex is open, Malpensa Shuttle also offers direct connections with Fiera Milano Rho-Pero.

Linate airport has connections to Centrale railway station every 30 minutes, with a stop in Piazza Dateo. The connections are offered by companies **Air Bus ATM** (*€5; www.atm-mi.it*) and **Starfly** (*€5; www.starfly.net*), but there is also a regular ATM city bus-line (**number 73**, every 10 mins) or the **X73** (every 20 mins, one stop only in Piazza Tricolore) with terminus in Piazza San Babila, where there is a connection with the M1 metro line (*€1.50; www. atm-mi.it*).

On fair days, the airport also runs connections to Fiera Milano Rho-Pero.

Coach connections are also available from Orio al Serio to Centrale railway station, operated by **Autostradale** (*€5; www.autostradale.it*) and **Orio Shuttle** (*€5; www.orioshuttle.com*)

Connections exist between Malpensa and Linate (*€13; www. malpensashuttle.it*) and between Malpensa and Orio al Serio (*€18; www.orioshuttle.com*)

By Train: the Malpensa Express (*www.malpensaexpress.it*) run by **Trenord** provides a connection between Terminals 1 and 2 at Malpensa with Cadorna, Porta Garibaldi and Centrale (*€12*) railway stations.

By Taxi: much more costly; from Malpensa to any address in Milan there is a fixed tariff of €90, from Linate to the center of Milan approximately €25, and between Malpensa and Linate there is a fixed cost of €100. Malpensa to the Fiera Milano Rho €65 and Linate to the Fiera Milano Rho €50.

By Car: car-hire companies are well represented at all the Milan airports.

By Train

Trains run to Milan from across much of northern Italy, the largest cities in the center and south of the country and some European cities in France, Spain, Germany, Switzerland and Austria. Milan's largest railway stations are the **Centrale** (*Piazza Duca d'Aosta 4*, connections with the M2 and M3 metro lines, trams 5, 9, 33, buses 42, 60, 81, 82, 87) and **Porta Garibaldi** (*Piazza Freud 1*, connections with M2, and bus 37).

Trenitalia (*www.trenitalia.com*) offers connections with high-speed trains (called Frecciarossa, Frecciargento and Frecciabianca), between Milan and the more important cities in Italy (e.g. Florence in 1h45 mins, Rome in 2h55 mins).

High-speed trains run by **Italo** (*www.italotreno.it*) run from the Milano Porta Garibaldi and Milano Rogoredo stations to Bologna, Florence, Rome, Naples, Torino and Salerno.

In addition to running a service to Malpensa, **Trenord** (*www.trenord.it*) connects Milan to various cities in northern Italy, including Alessandria, Bergamo, Brescia, Como, Cremona, Mantova, Monza, Novara, Pavia, Sondrio, Varese, Verona, and several towns on the lakes (*see p24*).

Thomas Cook European Rail Timetable gives European train timetables. Also check **Rail Europe** (*uk.voyages-sncf.com*) and **Italian State Railways** (*www.trenitalia.com*).

By Coach/Bus

National Express/Eurolines. *087 17 81 81 78. www.eurolines.co.uk*. Coach services from Victoria Coach Station, London.

By Car

Formalities

Citizens of the European Union require a valid **national driving license**. US citizens should obtain an **international driver's licence** from the American Automobile Association (*www.aaa.com*). The driver must have the vehicle's current **registration document** and a **green card** for insurance.

Main roads

Milan lies at the center of a network of roads and motorways. The city is circled entirely by a combination of three bypasses that connect with the center from all directions. The **west bypass (A 50 – Tangenziale Ovest)** runs from the northwest to the south of the city and connects with the following motorways: A8 Milan-Varese (to Malpensa airport), the A4 Turin-Trieste, the A7 Milan-Genoa and the A1 Milan-Naples.

The **east bypass (A 51 – Tangenziale Est)** serves the east side of the city and connects with the A4 Turin-Trieste, Linate airport, the A1 Milan-Naples and the west bypass.

The **north bypass (A 52 – Tangenziale Nord)** and the section parallel to the A4 Turin-Trieste complete the circle around Milan and give access to Monza, Como and the Canton Ticino in Switzerland.

Maps

Michelin Tourist and Motoring Atlas Italy and Michelin Maps *no. 705* Europe (1:3 000 000), *no. 735* Italy (1:1 000 000), *no. 562* Northeast Italy (1:400 000) and *no. 353* Lombardia (1:200 000) will make it easier to plan your route.

GETTING AROUND

The center of Milan is small enough to be explored on foot but, to avoid feeling too tired by the end of the day, it is better to use the ATM public transport system.

Public Transportation

Public transportation systems (bus, tram, metro) are run by **ATM** (*02 48 607 607; www.atm-mi.it*). ATM tickets of all kinds are valid across the entire transport network throughout the city.

For information and tickets, visit **ATM Points** (Mon–Sat 7.45am–7.15pm) in the following stations: Duomo (M1, M3), Centrale (M2,

M3), Cadorna (M1, M2), Garibaldi (M2), Loreto (M1, M2), Romolo (M2).

Tickets and Travel Cards

Tickets are on sale at multilingual automatic distributors in stations, and at ATM Points, newspaper kiosks, bars and tobacco shops (tabacchi). An ordinary ticket costs €1.50 and is valid for 90 minutes from the moment it is stamped, however, it is only valid for a continuous journey: for example, it is not possible to exit one metro station and enter another with the same ticket, even within the 90 minute period.

The best options for visitors to Milan are to buy either a day-ticket or two-day ticket. A day-ticket is valid for 24 hours from the time it is stamped and for an unlimited number of journeys (€4.50); a two-day ticket is valid for 48 hours (€8.25). Another solution is a book of 10 ordinary tickets, called a "carnet" (€13.80). ATM Points also sell a *RicaricaMI* electronic ticket (€2.50 with a ticket included) in which various types of tickets can be loaded and held at the same time. For further information on tickets and passes, visit **www.atm-mi.it**.

Timetables

The metro operates between roughly 6am and 0.30am. Trams and buses begin a little earlier and finish a little later (trams 4.30/6am–1/2.30am; buses 5.30/6am–0.30/1.45am). Buses follow the same routes as the metro lines 1, 2 and 3 from Monday to Friday, 5–6am and 0.30–3am.

Weekend night service

There is a weekend night service of buses (0.30–6am) that run every 30 minutes on Friday and Saturday nights. In addition to following the same routes as the metro lines, the service offers an additional 11 lines (map visible at **www.atm-mi.it**).

By Metro

This is the fastest way to move around the city. There are three lines in operation with two more under construction.

M1 (red) – Runs from the terminus (Sesto 1 Maggio F.S.) in the northeast across the city, splitting into two branches at Pagano station before continuing west. The trains running west alternate their destination between the two branches so check the noticeboards on the platforms and destination sign on the trains themselves: *Rho Fiera Milano* for stations to the north, *Bisceglie* for stations to the south.
Note also that the final two stations at two of the three ends of the line (Pero and Rho Fiera Milano, and Sesto Rondò and Sesto 1 Maggio F.S.) are not included in the network covered by the ordinary €1.50 ticket, and it is necessary to purchase a specific ticket for those destinations (€2.55 to Rho Fiera Milano, or €5 roundtrip).

M2 (green) – The line M2 branches south (Assago or Abbiategrasso) and north (Gessate or Cologno Nord). The ordinary ticket is only valid as far as Cascina Gobba in the north and Abbiategrasso in the south. To go to Assago or continue past Cascina Gobbo, a ticket for a specific destination is required.

M3 (yellow) – This line runs between Comasina in the north and San Donato in the south.
M5 (lilac) – The terminus is Bignami in the north. The lilac line is under construction and will run as far as SanSiro stadium.

By Bus and Tram

The bus and tram systems connect all the different areas of Milan and are indispensable where the city is not covered by the metro. Trams have run in Milan since the end of the 19C. Take a ride at least once on a tram, for example, on line **1** which runs through Piazzale Cadorna, past Castello Sforzesco (Piazza Cairoli), the Duomo (Via Cantù), Via Manzoni and Piazza della Repubblica. The stations on the individual lines are given at each stop. To see the full tram map, visit **www.atm-mi.it**.

By Bike

Practical and ecological, **BikeMi** is Milan's bike-sharing service. You can take a bicycle at one of the stations around the city and leave it at another. The center is almost completely flat and it is quick and easy to get around, although there are not always bike lanes available

and you must always be careful of the city's generally feverish traffic. To use BikeMi, a daily or weekly pass is required. You can take out a subscription in various ways: online at **www.bikemi.com**; by calling the Italian toll free number **02 48 607 607**; via WAP from your telephone (**wap.bikemi.it**); or at an ATM Point (*see p18*). Payment must be made by credit card (Visa and Mastercard; neither prepaid credit cards nor cash cards can be used). Prices: €2.50 for a day pass, €6 for the week pass: the first 30 minutes of use are free, then €0.50 for each 30 minutes up to a maximum of 2 hours; once the 2-hour limit has been exceeded, the cost is €2 for hour. All information is available at **www.bikemi.com**.

By Taxi

To get a taxi, call one of the city's taxi companies: **Radiotaxi** (*02 85 85*); **Taxi Blu** (*02 40 40*); **Yellowtaxi** (*02 69 69*). They can also be picked up at special parking areas signaled by luminous signs. It is much more difficult to flag a taxi down. The fixed basic starting charge is €3.20 (weekdays), €5.20 (holidays) or €6.20 (night from 9pm to 6am), and increases at €1.06 per km. Extra charges apply for luggage, night service and holiday service.

By Suburban Railways
Railway lines with the logo "S" connect the city of Milan with surrounding towns. They are run by Trenord (*www.trenord.it*).

By Car
In order to reduce road traffic and lower pollution levels, over the last few years Milan has created several schemes to discourage the use of cars in the city center: boosting public transport resources, bike sharing, and experimenting with paid access to a fairly large area in the center of the city (Area C, *see p21*). When one considers that the most annoying factor for car usage in Milan is finding a parking space, it is clear that for visitors the use of private transport to move around the center is unadvisable.

Car hire
Car hire agencies can be found not only at airports and Centrale and Porta Garibaldi railway stations, but also elsewhere in the city. The companies represented include **Avis** (*www.avis.com*), **Budget** (*www.budget.com*), **Europcar** (*www.europcar.com*), **Hertz** (*www.hertz.com*), **Sixt** (*www.sixt.com*).

Car sharing
Car sharing is common in Milan. Car2Go (www.car2go.com), E-vai (www.e-vai.com), Enjoy (enjoy.eni. com), EqSharing (www.eqsharing. it), GuidaMi (www.atm.it/it/ guidami/).

Parking
Blue lines indicate spaces permitted for general car-parking, while yellow lines indicate spaces reserved for residents. There are also numerous attended car parks in the center, which charge different prices but are never cheap. In general, blue-line spaces are paid by the hour from between 8am and 7pm but in certain zones, like the center, payment may have to be made until midnight. Payment can be made at parking meters on the street.

Area C
Area C is the area where the Congestion Charge is applied from Monday to Friday, 7.30am to 7.30pm (on Thursday, 7.30am-6pm). To pay for entering Area C (a fairly extensive zone called Cerchia dei Bastioni), an entrance coupon must be paid for before midnight of the following day. The cost is €5 per vehicle per day. Payment can be made in different ways: at a parking meter; on the site *www. areac.it* in the "Servizi on line" section; by calling number *02 48 68 40 01*; from authorized sales points (ATM Points, newspaper kiosks, tobacco shops, or tabacchi). Area C is still an experimental zone but the City Council plans to make it a permanent feature.

BASIC INFORMATION
Business Hours
Shops – Shops in the center of Milan are generally open continuously from 8.30 or 9.30am to 6.30 or 7.30pm, though some shops may remain open as late as 10pm. Those shops that do not remain open all day usually close for lunch between 12.30/1pm and

3pm. Some businesses are closed on Mondays.

Churches – Churches are generally open and free of charge between 7.30am and 6.30/7pm, though shut at lunchtime (often 12.30-2.30/3.30pm).

Communications

Although there are no longer any public phone booths on the streets of Milan, it's hard to walk more than a block without coming across either a cell phone store or a small international phone center (often called "internet points"), where you can make international calls quite inexpensively.

City codes – For calls within the city, include the 02 prefix code for Milan. For calls within Italy, enter the code for the town or district beginning with a 0, followed by the number. For international calls, enter 00 followed by the country code: 61 for Australia, 1 for Canada, 64 for New Zealand, 44 for the UK, 1 for the USA. The international code for Italy is 39. Note that in Italy, a "0" is the first digit of the area or city code.

Internet – Most good hotels provide internet access to guests. The city has many internet cafés and it is not unusual for bars to have a wifi service. The City of Milan also provides a **free wifi network** in the area of Piazza Duomo, Piazza della Scala, Piazza Cairoli and many other areas. Using a mobile computer, tablet or smartphone anyone can connect to the *openwifimilano* network and use internet free of charge. Each user has the right to download up to 300 MB of data per day: once this limit has been reached, 1 hour of connection time is permitted at high speeds, then the connection speed drops to 192 kb/s. Conditions return to normal starting the following midnight.

You must register with the service in order to access *openwifimilano*: if you have a SIM card from an Italian provider, you simply need to connect in an area covered by the signal, enter your portable phone number and follow the instructions. Otherwise, go to the ATM Point at Duomo metro station and register (you will need an ID card). Further information is available on the site *info. openwifimilano.it*.

Electricity

Voltage is 220 AC, 50 cycles per second; the sockets are for two-pin plugs. Bring an adaptor for hair dryers, shavers, computers and other electrical equipment.

Emergencies
Emergency Services:
✆112 and ✆113.

Mail

Post offices are generally open Mon–Sat 8.25am–1.35pm (Sat 12.35pm) but some are open until later. Post offices in the center can be found at Via dell'Orso 11 (Brera district), close to Cadorna station (Via Carducci 7), inside Centrale railway station (Mon–Sat 8.25am–7.10pm), and in the Navigli district (Viale Gorizia 6). Stamps (*francobolli*) are sold in post offices and tobacco shops (*tabaccheria*). For information *www.poste.it*.

Money

Euro are issued in notes (€5, €10, €20, €50, €100, €200 and €500) and coins (1 cent, 2 cents, 5 cents, 10 cents, 20 cents, 50 cents, €1 and €2).

Banks – ATMs (*bancomat*) are plentiful in Milan. Banks are usually open Monday to Friday, 8.30am–1.30pm and 2.30pm–4pm. Some banks remain open till 6pm. Some hotels will change travelers' cheques. Money can be changed in post offices, exchanges, train stations and airports. A commission is always charged. Money withdrawn from *bancomat* machines has a lower commission than from bank tellers.

Credit cards can be used at most shops, hotels, restaurants and gas stations.

Pharmacies

A pharmacy (*farmacia*) is identified by a green flashing electric cross, as well as by a red and white insignia. When closed, it posts the names of the nearest pharmacies that are open, as well as night pharmacies. The pharmacy inside Centrale station is open 24h/24 (*02 66 90 735*). Other pharmacies open at night can be found at Piazza Duomo 21, Via Boccaccio 26 (close to Cadorna station), and Corso Magenta 96.

Reduced Rates

Museums offer reduced rates, in particular for the young and seniors over 65.
The **MilanoCard**, can be used for public transportation and free entrance to museums for 24 hours (€6.50) or 3 days (€13), as well as offering various discounts.

You can buy the card online or at Autostrade offices in every airport, or at the TicketMi office in Centrale railway station.
Further information is available at *www.milanocard.it*.

Smoking

Smoking is officially banned in all public places, though some bars and cafés may have areas where it is possible to smoke.

Time

The time in Italy is the same as in the rest of mainland Europe (one hour ahead of the United Kingdom). The hour changes during the last weekend in March and and again in October, shifting between summer time (*ora legale*) to winter time (*ora solare*).

Tipping

Prices in restaurants include a service cost and *coperto* (cover charge for what is already provided on the table, for instance, bread or breadsticks). There is no obligation to leave a tip and it is quite normal to pay the exact charge only. Generally a tip may be left in restaurants where a better quality of service or food is offered, in which case a tip of €2 and up is normal.
Tips are not obligatory even for taxi drivers. Porters, hotel maids and toilet attendants should be tipped a few coins.

LAKES

WHEN TO GO

The Milanese often leave the city in search of milder temperatures in the lake regions, both in summer and in winter. The hills and mountains around the prealpine lakes protect the area from bitter cold while breezes and the large body of water temper summer heat. The only risks are from rain and summer thunderstorms. Rainfall is greater over Lakes Maggiore and Como than Lake Garda, where the rainiest seasons are in spring and autumn.

KNOW BEFORE YOU GO
Useful Websites

Information on lake timetables, fares, charters, cruises and trips, news and events is available at:
www.navigazionelaghi.it – Lake Maggiore, Lake Como and Lake Garda.
www.navigazionelagodorta.it – Lake Orta.
www.navigazionelagoiseo.it – Lake Iseo.
www.lakelugano.ch – Lake Lugano.

For tourist information, news and events:
www.illagomaggiore.com – Lake Maggiore and Lake Orta.
www.lakecomo.it – Lake Como.
www.visitgarda.com – Lake Garda.
www.iseolake.info – Lake Iseo.
www.luganoturismo.ch – Lake Lugano.

Visitor Information
Tourist offices

Lake Maggiore – Angera (Via Marconi 2, 0331 93 19 15); **Arona** (Largo Vidale 1, 0322 24 36 01); **Baveno** (Piazza della Chiesa 8, 0323 92 46 32, www.bavenoturismo.it); **Cannero Riviera** (Via Orsi 1, 0323 78 89 43, www.cannero.it); **Cannobio** (via Giovanola 25, 0323 71 212, www.procannobio.it); **Stresa** (Piazza Marconi 16, 0323 31 308, www.stresaturismo.it).

Lake Como – Bellagio (Piazza Mazzini, 031 95 02 04); **Cernobbio** (Villa Erba, 031 34 93 41); **Como** (Piazza Cavour 17, 031 26 97 12, www.lakecomo.it); **Lecco** (Via Sauro 6, 0341 29 57 20/21); **Menaggio** (Piazza Garibaldi 3, 0344 32 924); **Tremezzo** (Via Regina 3, 0344 40 493).

Lake Garda – Desenzano (Via Porto Vecchio 34, 030 91 41 510); **Garda** (Piazza Donatori di Sangue 1, 045 62 70 384); **Limone sul Garda** (Via IV Novembre 25, 0365 95 40 87); **Malcesine** (Via Capitanato 8, 045 74 00 044); **Sirmione** (Viale Marconi 2, 030 91 61 14).

Lake Lugano – Lugano (Riva Albertolli, 058 86 66 600, www.luganoturismo.ch).

GETTING THERE
By Train

The lakes can be reached cheaply by train from Milan and without having to worry about traffic conditions. Below is a list of connections: for the relative timetable, prices and further information, visit the **Trenord** site (*www.trenord.it*), which operates all these lines except Milano Centrale-Lugano, which is run by **Tilo** (Treni Regionali Ticino Lombardia, *www.tilo.ch*).

Lake Maggiore – From Cadorna: train to Busto Arsizio Nord (31min), change for Laveno (43min); from Centrale (53min) or Porta Garibaldi (1h14min) to Arona.

Lake Como – From Cadorna to Como Lago (1h3min); from Centrale to Lecco and Varenna (39min and 1h3min); from Porta Garibaldi to Lecco (1h).

Lake Garda – From Lambrate (northeast of the city center, M2 Lambrate) to Desenzano del Garda (1h19min) and Peschiera del Garda (1h29min) passing through Brescia.

Lake Iseo – From Lambrate to Brescia (1h12min), change for Iseo (30min).

Lake Lugano – From Porta Garibaldi to Varese (52min), bus to Porto Ceresio (50min) on the southwest Italian shore; from Centrale (1h) or Porta Garibaldi (1h52min) to Lugano.

Lake Orta – From Centrale to Novara (42min), change for Orta-Miasino (42min).

By Car
Main roads

Milan is connected to all the lake towns by highway and local roads. Due to the popularity of these places, these roads can be very busy on weekends, public holidays and during the summer months.

Lake Maggiore – From Milan to Laveno (79km/49.1mi, 1h36min); to Arona (65km/40.3mi, 1h14min).

Lake Como – From Milan to Como (50km/31mi, 1h10min); to Lecco (61km/37.9mi, 1h17min).

Lake Garda – From Milan to Desenzano del Garda (126km/78.2mi, 1h44min).

Lake Iseo – From Milan to Iseo (86km/53.4mi, 1h33min).

Lake Lugano – From Milan to Porto Ceresio (69km/42.9mi, 1h33min); to Lugano (77km/47.8mi, 1h21min).

Lake Orta – From Milan to Orta San Giulio (84km/52.2mi, 1h35min).

Maps

Michelin Maps *no. 562* Northeast Italy (1:400 000), *no. 561* Northwest Italy (1:400 000), *no. 353* Lombardia (1:200 000) will make route planning easier.

By Bus

Zani Viaggi (*02 86 71 31, www.zaniviaggi.it*) organizes daily tourist trips by bus, leaving from 76 Foro Bonaparte (M1 Cairoli), in front of Castello Sforzesco. Destinations include: Lakes Como and Bellagio (with panoramic lake cruise; Mon, Wed and Sat at 9am); Lake Maggiore (with visit to Stresa, lake cruise and visit to the Isole Borromee; Sun at 9am); Verona and Lake Garda (with visit to the Arena and most important sights in Verona, then Sirmione on Lake Garda; Fri at 7.30am).

GETTING AROUND
By Boat and Ferry

Information on ferries and boats for each lake can be found in the Lakes section of this guide. Transportation on Lakes Maggiore, Como and Garda is operated by the same company: **Gestione Navigazione Laghi.** (*toll free in Italy 800 55 18 01, www. navigazionelaghi.it*).

25

THE CITY IN HISTORY

Enjoy a brief overview of important moments in the history of Milan. From its start as a Roman settlement to the dukedom, the plague, occupying armies, the Kingdom of Italy and its current status as dream playground for contemporary architects.

Roman Mediolanum

Although Milan's origins are probably Gaulish, the development of *Mediolanum*, as it was then called, followed the Roman conquest in 222 BC. At the end of the 3C AD, Roman Emperor **Diocletian** declared Milan the capital of the Western Roman Empire, and it was here in AD 313 that **Constantine** issued the Edict of Milan granting Christians freedom of worship. In 375 **St Ambrose** (340–96), an amazingly eloquent orator, became Bishop of Milan, helping to build the city's prestige.

From the Lombard Kingdom to the Ghibellines

In the 5C and 6C barbarian invasions swept through the region, before the Lombards founded a kingdom with Pavia as its capital. The city was taken in 756 by **Pepin the Short**, King of the Franks, whose son Charlemagne was crowned with the Iron Crown of Lombardy in 774. Milan only regained its status as capital in the year 962. In the 12C Milan joined forces with neighboring cities to form the **Lombard League** in order to counter attempts by the Holy Roman Emperor Frederick Barbarossa to take control of the region, and went on to win autonomy at the Battle of Legnano. In the 13C the Ghibelline **Visconti** took control of the city. The most famous member of this noble family, **Gian Galeazzo** (1351–1402), was a cunning military strategist and a cultivated man of letters. He obtained the title of Duke of Milan in 1395, and built the **Duomo** and the **Certosa di Pavia**. His daughter Valentina married the grandfather of Louis XII of France, laying the foundations for a dynastic dispute that underpinned the Italian Wars.

Saint Carlo Borromeo

Sergey Kohl/Fotolia.com

The Rise of the Sforza Family

After the death of the last Visconti duke, Filippo Maria, the people proclaimed the Ambrosian Republic. Before long, however, the Sforzas were brought to power by Filippo Maria's brother-in-law, **Francesco Sforza**, son of a simple peasant who had become a *condottiere*. The most illustrious Sforza was **Ludovico Il Moro** (1452–1508), who transformed Milan into the "new Athens," attracting brilliant figures such as **Leonardo da Vinci** and **Bramante** to his court. In 1500, however, the city was conquered by Louis XII of France, who claimed to be the legitimate heir to the Duchy of Milan. France attempted to gain control again under **Francis I**, but his dream of conquering the Empire was stopped short in Pavia by the determined forces of Holy Roman Emperor **Charles V**.

From Spain to the Kingdom of Italy

Milan remained under Spanish control from 1535 to 1713. During this period, two great religious figures left their mark on the city: **Carlo Borromeo** (1538–84) and **Federico Borromeo** (1564–1631), both of whom distinguished themselves through their humanitarian work when the city was ravaged by the plague in 1576 and 1630. Under **Napoleon**, Milan became the capital of the Cisalpine Republic in 1797 and the Kingdom of Italy in 1805. In 1815 it became the capital of the **Kingdom of Lombardy-Venetia**.
After joining the **Kingdom of Italy**, Milan became a major economic, financial and cultural force within the country and a renowned European metropolis.

The Novecento (1900s)

In 1906 Milan hosted the Universal Expo. The Fascist movement, a party that would govern Italy for two decades starting in 1922, was founded in Piazza San Sepolcro in 1919. Milan was heavily bombarded by the Allies, mainly in 1943, when many neighborhoods were damaged and countless civilians lost their lives. The city was actively anti-Fascist during the war, and ultimately liberated on April 25, 1945. During the 1950s and 1960s Milan enjoyed economic boom times, but had to grapple with terrible political battles that erupted in terrorist strikes. From the 1970s onward the city consolidated its position as the cultural and economic capital of Italy.

Milan and tomorrow: towards Expo 2015

The city is currently experiencing a profound architectural shift, as formerly abandoned neighborhoods are reclaimed and transformed, and the city's economic vitality is invigorated by large-scale, ambitious architectural projects. These include the new Fiera di Milano, renovation of La Scala and the host of skyscrapers and parks around the Isola neighborhood known as the Porta Nuova project. Now the city is preparing fervently for Expo – Feeding the Planet, Energy for Life. The city's extensive new urbanization and transportation projects mean visitors are encountering a Milan that is markedly more cosmopolitan and international, while still retaining some of the Italianness that makes this country such a pleasure to visit.

MILANO

0   150   300 m

N

Via Paolo Sarpi

Corso Sempione

Arco della Pace ◆
Piazza Sempione

Parco Sempione

Torre Branca

Palazzo dell'Arte

Arena

Acquario Civico

Castello Sforzesco

see p 30

Viale XX Settembre

Pza Tommaseo

Conciliazione Ⓜ

Cenacolo Vinciano

S. Maria delle Grazie

Corso Vercelli

Palazzo Litta

Museo Civico Archeologico

S. Maurizio Maggiore

Pal. della Borsa Valori

S.Vittore al Corpo

Ospedale S. Giuseppe

Pinacotec Ambrosiar

S. Ambrogio

Museo della Scienza e della Tecnica

S. Ambrogio Università Cattolica

see p 50

Largo Carrobbio

S. Giorg Al Pala Triv

see p 55

S. Agostino Ⓜ

Piscina

Parco Solari

Mercato

S. Loren Maggio

Piazza del Rosario

Piazzale A. Cantore

Parco delle Basiliche

Porta Genova Ⓜ

Naviglio Pavese

Naviglio Grande

S. Eustorg Museo Di

Porta Ticinese

Ripa di Porta Ticinese

see p 64-65

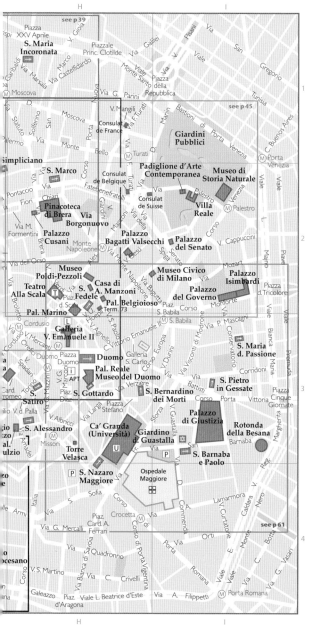

see p 39
see p 45
see p 61

Piazza XXV Aprile
S. Maria Incoronata

Piazzale Princ. Clotilde

Piazza della Repubblica

V. Mangili

Consulat de France

Giardini Pubblici

S. Marco

Consulat de Belgique

Padiglione d'Arte Contemporanea

Museo di Storia Naturale

Pinacoteca di Brera

Via Borgonuovo

Consulat de Suisse

Villa Reale

Palazzo Cusani

Palazzo Bagatti Valsecchi

Palazzo del Senato

Museo Poldi-Pezzoli

Museo Civico di Milano

Palazzo Isimbardi

Teatro Alla Scala

Casa di A. Manzoni

Palazzo del Governo

S. Fedele

Pal. Belgioioso

Pal. Marino

Term. 73

Galleria V. Emanuele II

Piazza Duomo

Duomo

S. Maria d. Passione

Pal. Reale
Museo del Duomo

S. Gottardo

S. Bernardino dei Morti

S. Pietro in Gessate

S. Satiro

S. Alessandro

Ca' Granda (Università)

Giardino d. Guastalla

Palazzo di Giustizia

Rotonda della Besana

Torre Velasca

S. Barnaba e Paolo

S. Nazaro Maggiore

Ospedale Maggiore

Porta Romana

MILAN

29

DUOMO AND CASTELLO SFORZESCO★★★

The two largest landmarks in Milan, the Duomo and Castello Sforzesco, dominate Milan's downtown area and are considered the city's most iconic landmarks. The intricate spiked silhouette of the gothic cathedral can be found on everything from postcards to potholders, and both buildings present romantic façades when lit up at night. Their iconic status has been centuries in the making. The Milanese say "as long as it took to build the Duomo" to describe any event that feels interminable, and various construction and renovation projects continue on site even today. Enjoy walking around these monuments, navigating the crowds and getting a feel for the rapid pace of urban life that defines this surprisingly contemporary corner of Italy.

Duomo★★★
Exterior

To the south of the Duomo, just beyond Palazzo Reale, you'll find the Duomo Info Point (Via Arcivescovado 1; 02 72 02 33 75; www.duomomilano.it). Here you can buy tickets to the roof, and to visit the baptistery and treasure; Combined Ticket €15 (visit to the roof with elevator) or €11 (on foot). A bristling Gothic marvel of white marble, the recently-restored Duomo is best viewed by the light of the setting sun. Its construction was a legendary affair. Begun in 1386 on orders from Gian Galeazzo Visconti, work continued through the 15C and 16C, but the cathedral wasn't completed until between 1805 and 1809. Walk around the edifice to view the east end with three bays of curved and counter-curved tracery and wonderful rose windows.

The view from the 7th floor of the nearby 🔎 **La Rinascente** store in Corso Vittorio Emanuele provides a close-up look at the architectural and sculptural features of the cathedral roof.

Seeing the Duomo and Castello Sforzesco

The enormous open piazza that extends outside the entrance to the Duomo is the epicenter of the city. The Milanese flood into this square to participate in important events, from sports victories to public protests. Bars under the porticos that line the piazza provide an excellent place for people watching. At the center of the piazza there is a large, late 19C statue of Vittorio Emanuele II by Ercole Rosa. Visitors can choose to explore a number of different routes through downtown Milan that extend outward from Piazza Duomo likes spokes on a wheel. At the southeast corner you can follow Corso Vittorio Emanuele to Piazza San Babila and Corso Venezia. Halfway along the northern side you can enter and cross through Galleria Vittorio Emanuele to see La Scala, Via Manzoni and explore the fashion district, or follow Via Verdi into Brera. At the northwest corner, you can follow pedestrian routes up Via dei Mercati and Via Dante, all the way to Castello Sforzesco.

Jose Fuste Raga/Prisma/age fotostock

Duomo

Interior

Open daily 7am–7pm. Clothes must be appropriate for a place of worship; no large bags and suitcases (the Cathedral does not have a bag checkroom); no photography or video cameras.

An imposing nave and aisles are separated by 52 tall pillars (148m/486ft). The mausoleum of Gian Giacomo Medici in the south arm of the transept is an excellent work by Leoni (16C). In the north arm you'll find an interesting statue of St Bartholomew (who was flayed alive) by the sculptor Marco d'Agrate. The Duomo's dimly-lit interiors are beautifully contrasted by its stained glass windows, the oldest of which date back to the 15C and 16C. Note their rich iconography, culminating in the apse where windows display a sun, the symbol of the Visconti family and Christ, and the eastern-facing direction of the church itself. On the left side of the transept, be sure to view the extraordinary Trivulzio candelabra, created by Anglo-Norman artists in the 13C.

The **crypt** (*cripta*) and **treasure** (*tesoro; Tue–Sun 10am–6pm. €6*)

house a silver urn containing the remains of St Charles Borromeo (1538-1584), the Bishop of Milan. On the way out you'll find the entrance to the early Christian **baptistery** (*battistero; Tue–Sun 10am–6pm. €6,*) and the 4C basilica of Santa Tecla, whose outline has been marked out on the parvis.

Visit to the roof★★★

Open daily 9am–6.30pm, Easter–9.30pm. Closed 1 May and 25 Dec. Elevator €12; on foot €7.

Be sure to take a walk along the cathedral roof, decorated with 2,245 white marble statues. The Tiburio, or central tower (108m/354ft), is topped by a gilt statue, the Madonnina (1774). Considered one of Milan's most distinctive symbols, for centuries the statue was the highest point of not only the cathedral, but the entire city. The Milanese believed it was bad luck to build anything higher than the Madonnina, so much so that when the 127-meter Pirelli building was completed in the early 1960s, workers placed a miniature replica of the statue on the roof of the skyscraper to ensure that Milan's "bela Madunina" would continue to preside over the cityscape.

Museo del Duomo★★

Piazza Duomo 12. Open Tue–Sun 10am–6pm; last admission 1hr before closing. €6. Closed 1 Jan, 1 May, 15 Aug and 25 Dec. 02 72 02 26 56. www.museo.duomomilano.it.

Scheduled to open in 2013 following renovations, the museum outlines various stages in the construction and restoration of the cathedral. Noteworthy artworks include the **Aribert Crucifix** (1040), the original support for the Madonnina (1772-73), and a wooden model of the cathedral built between the 16C and the 19C.

Museo del Novecento

FrenK58 /Fotolia.com

Museo del Novecento★★

Via Marconi 1. Open Mon 2.30–7.30pm, Tue, Wed, Fri and Sun 9.30am–7.30pm, Thu and Sat 9.30am–10.30pm; last admission 1hr before closing. €5 (entrance is free during the last two hours prior to closing and every Tuesday from 2pm). 02 43 35 35 22. www.museodelnovecento.org.

Located in the Arengario, an interesting modern building constructed in the 1930s, the museum displays a range of 20C artwork. The exhibits are organized chronologically, giving visitors an overview of Italian art movements from the beginning of the 1900s to the 1980s, and include works by Boccioni, Balla, Carrà, de Chirico, Burri, Fontana and Kounellis, as well as Giuseppe Pellizza da Volpedo's "The Fourth Estate." The world's largest collection of Futurist art is also on display. The large windowed façade offers a beautiful view over Piazza Duomo.

⚜ Palazzo Reale

Hours vary according to individual exhibitions. 02 87 56 72.

Located on Piazza Duomo opposite the entrance to Galleria Vittorio Emmanuele, Palazzo Reale was renovated and redesigned halfway through the 18C by Piermarini (1743-1808) at the behest of the Austrian court. Originally home to the city's municipal offices, today the building is used as a cultural center and exhibition space, and hosts most of Milan's most important temporary exhibitions.

Chiesa di San Gottardo in Corte

Via Pecorari. Mon–Fri 8am–6.30pm, Sat 9am–12.30pm, Sun 8.30am– 1.30pm. 02 86 46 45 00.

Built on orders from the ruler of Milan Azzone Visconti (1302-1339), the church hosts an interesting fresco from the Giotto school, and Visconti brought Giotto to Milan to create a fresco in his palazzo, though today this fresco has been lost. The character on the extreme left is quite expressive. Giuseppe Piermarini completely transformed the building's exterior during the neoclassical period (ca 1770), but the **bell tower★** has conserved its original structure, an octagonal layout designed by Francesco Pecorari, who also built the abbey bell tower at Chiaravalle.

33

🚶 Galleria Vittorio Emanuele II★

Connecting Piazza Duomo with Piazza della Scala, this enormous pedestrian gallery was designed by Giuseppe Mengoni and built beginning in 1865. At the center of the gallery, towards the west wing you'll find a well-worn mosaic of a bull. According to local legend, spinning around three times in the same direction with one foot on the bull brings good luck. Among the many different stores in the gallery you'll find a number of cafés and boutiques, including an entrance to the Ricordi Media Stores, which vaunts the largest collection of classical music in Italy, and is connected with a large Feltrinelli bookstore. Ricordi is the oldest Italian music publishing company still in business, and was founded in Milan by Giuseppe Ricordi in 1808.

🚶 Teatro alla Scala★★

Generally considered the most famous opera house in the world, La Scala was first completed in 1778 with six levels of boxes and seats for over 2,000 guests. The theater underwent a major renovation from 2002 to 2004, creating a larger stage and improving sound quality. Visitors are often surprised by the stark differences between the simple, almost austere white façade and the lavish brocade, velvet and stucco that distinguishes the interior. The Milanese, however, consider the theater a perfect expression of the city's character, similar to its many large buildings that present imposing, closed façades through which passersby can catch glimpses of lush gardens and lavish statuary hidden within.

Seats can sometimes be purchased last minute from the theater's ticket office. During the last hour before a performance is scheduled to start, any remaining tickets are sold at a 25% discount. **The Museo Teatrale alla Scala★** (*open daily 9am–12.30 and 1.30–5.30pm; €6; 02 88 79 24 73/74 73; www.teatroallascala.org*) displays Toscanini and Verdi memorabilia. From the museum, you can visit boxes and see the auditorium. The theater's simple and sober façade betrays little of the lavish decorations inside the theater, where red velvet, gold leaf and ornate stuccos reign.

Palazzo Marino

Palazzo Marino hosts Milan's municipal offices, and was designed and built by Galeazzo Alessi (1512–1572) for Tommaso Marino, a Genovese banker who lived in Milan. The balustrade that crowns the building is a typical Ligurian design. Walking down nearby Via Marino you can get a glimpse of the building's marvelous **courtyard★**, designed in a Renaissance mannerist style.

Chiesa di San Fedele

Piazza San Fedele. Mon–Fri 7.30am–4.30pm. 02 86 35 22 15.
An example of counter-reformation architecture, jesuits commissioned architect Pellegrino Tibaldi to build the church in the second half of the 16C. Inside you can view the *Visione di Sant'Ignazio* (ca 1622) by Giovanni Battista Crespi, and *Redentore* (1956), a ceramic sculpture by **Lucio Fontana**. Fontana became famous in the 20C for his cut canvases and Spatial Concepts (on display at the Museo del Novecento, *see p33*), but his religious sculpture remains

Galleria Vittorio Emanuele II

Ivan Floriani/Fotolia.com

relatively unknown. Today many of these enjoyable and surprising pieces are on display at the Museo Diocesano (see p66).

Casa degli Omenoni
Via degli Omenoni 3.
Behind San Fedele, take a quick look at this gem of a 17C building designed by sculptor and medallist Leone Leoni (1509-1590) as his personal residence. The eight enormous **statues★** "supporting" the façade are the *omenon,* a word that means "big men" in Milanese dialect. The design for these large sculpted figures was most likely heavily influenced by the artworks of Michelangelo, a close friend of Leoni's.

Casa di Alessandro Manzoni★
Via Gerolamo Morone 1. Tue–Fri 9am–4pm. 02 86 46 04 03. www.casadelmanzoni.it
Alessandro Manzoni (1785–1873) lived in this mansion for 60 years. The ground floor hosts the library and the writer's books and desk. On the first floor are memorabilia and illustrations of his most famous novel, *The Betrothed*. The bedroom

where he died has its original furniture.

Palazzo Belgiojoso
Located in the same elegant piazza as the Casa di Manzoni, this palazzo was designed by Giuseppe Piermarini in the late 18C. Today it is considered one of the best expressions of neoclassical architecture in the city.

🚶 Corso Vittorio Emanuele II★
Packed with pedestrians at all hours of the day, the Corso provides an ideal setting for a city stroll. There are numerous clothing, book, music and food shops, as well as movie theaters and cafés.

🚶 Towards Castello Sforzesco
Walking northwest from Piazza Duomo will take you along a busy pedestrian route that is packed with shops, restaurants and important architecture.

Via and Piazza dei Mercanti★
Piazza Mercanti provides a surprisingly calm and quiet corner amid the hubbub of downtown

35

Milan. The **loggia degli Osii** (1316) is decorated with insignias and statues of saints. The **Palazzo della Ragione**, built during the 13C and expanded in the 18C, is distinguished by its open portico ground floor, where Milanese citizens gathered for centuries to hear proclamations on civic and judicial matters. Note the image of the wild boar on the side of the building. According to legend, in 600 BC Gallic king Bellovesus fell in love with this area. He asked the gods where he should make camp, and they told him to stay where he found a sow half covered with wool. "Wooly sow," or "in medio lanae" is considered one of the early sources for "Mediolanum," the city's original name.

Piazza Cordusio

This piazza is the traditional economic epicenter of Milan, where the city's main banking and financial institutions have been located since the early 19C. The headquarters of the Banca d'Italia can be found here, as well as the original Milan stock market building, constructed between 1899 and 1901, now home to a central post office. The modern stock market building is located in nearby **Piazza degli Affari** in the imposing Palazzo Mezzanotte, inaugurated in 1932.

The location has stuck in people's heads ever since contemporary artist Maurizio Cattelan created a "dialogue" between his artwork and the bourse building, placing an enormous marble hand out front, at the center of the piazza, where it merrily raises its middle finger to the world.

Via Dante and Piazza Cairoli

Starting in the northwest corner of Piazza Cordusio, this monumental pedestrian avenue will take you straight to Piazza Cairoli and the entrance to Castello Sforzesco. **Milan's tourism headquarters** are located in the piazza directly in front of the entrance to the castle, on the corner of Via Beltrami.

Expo Gate

Expo Gate is located in the piazza Cairoli, in front of the castle. In the heart of Milan, Expo Gate introduces the public to Expo Milano 2015 and forms a bridge between the city and the Exhibition Site. From May 2014, Expo Gate is the stage on which Milan interprets the central theme of Expo Milano 2015: Feeding the Planet, Energy for Life. Open to residents and visitors, it offers a light and airy place to meet, learn and share ideas.

Foro Bonaparte

This curved, tree-lined avenue encircles the entrance to Castello Sforzesco and is characterized by elegant neoclassical apartment and office buildings. In 1801, a year after Milan was conquered by Napoleon Bonaparte, the architect Giovanni Antolini designed a circular piazza here that was to host a pantheon, thermal baths, Italy's national museum, stock market, theater and customs offices. Unfortunately political turmoil put an end to the grandiose project not long after the first foundation stones were laid. But Antolini's original plans for a large circular layout came back in vogue towards the end of the 19C, when the current semicircle of buildings were constructed.

Studio Museo Achille Castiglioni★

Piazza Castello 27. Guided tours by reservation Tue–Sat at 10am, 11 and noon. Thu eve 6.30pm, 7.30 and 8.30. Reservations 02 80 53 606 or info@achillecastiglioni.it. €10. www.achillecastiglioni.it.

Founded in 2006, this museum provides an inside look at the life, works and inspirations of Italian designer Achille Castiglioni (1918–2002). Visitors can see hallmark objects Castiglioni created, plus sketches, everyday objects, work spaces and more.

🏰 Castello Sforzesco★★★

The first bricks of this huge quadrilateral building were laid in 1368, when construction began on what would become the seat of the Sforza family, Dukes of Milan. The original castle was enlarged over centuries. Francesco Sforza (1450-1466) rebuilt it entirely, and during the Spanish era the star-shaped bastions were added. The main tower was originally designed by Filarete (1400-1469), though this was later destroyed. The current version is a faithful reconstruction by Luca Beltrami (1854-1933), completed in 1905.

Today the castle extends over a square layout. You will find the Ponticella, a sort of covered bridge attributed to Bramante, on the eastern side of the castle. The first large courtyard is the piazza d'armi, or weapons plaza, with the Bona di Savoia tower on the northern side. To the left, the Rocchetta courtyard was the Dukes' stronghold in the event of attack. The main tower, where the Sforza's treasures were stored, has a

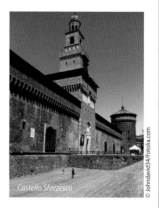
Castello Sforzesco

© Johndavid34/Fotolia.com

fresco by Bramantino (1465-1530). The ducal courtyard houses the "elephant portico," named after the fresco. This is where the castle's lord was appointed. Leonardo da Vinci painted a pergola in the Sala delle Asse. Within the enormous central courtyard, once the residence for the dukes of Milan, you will find the city's municipal art collection, subdivided into different sections known as the Musei del Castello. People often pose for pictures outside the main entrance and near the large circular fountain located out front, which the Milanese refer to – half in description and half as deprecation – as the "wedding cake."

Museums in the castle★★★
Open Tue – Sun 9am–5.30pm. Closed Mon, 1 Jan, Easter Monday, 1 May and 25 Dec. €5. 02 88 46 37 03. www.milanocastello.it.
The **Museo d'Arte Antica★★**'s minimalist layout includes Romanesque, Gothic and Renaissance works mainly by Lombard sculptors. Interesting works include the tomb of Bernabò Visconti (14C), the reclining figure of Gaston de Foix and statues

37

(1523) by Bambaia, as well as the unfinished *Rondanini Pietà* by Michelangelo.

The **Pinacoteca**★ (1st floor) displays works by Bembo, Foppa, Mantegna, Bellini, Luini, Bramantino, Lotto, Antonello da Messina, Correggio, Bronzino, Guardi, Canaletto and others. Located in the Rochetta courtyard, the **Museo degli Strumenti Musicali**★ boasts an extensive collection of stringed and wind instruments and keyboards.

The underground levels of the Ducal Courtyard (beneath the Rochetta courtyard) host two branches – Egyptian art and Prehistory collections – of the **Museo Civico Archeologico** (the main museum can be found in Corso Magenta, *see p55*). Here you can also admire the applied arts collection including tapestries, cloths, ceramics, glassworks, jewelry, scientific instruments and more dating from the medieval period to 20C. There are also numerous antique furnishings on display.

Parco Sempione

Frenk/Fotolia.com

🌳 Parco Sempione★

In this park, both Luigi Canonica's Arena and the Arco della Pace, the triumphal arch built for Napoleon I by Luigi Cagnola (1752–1833), take their inspiration from Classical Antiquity. The **Palazzo d'Arte**, designed by the architect Giovanni Muzio (1893–1982), is the home of the **Triennale**, an exhibition space and cultural center that is particularly active in the areas of architecture, urban planning, design and communication.

If you would like to kick up your feet and relax for a bit, the park hosts several popular watering holes. Inside the Triennale there is a **design café** that provides sandwiches and drinks. Note the vast array of famous designer chairs used around the tables. The **Bar Bianco** is a popular nightspot, while the **Just Cavalli Café** (located beneath the Torre Branca) is considered a place to see and be seen by the city's glitterati.

Triennale Design Museum★
Viale Alemagna 6. Tue–Sun 10.30am–8.30pm (Thu until 11pm). €8, €10 for entrance to the museum and all exhibitions. 02 72 43 41. www.triennaledesignmuseum.it.
This museum takes a scientific but entertaining approach to Italian design. Themed presentations change every year, hosting 🌳 **exhibitions** and events that highlight contemporary Italian design, urban planning, architecture, music and the applied arts. The museum's permanent collection includes a large number of hallmark objects from contemporary Italian design, like the Lambretta scooter, Bialetti's

© andrevillani/Fotolia.com
Arco della Pace

moka espresso maker and the luscious lip-shaped Bocca Sofa.

🏗 Torre Branca
Viale Alemagna. Open May–Sep 9.30pm–midnight (Tue, Thu and Fri 3pm–7pm and 8.30–midnight; Wed 10.30am-12.30 and 3-7 and 8.30–midnight; Sat–Sun 10.30am–2pm and 2.30–7.30pm and midnight). For hours during the rest of the year please call 02 33 14 120. €5.
Built in the 1930s by Gio Ponti, Cesare Chiodi, Tomaso Buzzi and Ettore Ferrari for the fifth Triennale, this slender metal structure stands 104m high and offers a magnificent 360-degree **panorama★★** of the city.

Arco della Pace
Located at the northwesternmost limit of the park, the Arco della Pace was designed by Luigi Cagnola but only completed in 1838, after his death. Napoleon ordered the arch built here to provide a triumphal greeting upon the French ruler's arrival from Paris, but when Austrian rule returned to the city the construction was dedicated to peace. The arch stands in a broad pedestrian amphitheater surrounded by popular bars and restaurants. Although you can stop here for a drink or bite to eat any time of the day, this corner of the city truly comes alive in the evenings, when the bars and cafés fill up for Milan's traditional aperitivo hour. The bronze statues atop the arch include a Minerva by Abbondio Sangiorgio, and the four horsemen of victory by Giovanni Putti.

Arena Civica
Designed by neoclassical architect Luigi Canonica, the Arena Civica is a Roman-style amphitheater that is now used for athletic events and concerts.

Acquario Civico
Viale Gadio 2. Open 9am–1pm and 2–5.30pm. Closed Mon. €5. 02 88 46 57 50. www.acquario civicomilano.eu.
This small but very enjoyable aquarium is housed in an Art Nouveau-style pavilion first built for the 1906 Universal Exhibition. Various activities are organized for children.

BRERA AND CORSO GARIBALDI★★★

Filled with art galleries, restaurants, clothing shops and boutiques of all kinds, Brera and Corso Garibaldi are the closest thing Milan has to an artist's quarter. By day, people come here to shop and sit down for lunch; by night, to enjoy drinks with friends and stroll through the romantic atmosphere created by suspended streetlamps, cobblestone alleys and the occasional cloud of *nebiùn*, Milanese dialect for the thick nocturnal fog that often invades the city's streets. In the early evenings, you'll see people crowded around bars covered with tray after tray of finger foods. This is the traditional Milanese aperitivo, where the price of a cocktail allows you to partake of a seemingly endless supply of tasty treats.

Palazzo Cusani
Via Brera 13–15.
A 17C building with an 18C façade, designed by Giovanni Ruggieri. The façade overlooking the garden was designed by Giuseppe Piermarini at the end of the 18C. Once the home of the noble Cusani family, today the building is the NATO headquarters in Milan.

Pinacoteca di Brera★★★
Via Brera 28. Open 8.30am–7.15pm. Closed Mon, 1 Jan, 1 May, 25 Dec. €6. 02 72 263 264 / 229. www.brera.beniculturali.it.
Hosted in the Palazzo Brera, the Pinacoteca is generally considered the most important museum in Milan. Though most people limit their visit to the art collection, this imposing, late-17C brick building comprises a series of institutes – the Accademia di Belle Arti (Fine Arts Academy), the Biblioteca Braidense (library), the Osservatorio Astronomico (observatory) and the Istituto Lombardo di Scienze, Lettere ed Arti (The Lombardy Institute of Science, Arts and Letters). At the center of the courtyard stands a statue of Napoleon (1809) by Canova depicting the French leader as a victorious Roman emperor.
A tour of the artwork starts with the Jesi collection, which introduces the main artistic movements of the first half of the 20C: note the sense of movement and dynamism

---

Seeing Brera and Corso Garibaldi

Brera, Corso Garibaldi and Corso Como are best enjoyed at a leisurely pace, with plenty of room in your schedule for window shopping, gelatos and sitting down at a local café or trattoria. On weekends there are often local arts and antiques stalls set up along Via Fiori Chiari. At night, palm readers, sketch artists and fortune tellers sell their skills to passersby along the small streets around the Pinacoteca. Many of the neighborhood's main streets – including Corso Garibaldi, Via Fiori Chiari, Via Fiori Oscuri, Via Madonnina and others – have been closed to through traffic, making a stroll that much more pleasant.

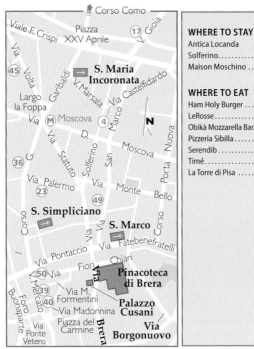

WHERE TO STAY

Antica Locanda
Solferino............. ④
Maison Moschino ...... ⑰

WHERE TO EAT

Ham Holy Burger ....㉓
LeRosse................㊱
Obikà Mozzarella Bar......㊴
Pizzeria Sibilla ....㊵
Serendib................㊺
Timé....................㊾
La Torre di Pisa ....㊿

in works by the Futurist painters (**Boccioni**'s *La Rissa*) and the clean geometry of the metaphysical works by **Carrà** (*The Metaphysical Muse*) and **Morandi** (*Still Life*). The sculpture collection is dominated by three artists: Medardo Rosso, Arturo Marini and Marino Marini. Along the passage to the left, it is possible to admire the Maria Theresa Room and the library, the Biblioteca Braidense.

The Cappella Mocchirolo gives a brief review of Italian painting from the 13C to the 15C (*Polyptych of Valle Romita* by **Gentile da Fabriano**).

Brera's collection of **Venetian paintings** is the largest and most important outside Venice.

Masterpieces include the *Pietà* by **Giovanni Bellini** and the famous *Dead Christ* by **Mantegna**, a meditation on death in which realism is given added pathos by the artist's skill in foreshortening. The collection also includes major works by **Tintoretto** (*Miracle of St Mark*), **Veronese** (*Dinner at the House of Simon*) and Giovanni and Gentile Bellini (St Mark Preaching at Alexandria in Egypt).

The **Lombard school** is well represented and includes important works like a polyptych with Madonna and Saints by Vicenzo Foppa and Mantegna in particular, and the Leonardo-esque *Madonna of the Rose Garden* by **Bernardino Luini**.

Pinacoteca di Brera

The museum also exhibits two Renaissance masterpieces from central Italy: the *Montefeltro altarpiece* by **Piero della Francesca**, in which the ostrich egg symbolizes both the Immaculate Conception and the abstract and geometrical perfection of form sought by the artist, and the *Marriage of the Virgin* by **Raphael**, in which graceful, delicate figures merge in the background with the circular Bramante-style building. **Caravaggio**'s magnificent *Meal at Emmaus* is a fine example of the artist's use of strong contrast and realism. You will also find *Rebecca at the Well* by **Piazzetta**, an exquisite portrayal of the girl's gaze of astonishment and innocence, as well as a series of paintings from the 19C and 20C, including *The Kiss* by Hayez.

Biblioteca Braidense★★
Via Brera 28. Open Mon–Fri 8.30am–6.15pm, Sat 9am–1.45pm. Closed holidays, 7 Dec. 02 86 46 09 07. www.braidense.it.
Hosted within the Pinacoteca and comprising over one million volumes, this library is one of the largest in Italy. The collection includes illuminated choral works, historical, literary, theological and legal publications as well as extensive general reference works. The library's interior furnishings are particularly beautiful and worth visiting in their own right: ornately carved wood paneling, ceiling frescoes and trompe l'oeil doors. This was the second library in the world, after the New York Library, to install electric lighting. At the time, lightbulbs were highly prized possessions, prompting the library's staff to have "Stolen from the Biblioteca Braidense" etched on each bulb it installed.

Chiesa di San Marco★
Piazza San Marco 2. Daily 7am–noon and 4–7pm. 02 29 00 25 98.
Rebuilt in 1286 over much older foundations, this church has an interesting black-and-white fresco by the Leonardo da Vinci school (north aisle) of a Madonna and Child with St John the Baptist that was discovered in 1975.

Basilica di San Simpliciano★
Piazza S. Simpliciano. 02 86 22 74.
Built in AD 385 for St Ambrose, Bishop of Milan, the church was expanded with successive

additions in the early Middle Ages and Romanesque period. The apse vaulting has a **Coronation of the Virgin** by Bergognone (1481–1522). Both San Simpliciano and San Marco often host special local events including music concerts, plant shows and antiques fairs.

🏛 In the Heart of Old Brera

Starting from San Sempliciano, you can walk back up Corso Garibaldi and into the heart of old Brera, once the preferred neighborhood for Milanese artists. Today the neighborhood is alive day and night, filled with restaurants, art galleries, antiques shops and boutiques. In Milan the neighborhood is considered a valid alternative to the fashion district, the sort of place where you can find craftsmen, artisans and small shops filled with delightful surprises.

🏛 Corso Garibaldi

Recently refurbished and closed to traffic, Corso Garibaldi is an excellent street for strolling and window shopping.

Chiesa di Santa Maria Incoronata

Corso Garibaldi 116. Open 8.30am–7pm. 02 65 48 55.
Located on Corso Garibaldi at number 116, this late-15C church has an unusual double structure. The cloister and library room (1487) are of special interest.

Corso Como

This wide pedestrian avenue is a particularly popular nightspot and meeting place. You can enjoy an aperitif while sitting on one of its garden benches, or walk along to the end of the avenue and look out over the bristle of skyscrapers that the city is building in preparation for the Expo. Towards the end of Corso Como you will find 🏛 **10 Corso Como**, an internationally-recognized art, fashion and design boutique.

Piazza Gae Aulenti

A new piazza opened to large crowds. This landmark new square is named after Gae Aulenti, and sits at the heart of the Porta Nuova Garibaldi development adjacent to Milan's main train station.

Renáta Sedmáková /Fotolia.com

San Simpliciano

FASHION DISTRICT AND CORSO VENEZIA★★

With an unusual mix of luxury boutiques, private homes turned into museums and manicured gardens, the fashion district and Corso Venezia offer you a tour of Milan's opulent underbelly. Within the labyrinth of small streets that make up the fashion quarter, you'll find shops offering best of modern Italian clothing, jewelry and design. Walking down Corso Venezia – the road that once led to Milan's easternmost gate – you'll see the elegant palazzi that have hosted the city's elite for generations and wind up in verdant public gardens.

🐾 Walking Tour

😊 **A bit of advice** – Purchase of a single, combined ticket (Casemuseocard, €15, valid for six months) provides access to all three of the small museums described in this itinerary (Museo Poldi Pezzoli, Palazzo Bagatti Valsecchi, Villa Necchi Campiglio).

Via Manzoni★

This sober, elegant street leads straight to the entrance to Milan's public gardens. Note the controversial stairstep statue "Monumento a Sandro Pertini," created by Aldo Rossi in 1990, located roughly halfway along the street. Giorgio Armani's hotel and flagship store can be found here.

Gallerie d'Italia★

Via Manzoni 10. Open 9.30am–7.30pm (Thu until 10.30pm); last admission 1hr before closing. Closed Mon, 1 Jan, 1 May, 25 Dec. Toll free in Italy 800 16 76 19. www.gallerieditalia.com.
Housed within the magnificent neoclassical **Palazzo Anguissola**, this collection of 19C Italian art includes beautiful bas reliefs by Canova as well as works by Boccioni and others.

Museo Poldi Pezzoli★★

Via Manzoni 12. Open 10am–6pm. Closed Tue, 1 Jan, Easter, 25 Apr, 1 May, 15 Aug, 1 Nov, 8 Dec, 25–26 Dec. €9. 02 79 48 89 / 63 34. www.museopoldipezzoli.it.
Attractively set out in an old mansion, the museum displays collections of weapons, fabrics, paintings, clocks and bronzes. Among the paintings are works by the Lombard school, portraits of Luther and his wife by Lucas Cranach and the famous *Portrait of a Woman* by **Piero del Pollaiolo**, a *Descent from the Cross* and a *Madonna and Child* by **Botticelli**, and a *Dead Christ* full of pathos by **Giovanni Bellini**. The other rooms are hung with works by Pinturicchio, Palma il Vecchio, Francesco Guardi, Canaletto, Tiepolo, Perugino and Lotto.

Via Montenapoleone

Only the elite can afford to shop here, but half the world has strolled its sidewalks. Via Montenapoleone is the Hollywood Boulevard of 🏛 Milan's fashion district, with star luxury boutiques lining the sidewalks, including Dolce & Gabbana, Versace, Prada, Gucci, Cartier, Bulgari and more.

Via Montenapoleone

Palazzo Bagatti Valsecchi★★
Via Santo Spirito 10 / Via Gesù 5.
Open 1–5.45pm. Closed Mon,
1 Jan, 6 Jan, Easter, 25 Apr,
1 May, 2 Jun, Aug, 1 Nov, 7–8 Dec,
25–26 Dec. €*9. 02 76 00 61 32 .*
www.museobagattivalsecchi.org.
The palazzo stands opposite the
current residence of the Bagatti
Valsecchi family. Its façade is divided
in two and linked by a loggia (first
floor) with a terrace above.

The piano nobile (first floor) was
home for Fausto and Giuseppe
Bagatti Valsecchi, brothers who
decided to decorate the interior in
the Renaissance style at the end
of the 19C, mixing genuine pieces
and high-quality replicas. You can
visit their two private apartments
and the reception rooms.

Fausto's apartment is made up of
the **fresco room** (named after the
fresco of the *Virgin of Mercy*, dating
from 1496), the **library**, with
its two magnificent 16C leather
globes and antiques such as the
17C German roulette wheel, and
the **bedroom**, with its splendid
bed carved with *Christ's Ascent
to Calvary* and battle scenes. The
labyrinth passage (look up at
the ceiling to see the reason for its
name) leads to the **dome gallery**,
which links the different areas of
this floor.

The Valtelline stove room (**Sala
della stufa valtellinese**) leads
into Giuseppe's apartment. The
woodwork here is adorned with a
sculpted frieze of anthropomorphic
figures, animals and plant motifs.

Seeing the Fashion District and Corso Venezia

Walking down Viale Manzoni towards the public gardens you'll pass a number
of interesting shops, including Alessi Design (no.14-16) and Gallo (no.16B),
where Milanese men buy their colorful and elegant socks. Starting at Via
Monte Napoleone you can zigzag through the fashion district, strolling down
the elegant Via Bagutta as you make your way to Piazza San Babila. If you feel
like a break, then turn right instead of left on Corso Matteotti and visit Café
Sant'Ambroeus at no.7, one of the most famous coffee houses in Milan. When
you're ready, continue down Corso Venezia, taking a side trip to visit Villa
Necchi Campiglio. You can finish your walk with a stroll through the public
gardens and a visit to the Villa Reale.

FASHION DISTRICT AND CORSO VENEZIA

Art Nouveau-style façade

The **red bedroom**, which belonged to Giuseppe and his wife Carolina Borromeo, contains children's furniture and a fine 17C Sicilian bed.

Returning to the dome gallery, you can move on to the reception rooms: a large **drawing room** with an imposing fireplace, the **arms gallery** (with its fine collection of close-combat weapons) and the **dining room** (17C ceramic ware), in which the walls are hung with a combination of 14C Flemish tapestries and paintings.

Via Bagutta

This narrow, charming street opens out into Piazza San Babila and provides a quiet alternative to the hubbub of downtown Milan. Small arts and crafts fairs are often held here.

Corso Venezia★

This broad boulevard is an extension of Corso Vittorio Emanuele II, lined by imposing buildings, including several examples of the **Art Nouveau style** that was in vogue in Milan in the early 20C, which is known in Italy as the Liberty style. Walking down Corso Venezia to the northeast, you'll see a number of interesting buildings. These include **Palazzo Fontana Silvestri** (no. 10), an attractive Renaissance building attributed to Bramante; **Palazzo Serbelloni** (no. 16), a late neoclassical palazzo designed by Simone Cantoni. Napoleon and Josephine lived here briefly; and at no. 47, near the Palestro metro station, you'll find **Palazzo Castiglioni**, considered Italy's finest example of a Liberty style building thanks to its size and the relationship between its architecture and sculpture. It was built between 1900 and 1903 by the architect Giuseppe Sommaruga and the sculptor Ernesto Bazzaro. Another noteworthy edifice is the "large arch" building over Via Salvini, built in 1930 by Piero Portaluppi.

Villa Necchi Campiglio★

Via Mozart 14. Open 10am–6pm; last admission 45min before closing. Closed Mon and Tue. €9 (visiting the garden is free). Guided visits: max 15 people every 30 minutes. 02 76 34 01 21. www.fondoambiente.it.

Built between 1932 and 1935 following a design by the Milanese architect Piero Portaluppi (1888–1967), with additions by Tommaso Buzzi, this villa stands discreetly on the elegant Via Mozart. Its rationalist architecture draws on decorative features that are inspired by Art Deco, but at the same time highly personal. The exterior, however, does not prepare you for the taste, restraint and modernity of the building as a whole, which includes a garden with a heated swimming pool and a tennis court.

Visitors will discover the lifestyle of a well-heeled, cultivated Milanese family, who were able to successfully combine functionality with good taste (dumb waiter, lift, intercom, wardrobe with automatic lighting, etc.). The house retains its very handsome furniture and an extensive **art collection** (including artworks by Sironi, De Pisis, Carrà, Casorati, Martini, Marino Marini, Marussig, Casorati, Morandi, De Chirico and Savinio as well as works by Canaletto, Rosalba Carriera and Tiepolo).

🐾 Indro Montanelli public gardens★

With 17ha/42 acres of paths, lawns and gardens, Milan's public gardens provide a welcome respite from the city bustle. There are cafés at the center and in the northern corner, as well as a merry-go-round and bumper cars near the museum.

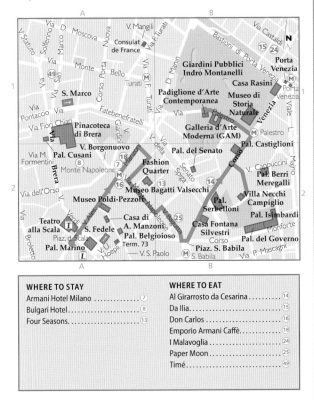

WHERE TO STAY	
Armani Hotel Milano	⑦
Bulgari Hotel	⑧
Four Seasons	⑬

WHERE TO EAT	
Al Girarrosto da Cesarina	⑭
Da Ilia	⑮
Don Carlos	⑯
Emporio Armani Caffè	⑱
I Malavoglia	㉔
Paper Moon	㉕
Timé	㊾

FASHION DISTRICT AND CORSO VENEZIA

Villa Reale

FrenK58/Fotolia.com

Civico planetario Ulrico Hoepli
Corso Venezia 57. 02 88 46 33 40.
This small planetarium was built by Piero Portaluppi, who drew inspiration for the design from Rome's Pantheon. It's open during conferences and planetarium shows (usually Sat and Sun at 3 and 4:30 pm).

Museo civico di Storia naturale★
Corso Venezia 55. Open 9am–5.30pm. Closed Mon, 1 Jan, 1 May and 25 Dec. €5 (free entrance Tue after 2pm). 02 88 46 33 37.
Interesting natural history collections covering geology, palaeontology and zoology. The educational presentation is brought to life with the help of numerous three-dimensional models, which will appeal to children.

Villa Reale – Galleria d'Arte moderna★★
Via Palestro 16. Open 9am–1pm and 2–5.30pm. Closed Mon (except holidays), 1 Jan, 1 May, 25 Dec. €5. 02 88 44 59 47. www.gam-milano.com.
This modern art gallery has been located in the 18C Villa Belgiojoso since 1921. It hosts the Carlo Grassi Collection, including impressive artworks by Gaspare Van Wittel, Pietro Longhi, Cézanne, Van Gogh, Manet, Gauguin, Sisley and Toulouse-Lautrec.
Behind the villa lies a small, attractive **English garden★** that can be accessed via an entrance to the left of the building. Though open only for parents with children 12 and under, no one will stop you from taking a peek. From the garden you can appreciate the rear façade of the building, with an impressive balustrade and windows lined with statues of classical divinities. The park has walking paths among cedars and cherry trees, as well as swings, see-saws and other games for children.

PAC – Padiglione d'Arte contemporanea
Via Palestro 14. Open 9.30am–7.30; Thu–10.30pm. €8. 02 88 44 63 59 / 60. www.pacmilano.it.
Located alongside Villa Reale, the PAC is an important exhibition space for contemporary art. Check with the website for exhibition content, dates and opening hours.

MUST SEE

CORSO MAGENTA AND SANT'AMBROGIO★★★

Prepare yourself to explore Milan's past. The area around Corso Magenta and Sant'Ambrogio is rich in history, with art, architecture and archaeological monuments that stretch from the Roman era to the 17C and beyond. You'll learn more about Saint Ambrose, the city's patron saint, and about Leonardo da Vinci, who spent a great deal of his life working here and left behind great artworks including *The Last Supper*. Enjoy chocolate delights along the way and see if you can smell the brimstone at the devil's column…

A Bit of History

Two historical figures loom large in this corner of the city: Sant'Ambrogio, or Saint Ambrose, and Leonardo da Vinci.

Saint Ambrose

Ambrose was born in Trier, in Germany. He chose to follow in his father's footsteps and become a magistrate. Ambrose became a consul in Milan, then the capital of the empire.

On December 7 of 374, while Catholics and Arians were arguing who had the right to nominate the city's new bishop, Ambrose was responsible for maintaining order in Milan and keeping the population from open conflict.

Saint Ambrose

Lorenzo Brasco/Fotolia.com

Seeing Corso Magenta and Sant'Ambrogio

Starting from Piazza Cadorna, make your way down Via Carducci, then right onto Via Boccaccio, lined with elegant apartment buildings. Turning down Via Caradosso will take you to S. Maria delle Grazie and the Last Supper. From there you can cross the piazza and walk down Via Zenale towards Via San Vittore and the Museo Nazionale della Scienza e della Tecnologia Leonardo da Vinci. Continuing down Via San Vittore and beyond the busy intersection with Via Olona and Via Giosuè Carducci will bring you to Sant'Ambrogio. From here you can walk along Via Lanzone, taking in the Università Cattolica. Walk up Via Luini to reach Corso Magenta and Palazzo Litta. Corso Magenta is lined with shops and cafés where you can sit and enjoy something to eat or drink. Continuing along the Corso, you will reach Palazzo delle Stelline.

Basilica di Santa Maria delle Grazie

Facing down rowdy crowds and speaking to the masses with authority and common sense, the unexpected happened: people began to shout "Ambrose for bishop!" The rest, as they say, is history.

As the city's new bishop, Ambrose began by distributing his earthly goods to the poor, and dedicating his energies to a systematic study of the sacred scriptures.

He learned to preach, becoming one of the most famous orators of his day, capable of enchanting even such a discerning intellectual as Augustine of Hippo. The man who would become Saint Augustine credited Ambrose for his conversion, and was baptized by the Milanese bishop in 387.

Saint Ambrose's influence over Catholicism in Milan can still be seen today, for example in liturgy and music (in Milan, the faithful follow the "Ambroseian rites").

He maintained close contacts with the emperor, but was unafraid to contradict the ruler when he felt it was necessary. Once Ambrose learned that Theodosius I ordered a violent and unjust repression in Thessaloniki, he didn't hesitate to demand the sovereign perform a public atonement.

Saint Ambrose left a permanent mark on Milan, especially in the city's moral and social life.

Leonardo da Vinci

In 1483 Leonardo da Vinci offered his services to the Duke of Milan Ludovico il Moro, presenting himself as an expert in machinery for work and war, a canal expert, painter, architect, sculptor and party organizer. For the next twenty years, his talents were tested and his services put to hard work in Milan. Leonardo painted many of his paintings during his stay in the city, not only the famous *Last Supper*, painted on the wall of the refectory in the Santa Maria delle Grazie convent, but also masterpieces like the portrait of one of the Duke's lovers, Cecilia Gallerani (known as the *Lady with an Ermine*, now on display at the Czartoryski Muzeum in Krakow). He painted a portrait of music theorist and composer Franchino Gaffurio (Pinacoteca Ambrosiana, see p57), then director of music in the Duomo, as well as the *Virgin of the Rocks* (at the Louvre in Paris). He crafted countless studies in order to create an enormous bronze statue of a horse to honor the memory of Francesco Sforza. The statue was never realized, but a contemporary copy based on his designs is now on display at the ippodromo at San Siro (*see p74*). He undoubtedly organized parties, designed stage sets, military machines and mechanized musical instruments, and acted as an architectural consultant. He furthered his scientific investigations and undertook new research in fields as varied as physics, natural sciences, optics and perspective.

When Ludovico il Moro was defeated by the French on March 16, 1500, Da Vinci was forced to leave Milan and move first to Mantua, and then to Venice. He returned to Milan in 1505, and there is ample documentation for the studies he conducted for canal locks and networks in Milan. He remained in the city, serving the French lieutenant Charles d'Amboise and studying water flow, anatomy and botany until 1512, when he left Milan for good and went to work mainly in Rome and, during the last years of his life, in the court of Francis I of France in Amboise.

ᐧ᛫ᐧWalking Tour

Piazzale Cadorna

The Cadorna train station, including Malpensa Express, the direct line to Malpensa international airport, is located on this busy piazza. Note the enormous, multicolored thread and needle, an artwork created by contemporary artists Claes Oldenburg and Coosje van Bruggen, threads its way through the piazza and is meant to symbolize Milan's hardworking character and its connections with clothing fashion and design. If you walk down via Boccaccio you can stop and enjoy a coffee with chocolates or a gelato at **Shockolat** (no. 9).

Basilica di Santa Maria delle Grazie★★
Piazza Santa Maria delle Grazie. Open daily 7am–noon and 3–7pm (holidays 7.30am–12.15 and 3.30–8.15pm). 02 46 76 111.

If you are following the walking tour, you will arrive at an alternate entrance via the apse of this Renaissance church, located on via Caradosso, where you'll have the best view of the east end and the **cloisters**. These marvelous porticos were designed by Bramante. If you happen to visit in the spring, you may be lucky enough to see the cloisters when the four *magnolie stellate* in the courtyard are in

The entrance to the Last Supper

F. Malerba

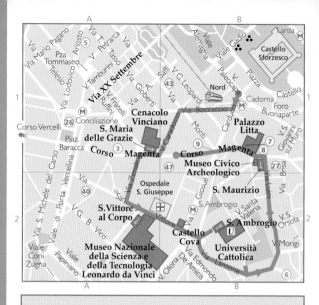

bloom, producing an explosion of white petals around a fountain decorated with small bronze frogs. Erected by the Dominicans from 1465 to 1490, construction on this church was completed by Bramante. The interior (restored) is adorned with frescoes by Gaudenzio Ferrari in the fourth chapel on the right, while its impressive **dome★**, gallery and cloisters are all by **Bramante**. You can leave the church via the main door, giving you a chance to view its impressive façade.

Cenacolo Vinciano★★★
Open 8.15am–7pm, by reservation only. Closed Mon, 1 Jan, 1 May, 25 Dec. €6.50 + €1.50 reservation. 02 92 80 03 60 (Mon–Sat 8am–6.30pm). www.cenacolovinciano.net.
In the former refectory of the monastery is **The Last Supper★★★** by Leonardo da Vinci, painted between 1495 and 1498 at the request of Ludovico il Moro. A skillful composition, it creates the illusion that the painted space is a continuation of the room itself. Christ is depicted at the moment

of the institution of the Eucharist: his half-open mouth suggests that he has just finished speaking. Around him there is a tangible sense of shock and premonition of imminent disaster with its intimation of Judas' betrayal. The technique used (Leonardo chose egg tempera, possibly mixed with oil, and placed the image on the coldest wall in the room), dust, WWII bomb damage and, more recently, smog have all contributed to the need for considerable restoration work (it's been restored 10 times). In fact the artwork's condition was already compromised in 1517.

In May 1999, after 21 years of restoration work, the Cenacolo was finally unveiled to show its original colors and use of chiaroscuro. Opposite is a *Crucifixion* (1495) by Montorfano, somewhat overshadowed by *The Last Supper*.

Chiesa di San Vittore al Corpo

Via San Vittore 25. Open Mon–Tue and Thu 7.30am–noon and 3.30–6pm; Wed 7.30am–noon; Fri–Sat 9.30–5.30pm and Sun 8am-1pm and 1.30–5.30pm. In Jul and Aug open only for functions. 02 48 00 53 51. www.basilicasanvittore.it.
The church and monastery were rebuilt in the 16C by Vincenzo Seregni and Pellegrino Tibaldi. The church structure dates to the 16C, while the decorations are 17C. The columns of the altar are a rich example of Lombard painting from this period, including works by Ercole and Camillo Procaccini and Daniele Crespi among others.

Museo Nazionale della Scienza e della Tecnologia Leonardo da Vinci★★

Via San Vittore 21. Open winter 9.30am–5pm (Sat and Sun until 6.30pm). Summer winter 10am–6pm (Sat and Sun until 7pm). Closed Mon except holidays, 1 Jan, 25 Dec. 02 48 55 55 58. www.museoscienza.org.
Welcome to the world of Leonardo da Vinci. This large museum exhibits interesting documents, sketches and models of the artist's inventions, while other areas deal with sciences like acoustics, chemistry, telecommunications and astronomy. Large pavilions have displays relating to railways, aircraft and shipping.

The museum is particularly oriented towards children, with original cars, locomotives and airplanes on display. You'll even find an original 1921 wooden teaching ship – the Nave Scuola Ebe – among the displays.

The exhibits are sure to elicit oohs and aahs from younger visitors. You can also visit the inside of a submarine – the **S-506 Enrico**

Detail of the Enrico Toti submarine

Marcodeepsub/Fotolia.com

Basilica di Sant'Ambrogio

Metrowebmilano/Fotolia.com

Toti – which served in the Mediterranean Sea from 1967 to 2000. (*Tickets available directly at the box office or by reservation at 02 48 55 53 30 –Tue and Fri 1.30– 4.30pm–, or via email, infototi@ museoscienza.it; €8*).

Basilica di Sant'Ambrogio★★★
Piazza Sant'Ambrogio 15. Open 10am–12 and 2.30–6pm (Sun and holidays 3–5pm). 02 86 45 08 95. www.basilicasantambrogio.it.
Built at the behest of Bishop Ambrose between 379 and 386 AD, the church was dedicated to Christian martyrs who were persecuted and killed (its original name was "Basilica Martyrum"). When the bishop died his body was laid to rest here, and the church's name was changed to the Basilica di Sant'Ambrogio in his honor. The building's current structure dates to the end of the 2C, when it was rebuilt according to the canons of Romanesque architecture. Benedictine monks oversaw the basilica's administration until the late 15C, when Cistercians took over. In 1799 the church was closed after Napoleon conquered the city, and wasn't reopened until his rule ended. Numerous renovation efforts were needed following the Second World War, when the basilica was heavily damaged by shelling. Today it remains a magnificent example of 11–12C Lombard-Romanesque style, with pure lines and a fine **atrium★** adorned with capitals. The façade pierced by arcading is flanked by a 9C campanile to the right and a 12C one to the left. The doorway has 9C bronze panels. In the crypt, behind the chancel, you will find the remains of St Ambrose, St Gervase and St Protase.

Inside the basilica there is a magnificent Byzantine-Romanesque **ambo★** (12C) to the left of the nave, and a precious gold-plated **altar front★**, a masterpiece of the Carolingian period (9C). In the chapel of San Vittore in Ciel d'Oro (at the end of the south transept) there are remarkable 5C **mosaics★**.

Access to Bramante's portico is from the end of the north transept. Outside in the piazza, to the left of the basilica and outside the gates, stands a column known as "**the devil's column**." The stone cylinder dates back to Roman times, when it was carried here from an unknown destination. Note the two holes in the column. According to legend, the column witnessed a battle between St Ambrose and the Devil. The Devil tried to spear the saint with his horns, but missed and wound up stuck in the column instead. After a great deal of struggling the Devil finally managed to break free and, frightened by the whole affair, fled the scene. They say that the holes still smell of sulphur, and that if you lay your ear on the stone and listen carefully, you can hear the sounds of Hell. In reality, this column was originally used for the coronation ceremonies of Germanic kings.

Università Cattolica
Rebuilt and expanded by Giovanni Muzio and Pier Fausto Barelli between 1929 and 1949, the university was originally a Benedictine monastery dedicated to S. Ambrogio. Renovation work involved many expansions, including the construction of new buildings and its monumental façade. If you visit on a weekday when students flood the campus, you can walk through the façade and look at the 15C cloisters designed by Bramante.

Chiesa di San Maurizio al Monastero Maggiore★
Corso Magenta 15. Open 9.30am–5.30pm. Closed Mon, Sun, 6 Jan, 1 May, 24–25, 31 Dec.
This is a monastery church built in the Lombard-Renaissance style (early 16C). The bare façade,

which often goes unnoticed on Corso Magenta, conceals an interior partially decorated with **frescoes★★** by **Bernardino Luini**, including one that depicts Ippolita Sforza Bentivoglio and Saints Agnese, Scolastica and Caterina d'Alessandria (located in the half-moon alcove in the partition wall), as well as the Cristo alla Colonna (in the Besozzi chapel). Your sense of perception may be fooled by the interiors: the church is actually twice as large as it seems. Note the partition wall at the fourth bay, where you'll see an unusual gallery walkway that separates the public area of the church from the area reserved only for monks. Walking to the chancel (where concerts are held), you can admire several additional frescoes by Luini and Simone Peterzano, who taught Caravaggio, as well as an organ from 1554.

Civico Museo Archeologico★
Corso Magenta 15. Open 9am–5.30pm. Closed Mon, 1 Jan, 1 May, 15 Aug, 25 Dec. €5. 02 88 44 52 08. www.comune.milano.it/museoarcheologico.
The museum housed in the extant buildings of the Benedictine monastery is divided into Roman and barbarian art on the ground floor and Greek, Etruscan and Indian (Gandhara) art in the basement, while the museum's Egyptian and Prehistoric collections are on display in the Castello Sforzesco (*see p37*). The most outstanding exhibits are the 4C **Trivulzio Cup★** cut from one piece of glass, and the **silver platter from Parabiago★** (4C) featuring the festival of the goddess Cybele. Opposite stands Palazzo Litta.

Palazzo Litta

Palazzo Litta
Corso Magenta 24.

This elegant 17C palazzo was designed by Francesco Maria Richini, while its 18C façade is the work of Bartolomeo Bolli.

In its heyday, the building played host to important parties and receptions for Spanish royalty as early as the second half of the 17C, and later for Elisabeth Christine of Brunswick-Wolfenbüttel, Maria Theresa, Eugène de Beauharnais and even French ruler Napoleon upon his arrival in the city. Part of the palazzo is currently under renovation, and eventually the public will be allowed to enter and view its marvelous 18C interiors, as well as its famous Mirror Room. Today Palazzo Litta hosts temporary art exhibits and a theater, and often has open-air movie showings during the summer months. If you visit around lunchtime, you can enjoy a tasty, inexpensive lunch at **Boccascenacafé**.

Palazzo delle Stelline

Originally the monastery complex of St Maria della Stella, in the early 17C St Carlo Borromeo turned it into a public institution designed to provide a home and education for orphan girls, then called "stelline," or little stars. Although the palazzo has undergone profound structural changes, many of the building's original features remain, including the stone staircases, the passages in the cloister and the magnolia in the center, which has become its symbol.

In 1986 the Lombardy region and the City of Milan established the Stelline Foundation in order to maintain and enhance the refurbished palazzo, as well as encourage the development of national and international social, economic and cultural enterprises. In recent years the foundation has hosted exhibitions devoted to photography, as well as contemporary and 20C art.

When you visit, be sure to take in the "**Leonardo Gardens,**" located behind the palazzo.

PINACOTECA AMBROSIANA★★★ AND VIA TORINO

The labyrinthine network of narrow streets that extend out from Piazza Duomo into this corner of the city host little treasures. Whether you're examining a bright fresco by Bernardino Luini or munching a brioche while you navigate the crowds on Via Torino, exploring this corner of Milan will make you feel a little less like a tourist and a little more like just another Milanese. At the pinacoteca you'll find drawings by Leonardo da Vinci and one of the world's first public libraries. Stroll down Via Torino to discover magnificent churches many others overlook.

Pinacoteca Ambrosiana★★★

Piazza Pio XI 2. Open 10am–6pm. Closed Mon, 1 Jan, Easter, 1 May and 25 Dec. €15. 02 80 69 21. www.ambrosiana.eu.
This 17C palace, built for **Cardinal Federico Borromeo** where the ancient Roman forum once stood, was one of the first public libraries (1609), and boasts Leonardo's **Codice Atlantico** drawings. An ardent bibliophile, Borromeo strove to make knowledge available to everyone. In addition to founding the library, he sent emissaries across Europe and the Far East to collect printed texts, manuscripts and codices of the most important literary and scientific texts available. The **Art Gallery** opens with an original body of work donated by the cardinal, as well as other acquisitions from the same period (15C and 16C).
Note the delightful *Infant Jesus and the Lamb* by **Bernardino Luini**. You'll also find the *Sacra Conversazione* by **Bergognone** (1453–1523), one of the most notable paintings of the Lombard School, with its Madonna dominating the composition.

WHERE TO STAY

Albergo Rio	24
Ariston Hotel	6
Hotel Gran Duca di York	14

WHERE TO EAT

Cantina della Vetra	11
Cracco	12
La Fettunta	29
Peck	42

Starting from the southwestern corner of Piazza Duomo, try taking a stroll down the righthand side of Via Torino, visiting first the church of S. Sebastiano, and then S. Giorgio al Palazzo. Then cross the street and wander back up the opposite side, stopping to visit the church of S. Maria presso S. Satiro on your way back. Via Torino is an attractive, stone-paved street with trams rumbling up and down its length, and you'll pass many different cafés, restaurants and food shops along the way where you can stop in for a drink or a bite to eat. Alternately, if you still have plenty of time left in your day, you can travel down Via Torino and continue past S. Giorgio al Palazzo, following the street all the way to Corso di Porta Ticinese and Milan's Navigli neighborhood (see Porta Ticinese and Navigli). Note that Corso Ticinese forks left off of Via Torino. Walking at a leisurely pace, it will take you roughly forty-five minutes to reach the Navigli area.

The *Musician* by **Leonardo da Vinci** has an unusually dark background. Da Vinci tended to create a strong relationship between the dominant figures and their surrounding space. The *Madonna Enthroned with Saints* by **Bramantino** is striking for the huge toad at the feet of St Michael (symbolising the dragon slain by the saint), which contrasts the grotesque swollen figure of Arius. *The Nativity*, a copy from Barocci, is pervaded by a glowing light which irradiates from the child. The splendid preparatory cartoons for *Raphael's School of Athens* (the fresco was painted in the Vatican in Rome) are the only surviving example of their kind. In **Caravaggio**'s *Basket of Fruit* shrivelled leaves and rotten fruit communicate the transitory nature of mortal life. The cardinal's collection includes Flemish **Jan Brueghel**'s remarkable *Mouse with a Rose*, painted on copper. Other rooms are mainly focused on painting from Lombardy. Of particular note are four portraits by **Francesco Hayez**.

The **library** houses masterworks of inestimable value, including Greek and Latin codices, as well as ancient Arabic and Oriental texts. It also has a collection of drawings, including Leonardo da Vinci's **Codice Atlantico**, which has studies the maestro created for Milan's canal locks.

Chiesa di San Sepolcro

Piazza San Sepolcro. Open noon–2.30pm. Closed Sat and Sun. 02 80 69 21.

The first church was built here in 1030 at the behest of Benedetto Rozone, a master minter. The original church was rebuilt in the 11C following the first crusades, with a design inspired by the Church of the Holy Sepulchre in Jerusalem (a narthex with two bell towers, three naves). Its current architectural form is the result of an 19C renovation, although the **crypt** is original and was considered so unusual that it inspired Leonardo da Vinci to draft several sketches of it. The sarcophagus is said to contain a little of the Holy Land brought back from the crusades, as well as a lock of Mary Magdalene's hair. The crypt also houses the *Lamentation of Christ* by Agostino de Fondulis. Carlo Borromeo wanted to turn this crypt into a small "sacred mountain," and though his desire was never realized, mute testimony to the ruler's dreams can be seen in the polychromatic terra-cotta scenes on display here: the Flagellation; Caiaphas tearing his clothes; Peter's denial; the Last Supper; and the cleansing of the feet.

Via Torino

This busy street is packed with pedestrians, buses and trams at all hours of the day. You'll find countless shops, as well as bookstores and movie theaters.

Chiesa di Santa Maria presso San Satiro★

Via Torino 17. Open Mon–Fri 7.30–11.30am and 3.30–6.30pm, Sat–Sun 10–12 and 3.30–7pm. 02 87 46 83.
With the exception of its 9C bell tower and façade dating from 1871, both the church and the **baptistery**★ are the work of Bramante, who dealt with the lack of space available for the church by employing a few clever architectural tricks, for example using a sly trompe l'œil décor in gilded stucco to create a marvellous **false choir**★★. The **dome**★ is another remarkable feature, and the basilica includes a small eastern-style chapel built on a Greek cross plan, a 15C Descent from the Cross in painted terra-cotta and 9C–12C fresco fragments.

Piazza Sant'Alessandro

This picturesque piazza hosts the **Arcimboldi School** (with a 17C façade) and a church distinguished by its sweeping stairs, where tourists and local university students alike enjoy stretching out in the sunlight. Here you will also find **Palazzo Trivulzio**, a building built in the 18C for the Marquise Trivulzio, father of the founder of the Trivulzian library, which was kept here until it was moved to Castello Sforzesco. Note the portal and balcony where the elephant's

Santa Maria presso San Satiro

Ph. Orain/MICHELIN

Sant'Alessandro

Ph. Orain/MICHELIN

head and faun statues create a framework for the family insignia. The courtyard is also worth a gander. Note the loggia with plaques, insignias and a 14C portal.

Chiesa di Sant'Alessandro★
Piazza Sant'Alessandro 1. Open daily 7am–noon and 4–7pm. 02 86 45 30 65.
This magnificent example of Milanese Baroque (17C) has a host of marble, gilding and frescoes as well as an interesting pulpit and main altar. The interior displays artwork typical of 17C Lombardy, with ceiling frescoes that portray biblical subjects, evangelists, prophets, patriarchs and important clerical functionaries. In the cupola, you can see the *Gloria di tutti i santi*, by Filippo Abbiati and Federico Bianchi. Other artworks worth noting include the *Decollazione del Battista*, by Daniele Crespi (in the third chapel of the left nave); the *Assunzione di Maria* and other artwork by

Camillo Procaccini (third chapel in the right nave). Note the confessionals, built in wood or marble and set with precious stones.

Chiesa di San Giorgio al Palazzo
Via Torino. Open 8.30am–noon and 3.30–6pm. 02 86 08 31.
Originally constructed in the 9C, the church was rebuilt during Roman times. According to legend the bodies of the three wise men were placed in the bell tower from that period (12C) in order to keep them out of the hands of Frederick I, the Holy Roman Emperor. Today, the church stands out for its series of **paintings★** by **Bernardino Luini** (third chapel on the right), which make up an articulated fresco depicting the Crucifixion, Flagellation and Ecce Homo. In the first chapel on the right you will find *S. Gerolamo con un donatore* by Gaudenzio Ferrari.

MUST SEE

AROUND PORTA ROMANA AND THE UNIVERSITY★

Beauties and a beast? This area of Milan offers an eclectic mix of sights ranging from small renaissance churches to a skyscraper some have called the ugliest in the world. You'll see the beautiful azure and gold façade of Milan's synagogue and the city's massive Justice building – a striking example of Fascist architecture. The Giardini della Guastalla provide a verdant vacation from busy city streets, while the broad brick façade of Milan's state university opens up to reveal the beauty of Bramante's architectural intuitions.

✍⠂Walking Tour

Piazza San Babila
In the northeastern corner of this busy central piazza you will find a small **church** of the same name, dedicated to the Bishop of Antioch. It was founded in the 11C but underwent extensive restoration in the early 20C.

Chiesa di Santa Maria della Passione★★
Via Conservatorio 14. Open 7.45am–noon and 3.30–6pm (Sun and holidays 9.30–12.30 and 3.30–6.30pm). 02 76 02 13 70.
One of Milan's largest churches, S. Maria della Passione, is located next to the Verdi Conservatory. The church was built in 1482, and its Baroque façade was added

in the 18C. Inside, you will find many works of art, including an impressive *Last Supper* by **Gaudenzio Ferrari** in the left transept, along with works by **Daniele Crespi**, **Bernardino Luini** and **Bergognone**, who also painted the splendid frescoes that decorate the sacristy.

Casa Campanini★
Located in via Bellini (no. 11) not far from S. Maria della Passione, this small palazzo was built by Alfredo Campanini at the beginning of the 20C, and is a striking example of Italian Liberty style. Take a moment to examine the curious details of the façade: multihued windowglass, floral motifs, wrought iron balconies and scupture.

Seeing the University neighborhood
Starting from Piazza S. Babila, follow Via Borgogna east as it becomes Via Pietro Mascagni. Take your first right onto Via Conservatorio, heading south past S. Maria della Passione and the Verdi Conservatory. Turning right on Via Passione and then left on Via Visconti di Modrone will bring you to S. Pietro in Gessate, after which you can turn left on Via Cesare Battisti and continue to the Palazzo di Giustizia. Turning left on Via San Barnaba will take you to the Rotonda, while turning right brings you to the Giardini della Guastalla. Weather permitting, you can take a break here before continuing around the university on Vias Francesco Sforza, Laghetto and Festa del Perdono. Follow via Osti and turn right on Corso di Porta Romana to visit the Torre Velasca.

Conservatorio Giuseppe Verdi
Via Conservatorio 12.
Originally the convent for S. Maria della Passione, the conservatory boasts one of the largest concert halls in the city and often hosts classical music concerts.

Chiesa di San Pietro in Gessate
Piazza San Pietro in Gessate. Open 7.30am–6pm (Jul–mid Sep –12pm. Sun and holidays 8.30am–12pm and 5–8pm). 02 54 10 74 24.
This 15C church contains the Grifi Chapel, decorated with attractive **frescoes★** detailing the life of St Ambrose. See if you can find, tucked into a lunette, the unusual tableau of a monkey staring at a grotesque, hanging torture victim.

Palazzo di Giustizia
Corso di Porta Vittoria.
Designed by Marcello Piacentini and Ernesto Rapisardi during the 1930s, this enormous marble cube of courtrooms, meeting halls and justice offices occupies an entire city block and has been decorated by numerous artists including Lucio Fontana, Carlo Carrà, Gino Severini, Giacomo Manzù, Arturo Marini and others.

Rotonda della Besana
Viale Regina Margherita.
Today used primarily as a display space for traveling exhibitions, during the 17C the Rotonda was originally part of the cemetery for Ca' Granda hospital, and is also called Foppone dell'Ospedale, which means "hospital grave" in Milanese dialect. "Rotonda" refers to the broad circular sweep of its external walls.

Hal Pand/Fotolia.com

Detail of the façade, Palazzo di Giustizia

Società Umanitaria
Via San Barnaba 48.
Built halfway through the 20C, this structure incorporates the refectory of the S. Maria della Pace convent, in which you'll find a 16C *Crucifixion* by Bernardino Ferrari. During the summer, the space is used for open air cinemas, creating a fascinating blend of modern and Renaissance.

Chiesa dei Santi Barnaba e Paolo
Via della Commenda 1. Open 6.45–11.30am and 4.30–6.45pm (Sun 9.30am–1pm and 3.30–6.30pm). 02 54 56 936.
This small church was designed in the 16C by Galeazzo Alessi, the same architect who designed Palazzo Marino (*see p34*), and hosts a *Pietà* by Aurelio Luini.

Sinagoga
Via della Guastalla 19. 338 25 03 042 (mobile). Guided visit to the Synagogue and permanent exhibition (75 min). €8. www.sinagogamilano.it.

The beautiful synagogue's façade wrought in gold and azure mosaics is the only part of the original structure that survived a firebombing in 1943. It was designed by Luca Beltrami and Luigi Tenenti.

Giardini della Guastalla

This elegant, tranquil corner of the city is the only Milanese example of a **Baroque garden** (Baroque basin, a 17C newsstand and a small neoclassical temple), and provides an excellent place to relax, read or just soak up some sunlight on a beautiful day.

Chiesa di San Bernardino alle Ossa

Piazza Santo Stefano. Open 7.30am –noon and 1–6pm (Sat and Sun only morning). 02 58 39 13 09.
Welcome to Tim Burton's dream church. Once the chapel for Milan's Brolo hospital, this octagonal church (completed in 18C) is most noteworthy for its extraordinary *memento mori*: a **chapel★** built with human skulls and bones as rather disturbing "decoration." Definitely a must for anyone visiting during Halloween.

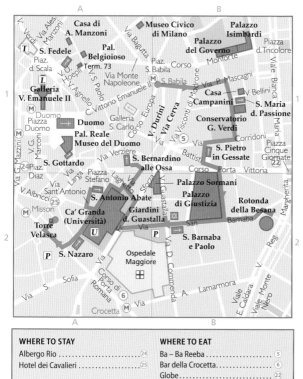

WHERE TO STAY		WHERE TO EAT	
Albergo Rio	24	Ba – Ba Reeba	5
Hotel dei Cavalieri	25	Bar della Crocetta	6
		Globe	22

Chiesa di Sant'Antonio Abate
Via Sant'Antonio 5. Open Mar–Oct 10am–6pm, Nov–Feb 10am–2pm. 02 58 39 13 09.

The façade of this church may not attract much attention, but **inside**★ you can enjoy a typical example of early Milanese Baroque. Its attractive cloister features Renaissance terracotta arcades.

Università Statale (Ca' Granda)★★
Today home to one of Milan's most important universities, this structure was originally a hospital, built in 1456 for Francesco Sforza based on a design by Filarete. It has been modified several times over the centuries, most notably by Guiniforte Solari. Note its lengthy brick façade adorned with pairs of windows, arches and sculpted busts in medallions. The inner courtyard was designed by Baroque architect Richini.

Torre Velasca (right)

Lorenzo Brasco/Fotolia.com

Basilica di San Nazaro Maggiore★
Piazza San Nazaro in Brolo 5. Open Mon–Fri 7.30am–noon and 3.30–6.30pm, Sat–Sun 8am–12.30pm and –7pm. 02 58 30 77 19.

This Romanesque basilica dates from the 12C, but the tower housing the **Mausoleo Trivulzio** was added by Bramantino for Marshal Gian Giacomo Trivulzio (who occupied Milan for King Louis XII of France) and his family. Inside, the Chapel of San Lino contains 12C and 15C frescoes.

Corso di Porta Romana
A continuation of the Roman decumanus, an east–west road, this street was originally lined with porticoes. Today it is a pleasant place to walk and window-shop, filled with shops, cafés and churches, and near Largo Richini, a distinctive piazza. The Corso ends with weathered arches that were once the Roman gates to the city (the decorations and epigraph of which are on display in the Castello Sforzesco museums).

Torre Velasca★
Piazza Velasca 5.

The world's ugliest skyscraper? Designed by Belgioioso, Peresutti and Rogers, this mushroom-like pink construction has been alternately dismissed as an eyesore and celebrated as a symbol of Milan ever since it was erected in 1956. The top nine floors project outwards, giving the reinforced concrete tower its distinctive shape.

PORTA TICINESE AND NAVIGLI★★

Crowded, chaotic, charming and cool… This corner of Milan is arguably the epicenter of the city's nightlife. In the evenings, groups of young people gather around Porta Ticinese, singing, drinking and having fun. The brightly-lit Parco delle Basiliche hosts impromptu guitar concerts on its benches, while people peddling everything from fake designer handbags to lighters and party wigs vie for your attention as you thread your way through crowds along the Navigli. Music pours out of the cafés and open restaurants, while calm, silent canal waters sparkle with reflected light.

Corso di Porta Ticinese

Lined with odd shops and unusual boutiques, this thoroughfare leading down to Milan's canal district is full of trendy fashions and crowded bars. If you come at night, be prepared to brave crowds and wander with a drink in hand.

Basilica di San Lorenzo Maggiore★★

Corso di Porta Ticinese 35. Open Mon–Sat 7.30am–6.45pm, Sun 9am–7pm. 02 89 40 41 29. 02 89 40 41 29.

Founded in the 4C and rebuilt in the 12C and 16C, the basilica has retained its original octagonal layout. In front of the façade is a majestic **portico**★ of 16 columns, all that remains of the Roman town of Mediolanum. In 1939 a bronze copy of the emperor Constantine (the 4C original can be found in Rome) was set in the parvis. The church's imposing cupola, built in 1619, is the largest in Milan. The Byzantine-Romanesque interior has galleries exclusively reserved for women. From the south atrium go through the 1C Roman doorway to the 4C **Cappella di Sant'Aquilino**★, which contains paleo-Christian mosaics.

Basilica di San Lorenzo Maggiore

Frenk58/Fotolia.com

Parco delle Basiliche

This odd and unexpected oasis of green in the middle of busy downtown Milan functions as a botanical "bridge" between the basilicas of S. Eustorgio and S. Lorenzo. The park is particularly suggestive at night, when lights illuminate the ancient walls and medieval gates, creating a pleasant harmony between nature and architecture.

Museo Diocesano

Corso di Porta Ticinese 95. Open Tue–Sat 10am–6pm. 02 89 42 00 19. www.museodiocesano.it.
Inaugurated in 2001, this museum boasts a contemporary design and displays a range of artworks and liturgical elements. If you're visiting during summer months, note that entrance is free from the end of June to the beginning of September (*7pm–midnight*), when the museum offers a number of temporary exhibitions, concerts and children's activities.

Basilica di Sant'Eustorgio★

Piazza Sant'Eustorgio 1. Open daily 7.30am–noon and 3.30–6.30pm. 02 58 10 15 83.
Used by the Inquisition prior to moving to Santa Maria delle Grazie in 1559, this church was originally attributed to Eustorgius I, bishop of Milan from 344 to 350. But its oldest foundations, visible beneath the apse, date back to the 6C. The church underwent significant expansion in the 13C during the Romanesque period, but was repeatedly damaged and rebuilt over the centuries. The **Cappella Portinari★★** is dedicated to St Peter Martyr, the inquisitor,

murdered in 1252. This chapel is a Lombard-Renaissance jewel, with a magnificent marble ark★★ sculpted by Giovanni di Balduccio (1336–39) that contains a reliquary with the clothes of San Pietro Martire, as well as an extraordinary series of paintings by Milanese artist **Vincenzo Foppa**. *The Annunciation* and *Assumption* are near the entrance. On the right you'll see St Peter, preaching alongside a scene of the devil assuming the guise of the Madonna and Child. Other scenes depict the saint healing a boy's foot, and wandering within the Barlassina woods, where Peter's earthly story reaches its conclusion. On January 6 of every year, a large group of Milanese take part in the **Corteo dei Magi** (*see p12*), walking from the Duomo to this basilica, where a burial urn contains a small part of the reliquaries of the three Wise Men.

WHERE TO EAT

Al Pont de Ferr .... ①
Al Porto.............................. ③
Be Bop................................ ②
Carlo e Camilla in Segheria - off map (A1)
C'era una volta una Piada............... ⑩
Cantina della Vetra.................... ⑪

Langosteria 10 35
Premiata Pizzeria 33
La Scaletta......................... 34
202 The Grill....................... 35
Trattoria Madonnina - off map (B1)

Chiesa di Santa Maria presso San Celso

Corso Italia 37. Open 7am–noon and 4–6pm (Sun and holidays 8.30am–noon and 4–7pm). 02 58 31 31 87.

The eye is immediately drawn to these two churches sitting side-by-side, the Romanesque S. Celso and the 16C S. Maria dei Miracoli. The latter contains a number of important artworks, including the *Caduta di S. Paolo* by Moretto, and paintings by Bergognone and Cerano. Work on S. Maria dei Miracoli was conducted by Gian Giacomo Dolcebuono, Giovanni

Amadeo, Antonio da Lonate, Cristoforo Solari (who designed the square portico) and Cesare Cesarino. The façade was built by Galeazzo Alessi and Martino Bassi.

Porta Ticinese

The "porta," or door you are seeing is the result of restoration work conducted on this medieval door in the 19C by Camillo Boito. Usually city gates like these were equipped with double doors. Porta Ticinese is unusual in that it has only one door, perhaps the result of work overseen by Azzone Visconti during the 14C. Just a few

Seeing Porta Ticinese and Navigli

More so than other sections of the city, the Porta Ticinese and especially Navigli areas seem custom designed for walking. Starting from Porta Ticinese you can stroll down one side of either the Naviglio Grande or Naviglio Pavese. There are numerous footbridges rising every few hundred meters along both, and when you feel you've walked far enough it will be easy to cross over to the other side and walk back. Note the way the cityscape changes the further you walk along the canal. At the beginning of your walk countless shops, cafés and stores draw your attention away from the canal waters. But before long the buildings thin out and the landscape opens into the broad Lombardy plains. At the far end of your walk you may even catch a glimpse of one of the white egrets or great blue herons that habitually haunt these waterways, searching for frogs or fish to snack on.

meters beyond the door, you'll find the remains of a 1C Roman amphitheater.

🏛 The Navigli★

Once Milan's primary means of transportation, the navigli that crisscrossed the city created a canal network rivalled only by Venice. Today most of Milan's original canals have been filled and paved over, but those that remain paint a suggestive picture of what the city once looked like. The **Darsena**, Milan's former harbor, lies just beyond Porta Ticinese, and from here two canals extend almost at right angles: Naviglio Grande (50km/31mi) and Naviglio Pavese (33km/20.5mi). These two canals remain almost exactly as they were when Leondardo da Vinci helped design parts of the original network in the 16C. This appealing district is now one of Milan's key nightlife areas, with a plethora of restaurants and bars. It is popular with people who work in fashion and design, and especially with young people from the city and its outskirts, who flock here in droves at night. A large and varied antiques market is held here on the last Sunday of every month.

Naviglio Grande

MUST SEE

Naviglio Grande

Alzaia Naviglio Grande runs alongside the first of the two canals, and is lined with colorful houses and picturesque bridges. If you walk along this naviglio, take a look inside the courtyard of no. 4, where the navigli association and several long-standing craftsmen studios are located. The ⛵ *Itinerario delle Conche*, a 55-minute boat ride along the Naviglio Grande and Naviglio Pavese (*Fri-Sun, €12, see also p103*) starts from here. You will also see the **Vicolo dei Lavandai**, where "lavandaie," or clothes-washers, once plied their trade on slabs of stone worn smooth from use. Walk roughly 800 meters further and you'll find **San Cristoforo**, a charming complex of two brick churches dating to the 12C and 14C–15C. On the far side of the church there is a **bike path** that runs all the way out of the city to Abbiategrasso and beyond.

Naviglio Pavese

This canal connects Milan with Pavia, and is lined with bars and restaurants, including some housed in floating barges moored along the banks of the canal. It was once the most heavily traveled naviglio in the city, and continued to host transport barges as late as the mid-20C. Today it functions mainly as an irrigation canal for agriculture, releasing an estimated two-thirds of its water into the many fields it crosses through. You can travel to the naviglio on foot, or sit comfortably aboard the canal ferry that departs from Naviglio Grande and travels to the "Conchetta," the first and smallest of the fourteen locks that lie between Milan and Pavia (at the intersection of Alzaia Naviglio Pavese and Via Darwin, roughly 750 meters from the Darsena). After having carefully studied the lock system on the Navigli, Leonardo da Vinci made several adjustments to improve it, as you can see in the drawings included in the Codice Atlantico on display at the Pinacoteca Ambrosiana.

Parco Solari

Originally a large stockyard for shipping trains, the architect Enrico Casiraghi turned this area into a public park in 1935, creating a much needed island of green for the city, and placing a large circular fountain at its center. The park makes a nice picnic area from which to continue to tour this part of the city. On Tuesdays and Saturdays nearby Viale Papiniano hosts a large **market** full of stalls selling different foods.

Via Savona and Via Tortona

Today Via Savona and Via Tortona are the frontier of Milanese and Italian design. The numerous industrial buildings that crowd this neighborhood have been renovated and repurposed as lofts, exhibition spaces, showrooms, ateliers and outlets for trendy design products. A perfect example is the **Teatro Armani**, designed by Tadao Ando in what was once the Nestlé factory building. The neighborhood is particularly active during the Salone del Mobile, Milan's mid-April furniture and design fair that draws people from all over the world.

PORTA NUOVA AND ISOLA

Welcome to the Milan of tomorrow, a sort of mini-Manhattan that the Milanese are learning, and leaning backwards, to appreciate. While wandering around other neighborhoods in the city will put you in touch with Milan's rich history, here you're given a look at its future: the 2015 expo, newly-planted parks and skyscrapers that unite design with heights unseen elsewhere in the country. Less Renaissance and more rebirth, with a new neighborhood rising out of what were until recently abandoned buildings and decadent railway yards.

The "Porta Nuova" Project

The project covers an area extending roughly from Garibaldi train station at its westernmost point to Porta Nuova and Piazza della Repubblica in the southeast and Via Pola in the north.

This enormous urban requalification effort is changing the face of Milan, connecting three different neighborhoods – Garibaldi, Varesine and Isola – through the creation of an almost 300,000 square meter mixed urban space that includes stylish skyscrapers, apartment buildings with hanging gardens, small grassy areas, piazzas, bridges, cultural centers and a hotel.

It includes an approximately 90,000-square meter park (**Giardini di Porta Nuova**) that will be one of the biggest in the city and landscaped as a "tree library," with pedestrian paths that weave among numerous different botanical species. It also includes over two kilometers of bike paths, some of which are already open and lead bicyclers to the nearby Martesana Naviglio bike route. If you come to the city by car, you'll note the first skyscrapers to be completed for the project rising up high above the existing city, providing Milan with an entirely new skyline. These towers, which can also be seen from the roof of the Duomo and from atop the Torre Branca (*see p39*), include the **Hines Tower**, designed by famous Argentine architect **César Pelli** (2011), capped by an 84m/275ft

Seeing Porta Nuova and Isola

With no specific monument or tourist sight to anchor it, the Porta Nuova and Isola neighborhood are open to exploration. Starting from Garibaldi station, you can walk around the area comprising the Porta Nuova project, threading your way between completed skyscrapers and buildings still under construction. Otherwise you can head north, into the older section of the Isola, perhaps in the evening when you'll have a chance to sit and have a drink in a wine bar or listen to live music. Via Paolo Sarpi, which used to be dedicated almost exclusively to commercial activity, now constitutes an interesting destination thanks to various cultural initiatives and a number of locales open in the evening hours.

Milan's new skyline

spire that brings the building's overall height to 231m/757ft, making it the tallest building in Italy. The Hines Tower is just one of three in a complex that encircles a large pedestrian plaza, also designed by César Pelli. You'll also see the **Palazzo Lombardia** (2011, at the newly completed n. 1 Piazza Città di Lombardia). This building complex includes a 161m/528ft tower, and was designed by Pei Cobb Freed & Partners in New York and Caputo Partnership and Sistema Duemila in Milan. It functions as the new regional headquarters for Lombardy. A copy of the golden Madonnina that crowns the cupola of the Duomo was placed on its roof and officially blessed by the cardinal of Milan Dionigi Tettamanzi. You'll also see the **Torre Diamante** (2012, between Viale della Liberazione and Via Galilei). The Torre Diamante (literally diamond tower) was given this name thanks to its multifaceted, diamond-like façade, and stands 140m/459ft tall, designed by the Kohn Pederson Fox studio. The Porta Nuova project is scheduled for completion in 2015.

Stazione Centrale★
Piazza Duca d'Aosta.

The second busiest train station in Italy, this massive, imposing edifice was designed and built by Ulisse Stacchini between 1912 and 1931. Dressed in marble and limestone, the façade echoes the Liberty style that can be seen across Milan, though its numerous and eclectic decorative elements make the building difficult to pin down to any one architectural style. A massive five-year renovation effort was completed in 2010, adding several new underground levels of shops and kiosks, as well as escalators and mobile walkways that bring travelers directly up into the station's massive main hall.

Grattacielo Pirelli★★
Piazza Duca d'Aosta 5.

This skyscraper, currently an administrative building for the Lombardy region, can be seen from many places across the city, and looms over the piazza directly in front of Stazione Centrale. The 127-meter-tall edifice was built halfway through the 20C, with design contributions by various architects, most notably

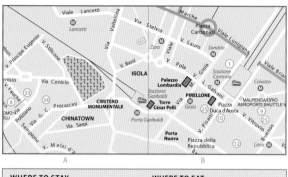

WHERE TO STAY	
Hotel Albert	①
Hotel Charly	⑨
Hotel Colombia	⑩
Hotel Salerno	㉕

WHERE TO EAT	
Bon Wei	⑧
Casati 19	⑫
Kanji	㉕
La Rosa dei Venti	㉝
Osteria Opera Prima	㉞

Gio Ponti. When the skyscraper was completed, workers installed a miniature replica of the Madonnina on the rooftop to honor a Milanese tradition that no building should rise above the famous golden statue that crowns the Duomo (see also p31).

The Isola neighborhood

This neighborhood extends roughly from Garibaldi train station in the south to Viale Stelvio and Via Sauro in the north, Via Valtellina in the west and Via Gioia in the east.

True to its name the Isola, or "island" neighborhood, remains strangely isolated from the rest of the city. But this is destined to change with completion of the Porta Nuova project. The neighborhood developed between the end of the 19C and the beginning of the 20C around the railway lines that crisscrossed this corner of the city. What began as little more than a transfer point for cargo trains and

merchandise started to develop various industrial and craftsman activities, and up until the late 20C Isola remained a working class neighborhood. Today Isola is anchored by the busy Garibaldi train station, and attracts Milanese from all over the city thanks to its combination of cultural and entertainment facilities. Completion of the Porta Nuova project is expected to reconnect Isola with the rest of Milan's urban fabric, putting an end to its relative isolation.

For the moment the neighborhood's main attractions include **Blue Note** (*Via Borsieri 37*), the Milanese branch of the internationally-famous jazz club, and the nearby **Nordest Caffè**. Blue Note offers a rich performance schedule year-round, including many world famous jazz artists. The club also offers a sumptuous Sunday brunch buffet that attracts people from all over the city.

Visitors to this neighborhood may also want to stop by **S. Maria alla Fontana** (Via Thaon di Revel). Designed by Antonio Amadeo between the 15C and 16C under orders from the governor of Milan Charles Chaumont d'Amboise as the city's third hospital after the Maggiore and Lazzaretto hospitals, it includes a chapel erected near a spring that housed an image of the Madonna many considered miraculous.

Cimitero Monumentale★

Piazzale Cimitero Monumentale. Open 8am–6pm. Closed Mon except holidays. 02 88 46 56 00. www.comune.milano.it/ monumentale

This vast cemetary is the final resting place for many famous Italians, including writer Alessandro Manzoni, conductor Arturo Toscanini and painter Francesco Hayez. The cemetary's primary neogothic façade was designed by Carlo Machiachini and built during the second half of the 19C. Countless funereal artworks make the cemetary a sort of open air museum, where visitors can view works by Mosè Bianchi, Medardo Rosso, Francesco Messina, Pietro Cascella, Giacomo Manzù and others.

Chinatown

Although many visitors – and even many Italians – are unaware of it, Milan has been home to a significant Chinese immigrant population since the 1920s. Today their presence amounts to an authentic Italian Chinatown, where countless Chinese businesses are concentrated on Via Paolo Sarpi and surrounding streets. To walk down Via Paolo Sarpi is to exit Italy and enter China. A dragon-led procession is held here to celebrate the Chinese new year, as well as a China Film Festival, with Chinese films subtitled in Italian. There are many Chinese restaurants, ranging from inexpensive dumpling stalls to elegant eateries. Several different Chinese language newspapers have their headquarters along this street, including *Europe China News*, distributed across Italy and Europe.

Cimitero Monumentale

E.Zane/MICHELIN

SAN SIRO

For soccer fans the world over San Siro is synonymous with the successful A.C. Milan and F.C. Internazionale teams. The area around the stadium is an elegant residential area, and the Milan ippodromo horseracing track is located nearby.

🏟 Stadio Giuseppe Meazza

The original foundations for this stadium date back to 1925, while the current version was significantly renovated and expanded from 1986 to 1990. Recognizable to soccer fans all over the world thanks to its four imposing 50m towers, the stadium can host up to 86,000 spectators. Visitors to the stadium can take a special **tour** through the VIP seats, lounges, interview rooms and player locker rooms, as well as the Inter and Milan museum.

Inter and Milan Museum

Enter the stadium through gate 14. Open daily 9.30am–6pm. Guided tours of the stadium and museum available in English every 20 min. Ticket museo + tour €17. 02 40 42 432. www.sansiro.net.

Located inside the stadium, the museum covers the full history of each team, with displays that include famous jerseys, trophies and awards, fan scarves, soccer memorabilia and more.

Leonardo's Horse

Piazzale dello Sport 6.

This 7m bronze statue was created following the original sketches by Leonardo da Vinci, who designed the horse for Francesco Sforza. Da Vinci only managed to complete the terracotta cast from which he intended to make the bronze statue, but this was ultimately destroyed by the French in 1499. His drawings, however, resist to this day.

The sketches served as inspiration to American **Charles Dent** who, beginning in 1977, worked to have a final bronze copy made. Although Dent passed away before the statue was finished, he established a trust fund to continue his life's work, and the statue was ultimately completed and installed outside the ippodromo.

Parks

Proceeding past the stadium along Via Novara (bus 72), you will reach the **Parco di Trenno** and the **Bosco in Città** (literally "Forest in the City"), two verdant oases that are popular with the Milanese.

Seeing San Siro

There are several ways to reach the stadium. On the M1 subway (the red line), exit the metro at Lotto and walk along Via Caprilli to the stadium. Alternatively, you can take bus 49 from Piazza Tirana (San Cristoforo train station) to Piazzale Lotto and walk up Viale Caprilli; or take the tram 16 from Piazza Fontana (Duomo) to San Siro, last stop Via Dessiè. For information on match tickets, visit: www.inter.it (for Inter) or www.acmilan.com (for Milan).

RHO-PERO CONVENTION COMPLEX

While hardly a tourist hotspot, Milan's new Rho-Pero fair and convention complex attracts hundreds of thousands of travelers every year from Italy and abroad, especially during its premiere fairs dedicated to fashion, craftsmanship, furniture and design.

The new Rho-Pero exhibition space★

Toll free in Italy 800 82 00 29, or 02 49 971. www.fieramilano.it.

On the edge of Milan, between the outlying towns of Rho and Pero, an enormous new convention, fair and exhibition space is taking shape thanks to the creative input of numerous architects and designers, including Massimiliano Fuksas and Dominique Perrault. Characterized by contemporary forms, glass and green spaces, the new Fiera Milano exhibition venue includes 20 large pavilions located on either side of a pedestrian walkway over 1 kilometer long. The site offers 345,000 square meters of covered exhibition space and 60,000 sq meters of outdoor exhibition space. Much of the 2015 Universal Expo will be held in or around the Fiera's

Recury/Fotolia.com

spaces. There are three public entrances: East Gate (Porta Est), where the Red subway line arrives (Rho Fiera Milano); West Gate (Porta Ovest), where the the major car parks are located; and South Gate (Porta Sud), the most convenient entrance for the convention center, service center and Fiera Milano offices.

At the website www.fieramilano.it you can download the official Fiera Milano app for iPhone and Android.

Seeing the Rho-Pero convention complex

Milan's new fair and convention complex can easily be reached via the metro on M1 (the red line). Remember that the red line divides at the Pagano station, so you'll need to take trains traveling to Rho Fiera Milano (each train's destination is marked on the front of the train and broadcast on digital signs at each stop). Get off at Rho Fiera Milano. Note that the ordinary €1.50 ticket is not valid for this route, so purchase a €5 round trip ticket or a €2.50 one way ticket for this station. For further information visit www.atm-mi.it, www.fieramilano.it. If you are staying in a hotel near one of the Suburban Railways (designated by the logo "S," run by Trenord, www.trenord.it), you can get on either train S5 or S6 at the Dateo, Porta Venezia, Repubblica, Porta Garibaldi, Lancetti, Villapizzone or Certosa stations and ride all the way to the Rho Fiera Milano station. One way tickets cost €2.10. On the days that special events are being held in the complex, there are direct bus connections available from both Linate and Malpensa airports (see p16).

Simione, Lake Garda

FrankvFotolia.com

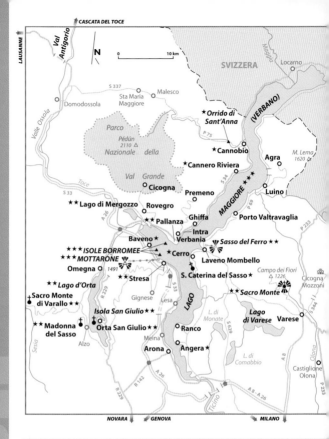

★ CASCATA DEL TOCE

N

0 _____ 10 km

SVIZZERA

Locarno

(VERBANO)

Maggia

S 337

Sta Maria
Maggiore

Malesco

Domodossola

Valle Ossola

★ *Orrido di
Sant'Anna*

P 75

Parco

Pédún
2110 △

Nazionale della

★ *Cannobio*

Agra

M. Lema
1620 △

★ *Cannero Riviera*

S 34

Val Grande

○ Cicogna

★★ Lago di Mergozzo

Toce

S 33

A 26

Rovegro

Premeno

MAGGIORE ★★★

Luino

P 69

★★ *Pallanza*

Ghiffa

★ Porto Valtravaglia

P 233

Baveno ★

Intra
Verbania

▲ *Sasso del Ferro* ★★

★★★ *ISOLE BORROMEE*
★★★ *MOTTARONE* ▲

1491

★ *Cerro*

Laveno Mombello

Campo dei Fiori
△ 1226

Cicogna
Mozzoni

Omegna ○

★★ *Stresa*

S. Caterina del Sasso ★

S 629

S 344

★★ *Sacro Monte*

★★ *Lago d'Orta*

Gignese

† Sacro Monte
di Varallo ★★

Lesa

L. di
Monate

*Lago
di Varese*

Varese

A 8

★★ *Madonna
del Sasso*

† ○ *Isola San Giulio* ★★

Sesia

Alzo

○ *Orta San Giulio* ★★

Meina

○ Ranco

Angera ★

L. di
Comabbio

A 8 - A 26

Castiglione
Olona

P 233

Olona

R 229

R 142

A 26

Arona ○

TICINO

Isola San Giulio, Lake Orta

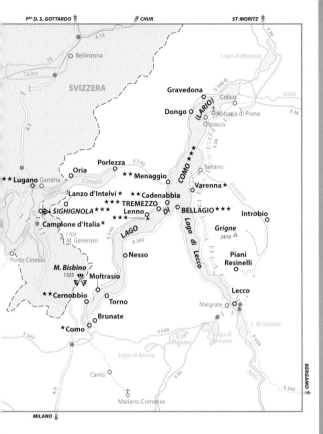

Bellinzona

SVIZZERA

Ticino

Lago di Mezzola

Adda

Gravedona

Colico

Dongo

Abbazia di Piona

(ILARIO)

Olgiasca

★★ Lugano Gandria

Oria   Porlezza

★★ Menaggio

COMO ★★★

Bellano

Lanzo d'Intelvi ★   ★★ Cadenabbia

Varenna ★

◆ SIGHIGNOLA ★★★   ★★★ TREMEZZO

DI

Lenno   BELLAGIO ★★★

Introbio

Campione d'Italia ★   ★★★

1703
M. Generoso   LAGO

Grigne
2410 △

Porto Ceresio

Nesso

Lago di Lecco

Piani
Resinelli

M. Bisbino
1325

Moltrasio

★★ Cernobbio

Torno

Lecco

Brunate

Malgrate

L. di Garlate

★ Como

L. di
Pusiano

Lago di
Annone

Lago di Alserio

Cantù

Mariano Comense

BERGAMO

MILANO

Lotharingia/Fotolia.com

LAKE MAGGIORE★★★

Nestled like a jewel amid lush snow-capped Alps, Lake Maggiore is one of the most beautiful lakes in Italy. Its waters are jade green in the north and deep blue in the south. The lake enjoys a mild climate, lush semi-alpine vegetation and beautiful natural and architectural landscapes, with mountainous slopes covered with castles, villas and vast terraced gardens. In the small towns along its banks, resorts and hotels peek out from between palm trees and magnolias. And amid them all, shining like a solitaire, the Borromean Islands represent the pinnacle of refinement and beauty.

Eastern shore and western shore

The eastern shore of the lake (the Lombardy region side) is less exposed than the western shore and markedly less touristy. The most important town is Luino can be charming to visit, especially on Wednesdays when there is a large open market. Mostly wild and natural north of Laveno, while more developed to the south, the eastern shore has a few attractions including the Santa Caterina del Sasso monastery (near Laveno), and the majestic Angera fortress. The western shore gets the most sunshine and hosts the lake's main points of interest, beginning with the magnificent Borromeo Islands.

Further north you'll find pretty resorts and villas between Stresa and Cannobio, where people have come for centuries to take in the tranquil beauty of lake and its surrounding countryside.

Angera★

65km/40.3mi NW from Milan, 5min by boat from Arona.
This wonderful holiday resort town stands in the shadow of the **Rocca Borromeo** (*open end of Mar–end of Oct 9am–5.30pm; €9; 0331 93 13 00; www.borromeo turismo.it*), a castle with sweeping panoramic views best seen from atop the Torre Castellana. Known since the days when Lombards crisscrossed these lands (8C),

---

🚢 Seeing Lake Maggiore by boat and car ferry

There are ferryboat connections for passengers between Arona and Angera (5min), Arona-Intra (2h 10min), Arona-Locarno (4h 15min), Stresa-Intra (55min), Cannero Riviera or Luino-Cannobio (39min) and Luino-Locarno (1h 25min). Ferryboats traveling between Stresa and Intra stop at the Borromee islands (Isola Bella, Isola dei Pescatori, Isola Madre) as well as Baveno and Pallanza. Stresa also has a second pier further south, in the town's Carciano neighborhood, where a direct Isola Bella ferry operates (5min). The ferry between Laveno Mombello and Intra also takes cars (20min). Day tickets for unlimited ferry travel are available, covering all standard ferry and boat routes. Prices vary based on 10 different distances, ranging from €6.90 (route 1) all the way (route 1) to €30 (route 10). Nighttime cruises are available during the summer months. For further information, contact **Navigazione Laghi** (*toll free in Italy 800 55 18 01; www.navigazionelaghi.it*).

Villa Taranto, Pallanza

© blende40/fotolia.com

LAKE MAGGIORE

the Rocca houses law courts decorated with admirable 14C **frescoes★★** depicting the life of Archbishop Ottone Visconti. The fortress also houses the **Museo della Bambola★**, boasting over a thousand exhibits detailing doll design since the 18C. If you would like to take a break, the museum café has a terrace with a wonderful view.

Arona

65km/40.3mi NW from Milan, 5min by boat from Angera.
Arona is the main town on Lago Maggiore, presided over by a gigantic statue, 🚶 **il San Carlone★**, of St Charles Borromeo, the Cardinal Archbishop of Milan who distinguished himself by the authority he showed in re-establishing discipline in the Church, as well as by his heroic conduct during the plague of 1576. Walk up the hill from Arona and climb up inside the statue for fantastic views (*open end of Mar–Sep daily 9am–12.30 and 2–6.15pm; Oct Sat–Sun 9am–noon and 2–6.15pm; rest of the year Sat–Sun 9am–12.30 and 2–4.30pm (Dec Sun); €4; 0322 24 96 69; www.comune.arona.no.it*).
At the summit of the old town the **church of Santa Maria** contains a polyptych (1511) by Gaudenzio

Ferrari. The Rocca, the town's ruined castle, offers a view of Lake Maggiore, Angera and its mountain setting.

Stresa★★

18km/11.2mi N from Arona.
This delightful resort town is active year-round, attracting artists, writers and tourists from all over the world. The town is idyllic, perched on the side of a steep slope on the west bank of Lago Maggiore, directly facing the Isole Borromee. The town's attractive center is riddled with small streets, and extends quite far along the lakefront, with numerous 20C villas. There is a lakefront park and boardwalk that affords you views of both the town and the Isole Borromee.
In town you can take a ride on the Mottarone alpine car, which rises up 1,491 meters above the lake in just 20 minutes, giving you a marvelous view from the height of both Lago Maggiore and Lago Orta. At the summit of Mottarone, you'll have a 360° 🚶 **view★★★** that includes the peak of Monte Rosa and the seven lakes: Maggiore, Orta, Mergozzo, Varese, Comabbio, Monate and Biandronno). The slopes of Mottarone are perfect for paragliding, hiking, mountain

---

🚶 From lake views to Swiss valleys…

Traveling by boat is not the only way to enjoy Lago Maggiore. You can also take a train and thread your way through the wild natural landscapes in the valleys between Domodossola and Locarno, with glimpses of towering bridges, woodlands and streams. The 🚶 **Lago Maggiore Express** (*0324 24 20 55 or 0322 23 32 00, www.lagomaggioreexpress.com*) offers various routes between Arona and Locarno that include travel by train and by boat, departing from various different locations. Every route includes stops at Stresa and Isola Bella.

Isola Bella gardens

Gilles Oster/Fotolia.com

biking and of course skiing during the winter months (*Piazzale Lido 8; Apr–Oct 9.30am–5.40pm, every 20 min; rest of the year 8.30am–4.50pm; last departure from the summit at 5.40pm; €19 roundtrip, supplement ticket with mountain bike, €9; 0323 30 295; www.stresa-mottarone.it*).
There's even an Alpine theme park, **Alpyland**, that boasts a rail car bobsled ride! (*open Mon–Fri 10am–5pm, Sat and Sun 10am–6pm; closed Nov; €5; 0323 30 295, www.alpyland.com*). Halfway down the Mottarone you can visit the **Giardino Botanico Alpinia**, which boasts more than 1,000 species of plants gathered from various different alpine altitudes. Access from the alpine car (*open daily Apr–Oct 9.30am–6pm; €4; 0323 30 295*).
Just outside the town you'll find **Villa Pallavicino★** and the adjacent wildlife park (*open mid Mar–Oct daily 9am–7pm; entrance ticket sold till 5pm. €9.50; 0323 31 533; www.parcozoopallavicino.it*).
8km/12.8mi SW from Stresa, at **Gignese**, you can visit the **Museo dell'Ombrello e del Parasole** (*open Apr–Sep 10am–noon and 3–6pm; closed Mon except holidays; €2.50; 0323 89 622; www.gignese.it/museo/ombrello*), an interesting museum institution that illustrates the history of the umbrella, with particular emphasis on the Lago Maggiore region and its celebrated umbrella-making tradition.

Isole Borromee★★★

Pick up an up-to-date timetable for ferry services in order to organize visits to the various islands. A ticket providing unlimited travel between the three islands costs €22.

A large area around the lake was given to the princely Borromeo family in the 15C, but it took the family centuries to purchase the islands in the tiny archipelago. In the 17C Charles III established a residence on **Isola Bella**, named after his wife, Isabella.
The Lombard-Baroque palace has several state rooms – a medals room, state hall, music room, Napoleon's room, ballroom and Hall of Mirrors. The most unusual

Statue holding the Borromeo symbol

Fulcanelli/Fotolia

of the Borromean Islands. In the center of town you'll find a baptistery with foundations laid in the 5C, decorated with Renaissance frescoes and located next to a Romanesque church, providing an interesting juxtaposition of different styles.

Lago di Mergozzo★★
7km/4.3mi NW from Baveno.
Separated from Lago Maggiore by little more than a thin spit of land, this small lake has conserved its discreet natural charm, with beautiful views of Lago Maggiore and the Alps reflected upon its surface. There is a 12C Romanesque church dedicated to San Giovanni here, as well as the Montorfano Antiquarium, a small museum-like structure that displays items recovered from archeological digs. In nearby Mergozzo you'll find the Candoglia quarries, where the marble used to build the Duomo in Milan was mined.

Pallanza★★
11km/6.8mi NE from Baveno.
Pallanza is an offshoot of **Verbania**, the most important municipality on Lago Maggiore. Verbania brings together a number of small towns, including Suna, Pallanza and **Intra**, a wonderful flower-filled resort town with has **quays** sheltered by magnolias and oleanders with lovely views of the lake. The area boasts many cafés and restaurants. At its center you'll find the charming Renaissance-style church **Madonna di Campagna**, built upon the foundations of a preexisting Romanesque church, Sancta Maria de Egro. Today, all

feature is the underground cave area, where palace residents could go to cool off on hot days. Outside you'll find an amphitheater set amid exotic gardens that form an amazing Baroque composition: a truncated pyramid of 10 terraces ornamented with statues, basins, fountains and architectural perspectives like stage sets. Boat trips are available to **Isola dei Pescatori**, which has retained its original charm, and **Isola Madre**, an island totally covered with a splendid flower garden that boasts dozens of rare and exotic plants. The **Palazzo** on Isola Madre (*open Mar–Oct daily 9am–5.30pm; €11; 0323 30 556*) hosts a **Puppet Museum** with items dating from the 17C and three puppet theaters.

Baveno★
4.5km/2.7mi NW from Arona.
This quiet holiday resort town, once visited by Queen Victoria, was established in the 19C. It boasts impressive Art Nouveau villas, and offers beautiful views

that remains of the original church is the 11C bell tower and a few walls. Walk through the gate to view several attractive 15C and 16C frescoes.

The **Museo del Paesaggio** showcases landscape paintings from the 20C and 21C, as well as a collection of 19C plaster casts. An archeological hall displays objects from Roman times. (*Via Ruga 44; open 10am–noon and 3–6.30pm; closed Mon, 1 Jan and 25 Dec; €5; 0323 55 66 21; www.museodelpaesaggio.it*).

Villa Giulia opens out onto a pleasant public garden (*Via Vittorio Veneto; open 9am–6pm*) and has a charming café and terrace overlooking the lake and snowcapped peaks of the Swiss Alps.

On the outskirts of the town on the Intra road you'll find **Villa Taranto★★**, enriched with gardens of azaleas, heather, rhododendrons, camellias and maples. The villa was bought in the 1930s by Captain Neil Mc Eacharn, who renamed it in honor of his grandfather MacDonald, named the first Duke of Taranto by the Emperor Napoleon (*open mid Mar–Oct daily 8.30am–6.30pm; €10; 0323 55 66 67; www.villataranto.it*).

Laveno Mombello

20min by car ferry from Intra.
A cablecar departs from this charming little lakeside town and climbs all the way to the summit of **Sasso del Ferro★★**, where you can enjoy an excellent panoramic view. *Cableway open Mar–Oct, 11am–6.30pm (Sat –10.30pm, Sun and holidays 10am–10.30pm). €10 roundtrip. 0332 66 80 12. www.funiviedellagomaggiore.it*. If you feel like having a bite to eat, the restaurant provides wonderful sunset views over Lago Maggiore.

Cerro★

3km/1.8mi SW from Laveno Mombello.
This peaceful lakeside village has a fishing port and a **ceramics museum**.

Scenari/Fotolia.com

Isola Madre

Santa Caterina del Sasso

Rifberlin/Fotolia.com

Eremo di Santa Caterina del Sasso★
4km/2.5mi SE from Cerro (about 500m/550yds from Leggiuno). Open Apr–Jun daily and mid Sep–Oct 9am–noon and 2–6pm; midi-Jun–mid-Sep 9am–6pm; Mar and Christmas period daily 9am–noon and 2–5pm; rest of the year Sat, Sun and holidays 9am–noon and 2–5pm. Donation welcome. 0332 25 20 71. www.santacaterinadelsasso.com.

This 13C hermitage was founded by an anchorite, Alberto Besozzo, and clings to a rock overlooking the lake. It is worth visiting mainly for the romantic views you're given of the site when arriving by boat.

Cannero Riviera★
13km/8mi NE from Intra.

Clinging to the slopes of Monte Carza, this town is named in honor of its mild climate, the warmest on Lago Maggiore. Along the slopes palm trees mingle with camellias, olive trees and lemon trees. The town has a pleasant lakeside promenade lined with magnolias, from which you can see the islands upon which the ruins of Malpaga castle (14C) still stand.

Cannobio★
6.5km/4mi NE from Cannero Riviera.

Visiting Cannobio you can tell you're near the Swiss border just by looking at the architecture, including its Palazzo della Ragione, located in the upper, more commercial section of town. This old town hall dates to the 13C and hosts many different exhibitions. In the lower section of town, near the lake, you'll find café terraces lined up underneath the arches, and the **Madonna della Pietà**, a church with Baroque interiors and a 16C alterpiece. During warm months you can stop for a swim on the beaches located outside the town to the west, near Traffiume. Upstream of the river (on the Malesco road) you'll find the **Orrido di Sant'Anna★**, an impressive gorge in which the river forms foaming cascades of rushing water.

LAKE ORTA★★

Less grandiose than Lake Maggiore for some, and more romantic for others, the smaller Lake Orta is separated from its cousin by the Mottarone massif and attracts fewer tourists. The landscape is delightful, with wooded hills and an islet, Isola San Giulio.

Orta San Giulio★★

84km/52.2mi NW from Milan.

This small resort town on the tip of a peninsula has alleyways lined with old houses adorned with elegant wrought-iron balconies. The **Palazzotto★**, or 16C town hall, is decorated with frescoes and often hosts temporary exhibitions.

Isola San Giulio★★

Boats leave from Orta San Giulio. Easter–first week of Oct Mon–Wed and Fri 9.55am–6.05pm, every 45 min; Sat, Sun and holidays 9.45am–7.00pm,every 25 min. Boats are also available on Sundays in Mar and Oct. €3.15 roundtrip. Ticket on board. Trip lasts 5 min. 345 51 70 005. www.navigazionelagodorta.it.

This village is best viewed by night, when dim lights and sparkling reflections on the lake's surface make this tiny island look like something from a dream half-forgotten. A mere 300m/330yds long and 160m/175yds wide, the island hosts the **Basilica di San**

🚢 Seeing Lake Orta by boat

Daily ferryboat connections available between Omegna, Oira, Ronco, Punta di Crabbia, Pettenasco, Orta, Isola San Giulio, Pella, San Filiberto and Lagna. For further information, contact **Navigazione Lago d'Orta** *(345 51 70 005; www. navigazionelagodorta.it).*

Giulio *(open 9.30am–12.15 and 2–6pm; winter –7pm)*, said to date from the 4C, when St Julius came to the island. Inside there is a lovely 12C **ambo★** decorated with frescoes by the Gaudenzio Ferrari school (16C). Note the shrine containing relics of St Julius.

Sacro Monte d'Orta★

1.5km/0.9mi from Orta.

Dedicated to St Francis of Assisi and set on a hilltop, this sanctuary is decorated in the Baroque style and comprises 20 chapels, with frescoes that serve as background to lifelike terracotta statues.

Chiesa della Madonna del Sasso★★

On the lake's opposite shore, 14 km/8.7mi from Orta San Giulio, 5km/3.1mi from Alzo.

The church terrace provides a magnificent view of the lake in its verdant mountain setting.

Varallo

25 km/15.5mi W from Alzo.

This industrial and commercial town in Val Sesia is famous for its pilgrimage to the **Sacro Monte★★** *(www.sacromontedivarallo.it)* with its 43 chapels. The **chapels★★★** are decorated with frescoes and groups of life-size terracotta figures (16C–18C) produced by a number of artists including Gaudenzio Ferrari (1480–1546), a local painter and pupil of Leonardo da Vinci.

LAKE COMO★★★

There's something magical about Lake Como. All along its shores, cypress, olive and palm trees mingle with rhododendrons and azaleas in a beautiful blend of Mediterranean flora.
Seduced by its unique atmosphere, art lovers and wealthy patrons have built sumptuous villas here, collecting artwork and statues to embellish terraced gardens full of roses and jasmine.
With snowy Alpine peaks in the distance, Lake Como combines elegance with natural and artistic beauty. In addition to internationally-famous towns like Como, Bellagio and Cernobbio, countless small towns and villages cling to the steep mountainsides that line the lake, some boasting resorts that attract movie stars and international jetsetters.

Como★

50km/31mi NW from Milan.
An important commercial and industrial center, Como extends well beyond its ancient city walls, though the most attractive parts of this small city are concentrated in its center. Already prosperous under the Romans, the town was the birthplace of naturalist Pliny the Elder and his nephew, Pliny the Younger. Como reached its zenith in the 11C. It was destroyed by the Milanese in 1127, then rebuilt by Emperor Frederick Barbarossa. The city's fortunes have been bound with those of Milan from the mid 14C onwards. The Maestri Comacini, known as early as the 7C, were masons, builders and sculptors who spread the Lombard style throughout Italy and Europe. Como has had a flourishing silk trade since the Middle Ages, and there are still a number of silk factories operating in this region.

Duomo★★

Piazza Duomo. Open 8–noon and 3–7pm. 031 30 06 10.
Begun in the late-14C, the cathedral was completed during the Renaissance and crowned in

---

🚢 Seeing Lake Como by boat and car ferry

A host of ferries depart from Como throughout the day for nearby towns (traveling as far as Torno), and some ferries that stop in Tremezzo, Bellagio and Menaggio travel on all the way to Varenna and Colico, on the lake's northern shore. There is a fast Como-Colico ferry service operating from June to September. Towns at the center of the lake (Lenno, Tremezzo, Bellagio, Varenna, Menaggio) are connected with one another via a number of daily local ferries as well. Car ferries are available for Bellagio-Cadenabbia, Bellagio-Menaggio, Bellagio-Varenna, Cadenabbia-Varenna and Menaggio-Varenna. Day tickets for unlimited ferry travel are available, covering all standard ferry and boat routes. Prices vary based on 8 different distances, ranging from €6.90 (route 1) all the way to €28 (route 8). Nighttime cruises are available during summer months. For further information, contact **Navigazione Laghi** *(toll free in Italy 800 55 18 01; www.navigazionelaghi.it).*

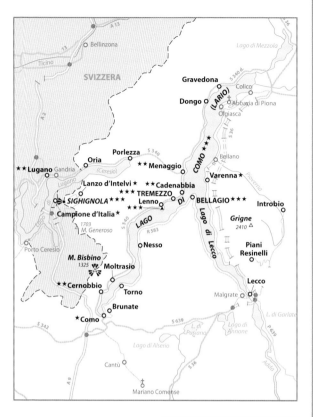

the 18C with an elegant dome by Juvarra. It has a remarkable **façade★★** that was richly decorated starting in 1484 by the Rodari brothers, who also worked on the north door, known as the "Porta della Rana." Note the frog (rana) carved on one of the pillars, and the exquisitely delicate south door.

The **interior** combines Gothic architecture and Renaissance decoration. Note the curious banners hung between the pillars, and the magnificent 16C–17C **tapestries★**. There are canvases

Duomo of Como

Steve Morvay/Fotolia.com

by **Bernardino Luini** (*Adoration of the Magi, Virgin and Child with Saints*), and Gaudenzio Ferrari (*Flight into Egypt*), in the south aisle as well as a *Descent from the Cross* (1489) carved by **Tommaso Rodari** in the north aisle. The cathedral has a five-part **organ** comprising 96 registers and 6,000 pipes. Various 17C artists were involved in its construction, although its current form is by organ makers Balbiani and Vegezzi-Bossi. Adjoining the façade is the **Broletto★★**, or 13C town hall, with a lovely set of triple-arched windows.

Basilica di San Fedele★
Piazza San Fedele. Open 8–noon and 3.30–7pm. 031 26 72 95. www. parrocchiasanfedelecomo.it.
In the heart of the old quarter, walking up Via Vittorio Emanuele II, the city's main commercial artery, you'll reach the ancient Roman forum, where this Romanesque-Lombard style church stands amid medieval homes and attractive arcades. The church's nave and two aisles are terminated by a polygonal Romanesque **chancel★** with radiating chapels.

Tempio Voltiano
Viale Marconi. At the time of writing, only the first floor can be visited. Open Apr–Sep 10am–noon and 3–6pm, Oct–Mar 10am–noon and 2–4pm. Closed Mon. €2. 031 25 25 50 / 57 47 05. museicivici.comune.como.it or http://cultura.comune.como.it/ tempio-voltiano.
Near the lake and the war memorial, the small, neoclassical Temple of Volta commemorates the scientist Alessandro Volta (1745-1827). Volta was born in Como, invented the battery and gave his name to the unit of measurement for electricity, the volt.

Basilica di Sant'Abbondio★
Via Regina Teodolinda 35. Open daily 8am–6pm (Winter 4.30pm). 031 30 45 18.
Located outside the city walls on what was once the Roman Via Regia, this masterpiece of Romanesque-Lombard architecture was consecrated in 1093. The noble **façade★** has a lovely doorway. The remarkable 14C **frescoes★** evoke the Life of Christ.

🚡 Brunate by cable car
If you'd like to enjoy a splendid bird's eye **view** of Como and the lake, hop on the alpine car for **Brunate**, a village located high above Como to the northeast.

Villa Olmo
3km/1.8mi N by the S 35 and then the S 340 to the right. Open Mon-Sat 9am–12.30pm and 2–5pm.Park 7.30am–7pm; summer –11pm. 031 24 25 43. www.centrovolta.it.
This large Neoclassical building is now a scientific institute. The gardens contain a small theater and a lovely **view★** of Como in its lakeside setting.

Torno
7km/4.3mi NE from Como and 22km/13.66mi SE from Bellagio.
On the outskirts of this attractive port, the 14C church of San Giovanni boasts a fine Lombard-Renaissance **doorway★**.

Villa del Balbianello

Bellagio★★★

31km/19.2mi NE from Como.
This elegant little town has attracted international jetsetters since before there were jets to set about in. Built on a promontory dividing dividing Lake Lecco from the southern arm of Lake Como, today Bellagio is a gracious resort town with a worldwide reputation for friendliness and excellent amenities. Salita Serbelloni is one of its main shopping thoroughfares. The church of San Giacomo is a good example of Romanesque-Lombard style, but the town's numerous elegant **villas** are its true treasures. Extraordinary gardens are packed with orange and lemon trees, cacti, rhododendrons and rose bushes, with ancient statuary on display almost everywhere you look. The splendid lakeside **gardens★★** of **Villa Serbelloni** (*1hr 30mins guided tours Mar–Nov Tue–Sun 11am and 3.30pm from tourist office, Piazza della Chiesa 14; €9; 031 95 15 55*) and **Villa Melzi** (*Via Melzi d'Eril 8, 1 km southwest of the center, open end*

Mar–Oct daily 9.30am–6.30pm; €6.50; 339 45 73 838; www. giardinidivillamelzi.it), are the main sights to visit in Bellagio. If you'd like to enjoy the lake from a unique perspective, go up to the hotel Il Perlo Panorama, located above Spartivento (or "wind divider") point.

Cernobbio★★

6km/3.7mi NW from Como.
This location is famous for the **Villa d'Este**, the opulent 16C residence now transformed into a hotel and surrounded by fine parkland (access to both the villa and the park is limited to hotel guests). The best view of the villa (from the ground) is from Piazza del Risorgimento, near the landing.

Villa del Balbianello★★★

Balbianello, in the Lenno municipality. Open Mar– Nov 10am–6pm. Closed Mon and Wed. €13. 0344 56 110. www.visitfai.it.
Set upon a promontory perched above Lake Como, Villa del

LAKE COMO

Varenna on Lake Como

Balbianello is surrounded by cypress trees and boasts enchanting terraced gardens, dominated by an elegant loggia with three arcades. This 18C villa was owned by a cardinal and later by explorer Guido Monzino (1928-1998), who filled the building with a rich collection of Chinese, African and pre-Columbian artwork, as well as 17C English and French furniture. The villa also has a small museum that exhibits documents, trinkets and memorabilia collected during its famous former owner's many voyages.

Isola Comacina★

Comacina island can be accessed by water taxi, or from Lenno (2km north) by ferry.

This little island was an important place of worship in ancient times, as evidenced by the archeological remains found here. The island was a place of refuge for Christians fleeing barbarian invasions, and many legends, including some connected with the Holy Grail, feature it. Today the island has become a haven for artists.

Tremezzo★★★

3km/1.8mi NE from Lenno.

A mild climate and a beautiful location combine to make Tremezzo a favorite place for a stay. The town's slopes are covered with cypress, palm and olive trees, making it one of the most photogenic sites in the area. You'll enjoy the peaceful terraced gardens in the **Parco Comunale★**, while the 18C **Villa Carlotta★★** (*Via Regina 2, entrance beside the Grand Hotel Tremezzo; open daily Apr–end Oct 9am–7.30pm, museum 6.30pm; end Mar and end Oct–mid Nov 10am–6pm, museum 5.30pm; €8.50; 0344 40 405. www.villacarlotta.it*) occupies an admirable site facing the Grigne Massif. The villa boasts a wonderful collection of 18C and 19C paintings and sculpture, including a copy of Canova's *Cupid and Psyche* by **Adamo**

Tadolini (1788-1868). Note the magnificent **views** from the balcony. The villa's main attraction is its beautiful **terraced garden**, particularly impressive in the spring, when its numerous rhododendrons and azaleas are in full bloom.

Cadenabbia★★

3km/1.8mi NE from Tremezzo.
This delightful resort town occupies an advantageous position opposite Bellagio. A handsome avenue of plane trees, Via del Paradiso, links the town with Villa Carlotta and Tremezzo. At the San Martino chapel (1hr 30min on foot there and back), you can enjoy a good **view** of Bellagio, lakes Como and Lecco and the Grigne.

Menaggio★★

3km/1.8mi NE from Tremezzo.
You'll see beautiful villas and gardens along the slopes of this lovely town. Menaggio has excellent restaurants, and you can catch the ferry to and from Varenna here.

Gravedona

17km/10.5mi NE from Menaggio.
This fishing village has an attractive Romanesque church, **Santa Maria del Tiglio★**. The 5C baptistery was remodelled in the Lombard style in the 12C.

Varenna★

36km/22.3mi S from Gravedona, 30km/18.6mi NW from Lecco.
The only real tourist attraction on the eastern shore north of Bellagio, Varenna is worth a ferry ride from Menaggio or Belaggio. Follow the pier for a pleasant walk overlooking the river. You'll reach the magnificent Renaissance **Villa Monastero**, a former convent, surrounded by cypress and palm trees. The villa's vast terraced gardens, decorated with sculpture and Renaissance columns, are planted with cypress, lemon trees, camellias and rhododendrons, and provide one of the most beautiful **views** of the lake. Inside the villa you'll find a museum that displays paintings, tapestries and furniture collected by the villa's owners over different periods. *Via Polvani 4. Villa open Aug 9.30am–7pm; Mar–Jul and Sep– Nov Fri, Sat, Sun and holidays 9.30am–7pm. €8. Gardens only €5 Mon–Fri. 0341 29 54 50. www.villamonastero.eu.*

Lecco

22km/13.6mi SE from Varenna, 61km/37.9mi NE from Milan.
Surrounded by tall mountains and steep hills that culminate in **Monte Barro**, which provides a magnificent panoramic view, Lecco has attractive lakeside paths and a charming historic center. Here you'll find the **Basilica di San Nicolò**, a neoclassical church. Note the 96m-tall bell tower, the symbol of Lecco. Construction on the bell tower was begun in 1864 and finished forty years later thanks to fundraising by the town's citizens.

LAKE LUGANO★★

Most of Lake Lugano is in Swiss territory. Lugano is wilder than lakes Maggiore and Como and its irregular outline communicates none of their grandeur or majesty. Nevertheless, its mild climate and steep mountain countryside make it an excellent place for a holiday.

Campione d'Italia★

27km/16.7mi NW from Como, 71km/44.1mi NW from Milan.

An Italian enclave in Switzerland, Campione is a colorful village, popular on account of its casino. A chapel, the oratory of San Pietro, is a graceful building dating from 1326. It was the work of the famous **Maestri Campionesi**, who vied with the Maestri Comacini in spreading the Lombard style throughout Italy.

Lanzo d'Intelvi★

15km/9.3mi NE from Campione d'Italia.

Set in the heart of a pine and larch forest, this resort town (907m/2,976ft) is also a ski destination in winter. Roughly 6km/3.7mi away you'll find the 🚡 **Belvedere di Sighignola★★★**, also known as "Italy's balcony" because of the extensive views it offers of Lugano, the Alps as far as Monte Rosa and, on a clear day, Mont Blanc.

🚢 **Seeing Lake Lugano by boat**

The wide choice of lake cruises includes lunch and dinner cruises, as well as a "Grande Giro del Lago" cruise (daily from Apr to mid Oct, departing from Lugano 2.40pm, returning 5.28pm). For further information, contact **Navigazione del Lago di Lugano** *(0041 91 97 15 223; www.lakelugano.ch).*

Lugano★★

In Switzerland, 21km/13mi NW from Lanzo d'Intelvi, 77km/47.8mi NW from Milan.

Lugano benefits from its beautiful physical setting on a dark, still bay between two wood-lined mountains (**Monte Brè★★** and **Monte San Salvatore★★★**, both accessible via cable railway). Lugano's attractions appeal to all tastes, with pedestrian areas, small squares, luxury shops in the center, boutiques and quiet walks in the surrounding countryside.

Piazza della Riforma is very lively thanks to its bars and, in July, the concerts given as part of its summer jazz festival. It is the setting for the city's striking Municipal Palace (1844). Interesting streets include **Via Petrarca** and **Via Soave**, as well as the narrow **Via Pessina**, lined with small food shops and inviting store windows. In **Piazza Cioccaro** (cable railway), the Baroque **Palazzo Riva★** (1671) hides an internal courtyard with a surprising wall decorated with a trompe-l'œil painting (*Via Soave 9*). South of the town's center, you'll find the **church of Santa Maria degli Angeli★★**, construction of which began in 1499. The church has three splendid **frescoes** by **Bernardino Luini** (1480-1532 ca). The most notable fresco decorates the separating wall in the choir: representing the Passion, it is striking for the extraordinary expressiveness of the Crucifixion scene.

LAKE GARDA★★★

Appreciated since ancient times for its mild climate, Lake Garda is the largest lake in Italy and considered one of its most beautiful. It is sheltered by Monte Baldo to the east, earning the lake the name "Il Benaco," or the Beneficial Lake. Garda straddles three different regions of Italy – Trentino, Lombardy and Veneto – and attracts tourists from all over the world, proving particularly popular with Germans, Austrians and the Swiss. More than other similar sites in Italy, Lake Garda has actively promoted mass tourism, though a short trip out on the water is all you'll need to find a little peace and quiet. Gourmets will appreciate the high quality wines, olive oils and fish dishes, while athletic visitors can take advantage of numerous windsurfing, mountain biking, rockclimbing, canoeing and hiking services.

Riviera degli Ulivi and Riviera dei Limoni

The western shore of Lake Garda from Sirmione to Riva del Garda is the sunniest and most pleasant, filled with lemon and lime trees. Cliffs drop sheer into the lake waters and the road curves high above the lake, providing wonderful views. Cypress trees shoot up among attractive architecture and stone villages. The eastern side of the lake, from Peschiera del Garda to Torbole, is known as the "olive shore." It could just as easily have been called the "grapevine shore," because its banks host important Bardolino

and Valpolicella vineyards. This side of the lake is the most touristy, with a number of tourist services and facilities concentrated on the waterfront. Traveling up above the shoreline you will quickly leave the crowds behind and be free to enjoy the picturesque scenery amid low lying mountains.

Sirmione★★

136km/84.5mi E from Milan.
Located at the tip of a narrow, 3.5 km peninsula, Sirmione was appreciated as far back as Roman times for its bubbling sulfur springs. The tradition of "taking the waters" in Sirmione continues

🚢 Seeing Lake Garda by boat and car ferry

There are daily passenger ferryboat connections that cover the entire lake, from Desenzano or Peschiera in the south all the way to Riva del Garda in the north (travel times range from 3h 40min to 4h 30min). You have the option of eating lunch on board. There are many more daily ferries available between Basso Lago (between Desenzano or Peschiera and Gargnano), or covering only the northern lake area (Malcesine, Limone, Torbole and Riva del Garda).

The ferry from Toscolano Maderno to Torri del Benaco and vice versa, and from Limone to Malcesine and vice versa, also takes cars (25/30min). Day tickets are available for unlimited ferry travel on different sections of the standard ferry and boat network: €34.30 for travel across the entire ferry network; €23.40 for travel in the lower lake area; €20.50 for travel in the upper lake area only. Nighttime cruises are available during summer months. For further information, contact **Navigazione Laghi** *(toll free in Italy 800 55 18 01, www.navigazionelaghi.it).*

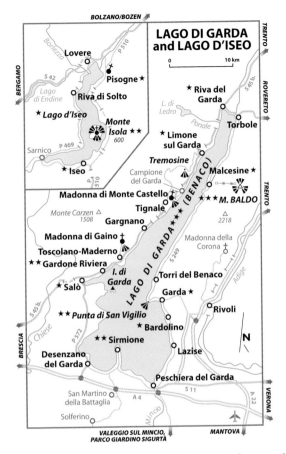

LAGO DI GARDA and LAGO D'ISEO

0 ——— 10 km

BOLZANO/BOZEN

TRENTO

ROVERETO

BERGAMO

Lovere

Pisogne ★

Riva di Solto

★ Lago d'Iseo

Monte Isola ★★ 600

Sarnico

Iseo ★

★ Riva del Garda

Torbole

L. di Ledro

Ponale

★ Limone sul Garda

Tremosine

Campione del Garda

Malcesine ★

Madonna di Monte Castello †

★★★ M. BALDO

TRENTO

Tignale

Monte Carzen △ 1508

Gargnano

△ 2218

Madonna di Gaino †

Madonna della Corona †

Toscolano-Maderno

★★ Gardone Riviera

I. di Garda

Adige

★ Salò

Torri del Benaco

L A G O   D I   G A R D A   (B E N A C O)

Garda ★

Rivoli

★★ Punta di San Vigilio

★ Bardolino

★★ Sirmione

Lazise

Desenzano del Garda

VERONA

Peschiera del Garda

San Martino della Battaglia

A 4

S 11

Mincio

A 22

Solferino

N

BRESCIA

Chiese

VALEGGIO SUL MINCIO, PARCO GIARDINO SIGURTÀ

MANTOVA

today, with many people traveling here to relax, reinvigorate the senses and cure respiratory diseases (www.termedisirmione.com). The town is charming and welcoming, with numerous hotels and campsites (see the Colombare tourist area), and a castle perched near the end of the peninsula. Outside the hotel area, the town is clustered around the 13C-15C **Rocca Scaligera★** (*open 8.30am–7.30pm; closed Mon; €4; 030 91 64 68*). This beautiful crenellated

castle has interesting frescoes and views of the ancient dungeon. Visit the outermost tip of the peninsula you'll find the suggestive ruins of an ancient Roman villa. According to local legend, this archeological zone is home to the remains of Roman poet Catullus (c. 87-54 BC), who composed elegies inspired by his turbulent love affair with Clodia. Known as the **Grotte di Catullo★★** (*open Mar–Oct Tue–Sat 8.30am–7.30pm, Sun 9.30am–6.30pm; rest of the year*

Tue–Sat 8.30am–5pm, Sun and holidays 8.30am–2pm; closed Mon except holidays, 1 Jan, 1 May, 25 Dec; €6; 030 91 61 57), here you'll find a small museum that charts the history and evolution of excavations conducted in the area. On a nearby hill you'll find the church of San Pietro in Mavino, built atop an ancient Roman temple. The 13C-16C church boasts a series of beautiful frescoes.

Desenzano del Garda
9.5km/5.9mi SW from Sirmione.
The old port, picturesque Piazza Malvezzi and the neighboring historic quarter are all good places for a stroll. The 16C parish church, the **Parrocchiale Santa Maria Maddalena**, has an intense **Last Supper★** by **Giambattista Tiepolo**. To the north of the town in Via Scavi Romani, the **Villa Romana** boasts remarkable multicolored **Roman mosaics** (*open Mar–Oct Tue–Sat 8.30am–7pm; rest of the year Tue–Sat 8.30am–5.30pm, Sun 9am–4.30pm; closed 1 Jan, 1 May, 25 Dec; €2; 030 91 43 547*).

Salò★
20km/12.4mi N from Desenzano del Garda.
Sheltered at the foot of a lovely bay, this peaceful market town boasts a beautiful lakeside location, and was the seat of the Venetian Captain under the Venetian Empire.
Magnolias shade a pleasant pedestrian promenade. Beneath Art Nouveau façades, cafés and restaurants open out onto terraces overlooking yachts and motorboats moored to the quays. You can depart from here on boat trips to visit various villages around the lake. Inside the town, the 15C Duomo hosts a large gilded **polyptych★** (1510) and works by Moretto da Brescia and Romanino. Near the church, the **Palazzo Fantoni** (15C) boasts one of the richest libraries in Italy.

Gardone Riviera★★
4km/2.5mi NE from Salò.
The village consists of two sections. The area near the lake is a sunny resort neighborhood, characterized by hotels and

Tower of Gardone

Steheap/Fotolia

Riva del Garda

tourist facilities. Higher up, the village known as Gardone di Sopra provides a more picturesque setting. Here you can visit the **Vittoriale degli Italiani★**, the large property once owned by Italian poet Gabriele D'Annunzio (1863-1938). This vast area is surrounded by gardens and provides beautiful **views★** of the lake. The property is a sort of sanctuary, celebrating poetry, patriotism and the heroic warrior ethos this writer embraced amid the Fascist movement popular during his lifetime. The Neoclassical villa, La Priora, expresses the curious atmosphere that this writer aesthete cultivated so ardently. The museum and park display mementos of his turbulent life. *Gardens: open Apr–Sep 8.30am–8pm; Oct–Mar 9am–5pm. Villa and museum: Apr–Sep 8.30am–7pm; Oct–Mar 9am–4pm. Closed Mon (museum), 1 Jan, 24–25 Dec. €8 (gardens); €16 villa, museum and gardens. 0365 29 65 11. www.vittoriale.it.*

Gargnano
12km/7.4mi NE from Gardone Riviera.

This charming resort is famous for its lemon trees. The **church of San Francesco** has 15C cloisters with curious Moorish-style galleries featuring capitals carved with oranges and lemons, recalling the fact that Franciscan monks were most likely the ones who introduced citrus fruits to this area. The lakeside promenade leads to **Villa Feltrinelli** (now a hotel), which served as Mussolini's headquarters during the Fascist Republic (1943–45).

Tignale
10km/6.2mi NE from Gargnano.

Here slopes are lined with spectacular terraces and characterized by the stone pylons used to cultivate lemon trees during the 18C. Heading north, walking away from the shore, you can work your way up above Tignale to **Tremosine**, enjoying exceptional **views★★★** of the lake on the way. At the height (800m) you'll find the Madonna di Monte Castello sanctuary, which boasts attractive frescoes from the Giotto school.

Limone sul Garda★
20km/12.4mi N from Tignale.
Whether you wander along the shoreline or wind your way through the mountains, you will eventually reach Limone (Lemon), where terraced slopes, greenhouses and private gardens are rife with the scent of lemons and citrus flowers. This picturesque village is nestled at the foot of impressive limestone cliffs lined with hanging vegetation that sometimes reaches all the way down to the lake's surface. The spectacular setting is enjoyed by many, and here you'll find that hotels may well outnumber lemons!

Riva del Garda★
11km/6.8mi NE from Limone sul Garda.
Located at the northernmost end of the lake, this resort town was already popular in antiquity. Its charming, storied streets are lined with shops, and countless bars and pubs come alive in the evening with crowds of boisterous revelers. Near the lakefront the town's Rocca (fortress) still conserves its original medieval towers. 3 km away, the **Parco Grotta Cascata Varone** provides visitors a chance to tour caves and waterfalls, and take relaxing walks through its botanical gardens (*open May–Aug 9am–7pm; Apr and Sep 9am–6pm; Mar and Oct 9am–5pm; rest of the year Sun, holidays and Christmas time 10am–5pm; €5.50; 0464 52 14 21; www.cascata-varone.com*).

Anyone visiting this corner of Lake Garda can choose from a wide range of sports activities: sailing and windsurfing on the lake, mountain biking and hiking in the mountains, plus trekking, paragliding, golf, fishing, horseback riding, canoeing and more. Activities are available for people of all ages and skill levels. Inquire with the local tourist office for further information.

Torbole
4km/2.5mi SE from Limone sul Garda.
Colored houses hug the bay of this pleasant resort town on the eastern bank of Lake Garda. Torbole is popular with windsurfing and sailing enthusiasts.

Malcesine★
14km/8.7mi SW from Torbole.
This attractive town stands on a promontory at the foot of Monte Baldo and is dominated by the crenellated outline of the **Castello Scaligero★** (*open Nov–Mar 11am–4pm; Apr–Oct 9.30am–7pm; €6; 045 657 03 33*), a 13C–14C fortress that once belonged to the Scalider family of Verona. Inside you'll find a small archeological and natural science museum, as well as memorabilia connected with the poet Goethe, who spent several years in Malcesine – including a spell as a prisoner while accused of espionage! The Venetian-style 15C **Palazzo dei Capitani** stands on the edge of the lake.
From the summit of **Monte Baldo** (accessible via cablecar) you can enjoy a splendid 🔺**panoramic view★★★** of the lake and the Brenta and Adamello massifs.

99

Take a ride on the cablecar.
€20 round trip. 045 74 00 206.
www.funiviedelbaldo.it.

Torri del Benaco
21km/13mi SW from Malcesine.
This attractive fishing village is
so popular during tourist season
that it can become difficult to find
your way through the crowds.
Numerous houses grouped
together around the remains of the
town's 14C castle contribute to the
location's particular charm.

Punta di San Vigilio★★
4km/2.5mi SW from Torri
del Benaco.
Though crowded and busy,
the Punta di San Vigilio forms
a charming tableau, capped by
the Venetian Villa Guarienti (16C,
not open to visitors). There is a
pleasant café overlooking a small
dock on the lakefront.

Garda★
3km/1.8mi E from Punta di
San Vigilio.
The lake is named after this
popular resort town, where you
can still see signs of a strong
Venetian influence. Both the
Palazzo dei Capitani and the
Palazzo Fregoso are 15C.
A path leads to the **Punta di San
Vigilio** (for further information
and maps inquire with the local
tourism office).

Bardolino★
3.5km/2.1mi SE from Garda.
This small town has given its name
to the famous red and rosé wines
cultivated here and available
in bars, cafés and restaurants
throughout the region. The historic
center is by the lakeside, where
you'll find a charming 11C church
and narrow streets lined with
inviting shops. In the evening
these streets fill up with people out
for a good time in one of the many
bars and nightclubs.
At the **Museo del Vino** you'll be
given a comprehensive overview
of the history of Bardolino wine
and its production throughout
the region, from past methods to
modern cultivation techniques.
(*Via Costabella 9; open Mid Mar–
Oct 9am–1pm and 2–7pm; 045
62 28 331; www.museodelvino.it,
www.zeni.it*).

Peschiera del Garda
14km/8.7mi S from Bardolino,
11km/6.8mi SW from Sirmione.
Set up over the mouth of the
Mincio, Peschiera has retained
its star-shaped fortifications and
encircling moat, originally built to
protect the town from Venetian,
then Napoleonic and Austrian
invasions. While it is pleasant to
take a walk along the canal, the
town is often overrun with tourists,
who are drawn to the large parks
established at the lake's southern
end (*see p132*).

LAKE ISEO ★

The southern reaches of the lake's western shore are industrial, while the landscape becomes more picturesque to the north. The prestigious Riva boats, wood-hulled motoryachts designed for freshwater navigation and popular with members of the jetset like Brigitte Bardot, Richard Burton and Aristotle Onassis, are built on the shores of this lake.

Iseo★

Iseo is a charming lakeside resort town with a lively promenade lined with inviting cafés and gelato shops. The Romanesque church of Sant'Andrea has retained its 13C bell tower.

Monte Isola★★

Boats leave from Iseo, Sulzano, Sale Marasino. Frequent connections. €3.60 round trip. 035 97 14 83. www.navigazionelagoiseo.it.
Crowned by the church of the Madonna della Ceriola, which provides a sweeping **panoramic view★★** of the lake and the Alps near Bergamo, Monte Isola is the largest lake island in Italy and a relatively unknown jewel. You can travel around the island on foot, by bus or by bicycle (available for rent in Carzano Peschiera). Its two main towns, and Carzano Peschiera in particular, are charming attractions where local fishermen still spend time drying their catch in the warm Italian sunlight. Take time to stroll through the countryside, crossing through olive groves and climbing up the Madonna della Ceriola for the view.

Pisogne★

This small port town has an attractive lakeside setting. The church of Santa Maria della Neve is adorned with 16C **frescoes★** by Romanino da Brescia.

Valcamonica

The Valcamonica follows the River Oglio as far as Lago d'Iseo. The main access road from Bergamo is the S 42. The valley, which stretches from Lovere to Edolo, and is linked to Valtellina by the **Passo di Gavia**, is relatively industrial at its lower reaches, but becomes more picturesque the higher you climb, dotted with castle ruins. A number of UNESCO World Heritage prehistoric and early **Roman rock carvings★★** (*Parco Nazionale delle Incisioni Rupestri di Naquane, access from Capo di Ponte; open Tue–Sun 8.30am–1.30pm; closed Mon; €4; 0364 42 140; www.parcoincisioni.capodiponte.beniculturali.it*) can be found over a 60km/37.3mi stretch of the valley. Eroded by alpine glaciers, the rocks of the Valcamonica have highly polished surfaces, making them perfect for figurative engravings. The carvings were created by tapping or scratching away at the stone, and are a testament to the daily life of the hunting people who lived here during the Palaeolithic era (c.8000–5000 BC).

> ### Seeing Lake Iseo by boat
> Tours of the lake's islands available in summer; 1hr 30min from Iseo, Sale Marasino; 1hr from Sulzano or Monte Isola. For information, contact **Navigazione Lago d'Iseo** (*035 97 14 83; www.navigazionelagoiseo.it*)

101

TRADE FAIRS AND EVENTS

From fashion to furniture, Milan hosts a number of internationally important fairs and conventions that enliven the city for a few days and can make an engaging side trip during your visit.

What's On?

To view a calendar of the ⚓ **international fairs** held in Milan's new Rho-Pero convention complex (*see p73*), or in **fieramilanocity** (🚇1 *Lotto-fieramilanocity or Amendola*) as well as other practical information on fairs and conventions: *toll free in Italy 800 82 00 29, or 02 49 971; www.fieramilano.it*. Here's a look at the main fairs and events held in Milan during the calendar year.

HOMI – Home Show

Salone Internazionale della Casa, late January and early September, www.homimilano.com
Furnishings, decor and interior design for homes, with particular attention paid to Italian style.

Bit – Tourism Exchange

Borsa Internazionale del Turismo, mid February, www.bit.fieramilano.it
Bit is Italy's most important industry event for tourism.

⚓ Fashion Weeks

Settimana della Moda, one week in February–March and one week in September–October, www.milan fashionweek.buzz. During fashion week all the world's foremost clothing designers hold fashion shows in the city, presenting their collections for next season.

TheMicam – ShoEvent

Mostra Internazionale della Calzatura, early February and
September, www.micamonline.com
A convention concentrating on footwear. Here you can take a look at next year's collections.

MiArt

Early April, www.miart.it
International modern and contemporary art fair.

Furniture Fair

Salone Internazionale del Mobile, mid April, www.cosmit.it. The world's most important furniture and domestic design event.

⚓ Design Week

FuoriSalone (literally "outside the Salone," held during the weeklong Salone del Mobile, www.fuorisalone.it
In some ways, design week draws more visitors than the fair itself. During the week, companies, museums, stores and other institutions organize shows and events dedicated to design in locations across the city.
Even the Milanese consider this one of the most vital and energetic weeks of the year, during which the city becomes the global epicenter of creativity for designers and visitors from all over the world.

Eicma – Motorcycle Exhibition

Esposizione Internazionale del Motociclo, mid November, www.eicma.it

THE NAVIGLI

The Naviglio Grande and the Naviglio Pavese provide tangible proof of the enormous waterworks designed in part by Leonardo da Vinci in the 16C that served as Milan's main transportation routes for centuries. This is a fascinating area of the city, where tradition, artisan shops, little street markets and antiques fairs enliven the streets by day, while crowded locales filled with young people energize its nights.

A Bit of History

Although it is not obvious today, Milan was once a waterfront city, connected to the rest of Italy via canals that, according to tradition, exceeded even those of Venice in overall length. For centuries these canals were the main transportation route for moving around the city. Most of these canals were filled and paved over during the 1930s. The Naviglio Grande was built in the 12C in order to defend Milan from Pavia, allied with Frederick I, Holy Roman Emperor. It was turned from a watery defense into a navigable channel, and used primarily to carry marble from Candoglia into the city to build the Duomo.

Although they have suffered from years of neglect, today the Navigli are experiencing a sort of renaissance thanks to various clean-up projects and a renewed interest in what were for centuries defining elements of Milanese life. Bicycling paths have been built alongside many Navigli, including one that flanks the Naviglio Martesana for over 21 kilometers, extending all the way to Trezzo sull'Adda.

🚣 Boat rides along Navigli

The simplest route, called the "Conche" itinerary (*see also p67; Fri–Sun; €12; 02 92 27 31 18 or 02 33 91 07 94; www.navigareinlombardia.it, www.naviglilombardi.it or ecomm.*

autostradale.it), travels along the Naviglio Grande and the Naviglio Pavese, giving visitors a chance to admire a suggestive 14C church complex, the bridge and washing basins of San Cristoforo, as well as look out over the Darsena, originally the merchant port for trade with Lake Maggiore.

You will also see the first of 14 locks, known as the "Conchetta," that made navigating these canals possible.

There are also shorter cruises available on different dates that often include culinary stopovers, giving people a chance to try some local specialties.

These often include a bus trip as well, for example bringing visitors out to romantic countryside towns like **Cassinetta di Lugagnano** and **Robecco sul Naviglio**, both famous for splendid villas lining the canals. (*Reservations required; 02 92 27 31 18; info@navigareinlombardia.it; www.naviglilombardi.it*).

Renovation of the Navigli

The major project for Expo 2015 will center on the Navigli: the plan is to "reopen" the canals with the creation of the Via d'Acqua-Parco Expo, a watercourse linking the two great parks located to the south and north of the city.

FOR KIDS

Fashionable and at times elegant to the point of appearing austere, Milan can feel a little adults-only. But don't let appearances deceive you. There are plenty of children in this city, and plenty of things to do with them. Here are a few options for the young and young at heart.

A bit of advice – For families with younger children, bear in mind that most restaurants have high chairs or seat-raisers and will bring them to the table if you ask. Public breastfeeding is not forbidden, but unusual and may be frowned upon. If you're bringing a baby carriage or stroller, make sure it has wide wheels and a rugged construction. Between uneven paving stones, high curbs and sunken tram lines navigating Milan with a kiddie carriage can become something of a challenge.

Milan by bus

Open-air bus tours like those offered by **City Sightseeing** (*www.city-sightseeing.com*) provide a chance to take in a large chunk of the city in a single day. When the sun is out, the open upper deck proves perfect for kids, who can sightsee and enjoy the city from a new perspective. The hop on, hop off format is also quite useful, since it allows families to leave the bus behind when they get tired of sitting or reach an area they want to explore on foot, then get back on another bus when they're ready to roll again. See also box p12.

Up to the top of the Duomo

While the prospect of looking at churches, arches and statuary can often make kids a little…less than enthusiastic, taking a trip up to the roof of the Duomo (*see p29*) will prove a worthwhile exception to the rule. Looking at gargoyles and gruesome faces carved in marble can be enjoyable in its own right, and the 360° views of the city available from atop the cathedral make the trip worthwhile on their own merits. If possible, make sure you visit on a cool, clear day (the day after a rainstorm is usually best). You'll be rewarded with clear views of the snow-capped Italian Alps in the distance.

Inter and Milan Museum

Even if there's no soccer game scheduled, the museum inside San Siro Stadium provides a healthy dose of soccer mania, exploring the glorious history of two of the most successful teams in Italy. If you take the **stadium tour** (*see p72*) your kids will get a chance to see private players' areas like the locker rooms, spa spaces and changing areas.

Tour Castello Sforzesco

Weather permitting, walking around the Sforzesco castle (*see p35*) can be fun for most kids. Make sure you visit the medieval weapons exhibit inside the guards room in the tower, which is guaranteed to elicit a few oohs and aahs.

Puppet shows

Carlo Colla and Sons is one of the most well-known marionette theater companies in the world, and has been performing marionette puppet shows for the public for almost three centuries. Although the performances are held in Italian, kids from all countries will enjoy the spectacle. Handcrafted puppets dance around onstage fighting, falling in love, dancing, laughing and singing during these long performances (1h 30 minutes/2 hours on average). Like the marionettes, the stage settings are built and painted by hand by the theater company, and enjoyable in their own right.

The theater-atelier in Via Montegani 35/1 (M2 *Abbiategrasso*), hosts a puppet show almost every Sunday at 4pm. This theater also plans a full year's calendar of events, bringing tales like *Pocahontas* and Shakespeare's *The Tempest* to life onstage (planned for the 2013 season). Some shows are performed at the **Piccolo Teatro Grassi**, in Via Rovello 2 (*see Entertainment*). To view an annual performance calendar, find out more about the theater or purchase tickets: *02 89 53 13 01; www.marionettecolla.org*.

Kid parks & playpens

Let's face it: sometimes there's no artwork, museum exhibit or monument that can satisfy a kid's basic desire for fun. If the day has rained on your parade, consider taking your kids to one of these special recreation centers. **Fun&Fun** (*Via Beroldo 2; M1/2 Loreto; 02 26 14 42 94; www. funefun.it*) have enormous netted kid parks that include tunnels, tubes, slides and more. There is a fixed fee for daily entrance, and a restaurant area inside if you'd like a bite to eat. You'll find Milanese

parents there, sitting and enjoying a coffee, a look of relief and relaxation on their faces.

MUBA

Opened in early 2014 at the Rotonda in Via Besana, MUBA (*Rotonda della Besana, via Enrico Besana 12; 02 43 98 04 02; www.muba.it*) is the first children's museum in Milan. It is a permanent center dedicated to cultural and artistic projects for the young, a place open to innovation that brings together the best of national and international culture, education, science and the arts to encourage creativity and creative thought. It includes many exhibitions and workshops.

⛲ The "hidden" park behind Villa Reale

Ostensibly forbidden for everyone except parents with children 12 and under, this little gem of a garden (*see also p46*) fills up with kids having fun on sunny days… And the parents seem to enjoy it too!

Toys

Just around the corner from *The Last Supper*, **Tofy Toys** (*Via Ruffini 9; M1 Conciliazione; www. tofytoys.it*) offers a selection of toys from all over the world. **La città del Sole** (*Via Orefici 13; M1 Duomo; www.cittadelsole.it*) is a toy shop where you can find toys from the past alongside ultra modern construction systems and kits for conducting physics experiments. **Torriani** (*Via Mercato 5; M1 Cairoli e M2 Lanza; www.labottegadelcarnevale.it*) is the kingdom of masks, costumes, wigs and trick gadgets. This is a historic Milanese store where everyday is Carnival.

ENTERTAINMENT

Milan enjoys a lively cultural and artistic scene, and is considered the epicenter of Italian theater and cabaret. The city hosts a number of musical events throughout the year, from classical music concerts to jazz, rock and pop, and many of the world's premiere musicians give concerts here. There are also many movie theaters to choose from.

What's Playing?

You can find ou out more about theaters, cinemas, concerts and other events in Milan by inquiring at the local **tourist offices** (*see p13*), or by visiting **www.turismo.milano.it**, or **www.visitamilano.it**.

Entertainment information for everything from movies to art exhibitions is published daily in the major newspapers as well, so if your Italian permits, you can browse the *Corriere della Sera* (visit **vivimilano. corriere.it**) or *La Repubblica*. Note that local culture pages are usually set apart at the center of the newspaper. You can also visit other websites dedicated to Milan's entertainment scene like **www.2night.it/milano/,** **www.milanodabere.it** and **www. milanotoday.it/notizie/**. For concerts featuring major international artists like Bruce Springsteen, Lady Gaga or U2, concert tickets are usually sold online at **www.ticketone.it**, **www. vivaticket.it** and **www.viagogo.it**. Please note that like major venues in any big city, tickets sell quite quickly and you'll need to plan ahead if you want to enjoy the show. In most areas of Milan, large posters announcing events are plastered on designated walls and billboards, so keep your eyes peeled.

Classical music and Opera

Milan boasts what is arguably the most famous operahouse in the world, La Scala, where some of the world's greatest musicians, directors and composers have presented their work to international audiences. Recent stars have included Maurizio Pollini, violinist Uto Ughi, Milanese conductor Claudio Abbado (who recently passed away) and conductors Daniel Barenboim and Riccardo Chailly, the ballet dancer Carla Fracci and international ballet star Roberto Bolle.

For information on opera programs and classical music concerts:

Teatro alla Scala – *Piazza della Scala (ticket offices in Via Filodrammatici 2 and Galleria del Sagrato in Piazza del Duomo).* Ⓜ 1/3 *Duomo or Tram 1. Information 02 72 00 37 44; Automatic Telephone Booking Service 02 86 07 75.* **www.teatroallascala.org**.

Rich and varied performance seasons are also held in the following locations:

Conservatorio Giuseppe Verdi – *Via Conservatorio 12.* Ⓜ 1 *San Babila. 02 76 21 10.* **www.consmilano.it**.

Auditorium di Milano – *Largo Gustav Mahler. Tram 3. 02 83 38 94 01/2/3.* **www.laverdi.org**.

Teatro Dal Verme – *Via San Giovanni sul Muro 2.* Ⓜ 1 *Cairoli. 02 87 905.* **www.dalverme.org**.

Please note that a number of churches in Milan also host interesting concerts (San Marco, San Maurizio, San Simpliciano).

Live music

Blue Note – *Via Pietro Borsieri 37. Tram 7 or* Ⓜ3 *Zara. 02 69 01 68 88. www.bluenotemilano.com*. This popular club is directly affiliated with the famous New York jazz club of the same name.

Le Scimmie – *Via Ascanio Sforza 49.* Ⓜ2 *Romolo. 02 39 81 10 39. www.scimmie.it.* Here you can enjoy live music and good food in an attractive canalside location.

Nord Est Caffè – *Via Borsieri 35. Tram 7 or* Ⓜ3 *Zara. 02 69 00 19 10.* Just around the corner from Blue Note, this locale is dedicated to jazz (year round on Thurs evenings at 9), as well as concerts during happy hour and Sunday brunch.

🎭 Theaters

Piccolo Teatro – *848 80 03 04 or 02 42 41 18 89 (from abroad). www.piccoloteatro.org.* Founded in 1947 by Paolo Grassi and Giorgio Strehler (1921-1997), this prestigious theater has three stages, all in the center of the city: **Teatro Strehler** (*Largo Greppi,* Ⓜ2 *Lanza*); **Teatro Studio** (*Via Rivoli 6,* Ⓜ2 *Lanza*); and **Teatro Grassi** (*Via Rovello 2,* Ⓜ1 *Cordusio*).

Teatro Carcano – *Corso di Porta Romana 63.* Ⓜ3 *Crocetta. 02 55 18 13 77. www.teatrocarcano.com.* This theater specializes in public readings and dance.

Teatro Franco Parenti – *Via Pier Lombardo 14.* Ⓜ3 *Porta Romana. 02 59 99 51. www.teatrofrancoparenti.com.* An interesting program of readings, dance and cultural encounters.

Teatro degli Arcimboldi – *Viale dell'Innovazione 20.* Ⓜ5 *Bicocca. Tram 7. 02 64 11 42 212 / 14. www.teatroarcimboldi.it.* Music performances, dance, classical and modern shows.

Teatro Nuovo – *Piazza San Babila.* Ⓜ1 *San Babila. 02 79 40 26. www.teatronuovo.it.* Music performances, shows and children's theatre.

Teatro Manzoni – *Via Manzoni 42.* Ⓜ3 *Montenapoleone. 02 76 36 901. www.teatromanzoni.it.* Comedies and classical theater.

Teatro Litta – *Corso Magenta 24.* Ⓜ1/2 *Cadorna. 02 86 45 45 45. www.teatrolitta.it.* Offering original, "non-conventional" performances.

Teatro Elfo Puccini – *Corso Buenos Aires 33.* Ⓜ1 *Lima. 02 00 66 06 06. www.elfo.org.* A contemporary art theater.

Teatro Leonardo da Vinci – *Via Ampère 1.* Ⓜ2 *Piola. 02 26 68 11 66. www.teatroleonardo.it.* Contemporary theater.

TeatroCinque – *Via Ascanio Sforza 37.* Ⓜ2 *Romolo. 02 58 11 45 35. www.teatrocinque.it.* Specializing in contemporary theater, music and children's performances.

Teatro San Babila – *Corso Venezia 2/A .* Ⓜ1 *San Babila. 02 79 80 10. www.teatrosanbabilamilano.it.* Plays and concerts.

Cinema

Several cinemas in Milan show **original language movies** (almost always in English) three nights a week: **Anteo** (*Via Milazzo 9;* Ⓜ2 *Moscova; 02 65 97 732; www.spaziocinema.info*) on Mondays, **Arcobaleno** (*Viale Tunisia 11;* Ⓜ3 *Repubblica; 02 29 40 60 54; www.cinenauta.it*) on Tuesdays and **Cinema Mexico** (*Via Savona 57;* Ⓜ2 *Porta Genova; 02 48 95 18 02; www.cinemamexico.it*) on Thursdays. You can visit, *www.mymovies.it* for an updated calendar of the films currently showing.

ENTERTAINMENT

FASHION AND DESIGN

Italy continues to influence global fashion, and Milan is its haute couture and design mecca. The city's biannual Fashion Weeks, during which new collections from all the world's most important clothing designers are presented, rank alongside those of Paris and New York in importance. If you're looking for an elegant outfit, there's no better place to find it than Milan's fashion district.

The Big Names

Today the big names in Italian fashion make a lot more than clothing, putting their signatures on perfumes, sunglasses, jewelry and even furniture.

Giorgio Armani, whose signature style is understated elegance, believes that clothes are made to be worn, not just seen. For quintessential Italian chic, an Armani suit lasts many seasons, and his Emporio Armani collection guarantees high quality clothing and accessories.

Laura Biagiotti is known for clean lines and elegant clothing. The Biagiotti name is particularly well-known for cashmere products.

King of 1960s haute couture, designer **Pierre Cardin** was born in Italy to French parents. He introduced geometric designs and experimented with unisex styles.

The designs of **Dolce & Gabbana** celebrate the female form. Renowned for their show-stopping eveningwear, the duo fashions daywear that is equally confident, with an emphasis on corseting, figure-sculpting pencil skirts and décolletage. The diffusion line, D&G, is good for well-cut jeans.

Luxury brand **Fendi** is best known for its leatherwork; for style kudos, look for bags, wallets and shoes with the classic Fendi logo.

Gucci has reigned for some as the must-have label for the fashion faithful. Its look is sexy, streetwise and expensive. A Gucci bag is a key investment: still considered shorthand for style in A-list circles.

The family-owned label **Missoni** is best known for sumptuous knitwear in colorful stripes. Its distinctive swimwear is popular with chic sunbathers on Mediterranean beaches.

The **Moschino** style has remained true to the ethos of the late designer. The Cheap and Chic line is always full of surprising designs, with bright colors and quirky detailing.

Miuccia **Prada** designs grown-up, stylish clothes fashioned from fine materials, which frequently dictate future fashion trends. Her understated bags and shoes are global bestsellers.

Trussardi favors simple lines and a focus on high-quality tailoring and finishing.

The designer **Valentino** recognized that women should cultivate their own style to enhance their self-confidence. His label's designs lean towards elegant and classical, many incorporating the famous "V" logo.

After her brother Gianni's murder in 1997, Donatella **Versace** has taken the family business to new heights. The Versace label is adored by rock and film stars, boasting a signature style that is glamorous and glitzy, with colorful prints, sequins, attitude and plenty of suntanned skin on show.

MUST DO

Design

Founded in 1912 on the shores of Lake Como, **Alessi** is Italy's premiere design company, producing objects that have become famous all over the world. Italian design truly took off in the 1950s. **Gio Ponti** (1891-1979) guided his design school Domus towards modernism. His Superleggera chair, designed for Cassina in 1955, earned him the coveted Golden Compass design award. **Gae Aulenti** (1927-2012), Carlo Mollino (1905-1973), Joe Colombo (1930-1971), Achille (1918-2002) and Pier Giacomo Castiglioni (1913-1968) also contributed to the vitality of their discipline. In 1976, Alessandro Guerriero (born in 1943) founded Studio Alchimia, which specialized in engaging, playful designs. Before joining Alchimia, **Ettore Sottsass** (1917-2007) created several products for Olivetti that would become icons, including his bright red portable typewriter, Valentine (1969). Sottsass left the studio in 1981 to form Alchimia Memphis and revive radical design. He produced eccentric furniture, ceramics and patterned fabrics that would play a decisive role in internationalizing postmodernism. Founded in Milan in 1949, the company **Kartell** specializes in manufacturing plastic products. Ten years later, another Milanese firm, Artemide, began creating furniture and lighting that would help cement Italian design's position at the forefront of global creativity.

Districts
Near Duomo
Furla B2 – *Corso Vittorio Emanuele II.* Ⓜ1/3 *Duomo.* *www. furla.com.* The Furla collections are characterized by superior quality,

clean lines, elegance, functionality and innovation. The company was founded in 1927 in Bologna.

Max Mara B2 – *Piazza del Liberty 4* Ⓜ1 *San Babila.* www.maxmara. com. A clothing design company distinguished by its signature casual style.

Prada B2 – *Galleria Vittorio Emanuele II.* Ⓜ1/3 *Duomo.* www.prada.com. Famous worldwide, Prada was founded in 1913 in this very shop in the Galleria. Opposite, it has recently (and partially) opened a new multifunctional store, with almost 5000 sq.m. dedicated to fashion and much more. Spaces for exhibitions, artistic events and a restaurant have been planned.

La Rinascente B2 – *Via Santa Radegonda 1.* Ⓜ1/3 *Duomo.* www.rinascente.it. This is the largest, most famous and exclusive department store in Milan. Here you'll find prêt-à-porter clothing from all the major clothing designers in the world, plus design objects for the house, gourmet foods and more. There is a café and restaurant on the top floor with beautiful views of the Duomo.

Tod's B2 – *Galleria Vittorio Emanuele II.* Ⓜ1/3 *Duomo.* www. tods.com. Tod's represents the best of Italian craftsmanship. Luxury brand of shoes and leather goods.

Brera and Corso Garibaldi
10 Corso Como off map (N) – *Corso Como 10.* Ⓜ2 *Garibaldi.* www.10corsocomo.com. This avant-garde, New York-style location includes an art gallery, library, restaurant, café and the store, which features all sorts of trendy items: eco products, fashion, design, jewelry, shoes and more.

🏬 Fashion District

Haute couture

Giorgio Armani B2 – *Via Montenapoleone 2.* Ⓜ3 *Montenapoleone.* *www.armani.com.*

Dolce&Gabbana B2 – *Via della Spiga 26 (women),* Ⓜ3 *Montenapoleone;* and *Corso Venezia 15 (men),* Ⓜ1 *San Babila.* *www.dolcegabbana.it.*

Krizia B2 – *Via della Spiga 23.* Ⓜ3 *Montenapoleone.* *www.krizia.net.*

Missoni B2 – *Via Montenapoleone 8.* Ⓜ3 *Montenapoleone.* *www.missoni.it.*

Trussardi A2 – *Piazza della Scala 5,* Ⓜ1/3 *Duomo; Via Sant'Andrea 5,* Ⓜ3 *Montenapoleone.* *www.trussardi.com.*

Versace B2 – *Via Montenapoleone 11.* Ⓜ3 *Montenapoleone.* *www.versace.com.*

Ermenegildo Zegna A2 – *Via Montenapoleone 27.* Ⓜ3 *Montenapoleone. www.zegna.com.*

Fashion and design
Alessi A2 – *Via Manzoni 14/16.* Ⓜ3 *Montenapoleone. www.alessi.com.* The company's flagship store, where houseware products designed by the biggest names in industrial design are displayed and sold.

DMagazine A2 – *Via Bigli 4.* Ⓜ3 *Montenapoleone. www. dmagazine.it.* This outlet store carries clothing from all the major fashion brands.

Driade A2 – *Via Manzoni 30.* Ⓜ3 *Montenapoleone. www. driade.com.* This beautiful store is considered a mecca of avant-garde Italian design.

Corso Venezia
Artemide off map – *Corso Monforte 19.* Ⓜ1 *San Babila. www.artemide.com.* The greatest names in architecture and design (De Lucchi, Magistretti, etc.) have worked for Artemide.

De Padova B2 – *Corso Venezia 14.* Ⓜ1 *San Babila. www.depadova.it.* This showroom has been featuring the best in Italian design (Castiglioni, Cerri, etc.) accessories and furniture for almost 60 years.

Corso Magenta and Sant'Ambrogio
Galleria Rossana Orlandi A2 – *Via Matteo Bandello 16.* Ⓜ1 *Conciliazione. www.rossana orlandi.com.* A former factory converted into an extremely trendy and eclectic space where you can find fashion and design products.

Around the Porta Romana and University
Danese A2 – *Piazza San Nazaro in Brolo 5.* Ⓜ3 *Missori. www.danese milano.com.* A reference point for lovers of design, featuring contemporary objects and famous pieces from all the big names in Italian industrial design.

Porta Nuova and Isola
Isola della Moda B1 – *Via Carmagnola 7.* Ⓜ2 *Garibaldi FS. www.isoladellamoda.net.* Located in a trendy, dynamic neighborhood, here you'll find shop-sharing workshops that bring together works from a range of interesting young designers.

Monica Castiglioni B1 – *Via Pastrengo 4.* Ⓜ2 *Garibaldi FS. www.monicacastiglioni.com.* The daughter of famous designer Achille Castiglioni designs marvelous jewelry, exhibited at MoMA New York and the Victoria and Albert Museum in London.

SHOPPING

While the famous designer clothing stores in Milan's vaunted fashion district need little or no introduction, shopping in this cosmopolitan city is hardly limited to Via Montenapoleone. You'll find competitive prices, quality Italian products and even the odd undiscovered gem on a web of busy commercial streets around the city.

🛍 Shopping streets

Via Dante (Ⓜ1 *Cordusio or Cairoli*, from Piazza Cairoli to Piazza Cordusio), and **Corso Vittorio Emanuele** (Ⓜ1/3 *Duomo or* Ⓜ1 *San Babila*, from Piazza Duomo to Piazza San Babila) are two main pedestrian streets where dozens of famous shops and stores can be found, including major global brands. Another important shopping street is **Via Torino** (Ⓜ1/3 *Duomo, tram 3*), starting from Piazza Duomo. Packed at all hours, the street is lined with various shoe and clothing shops, and makes a great route for window shopping. Prices are more affordable here than in Milan's trendier streets, and many everyday Milanese come here to shop. Visitors enamored of Italian style and ready to spend heavily to have it should make a beeline for streets like **Via Monte Napoleone**, **Via della Spiga** and **Via Sant'Andrea** (Ⓜ3 *Montenapoleone*). *See Fashion and Design for the addresses of major clothing designers.*

Corso Vercelli (Ⓜ1 *Conciliazione*), that runs between Piazzale Baracca and Piazza Piemonte, is a good mix of fashion, luxury and affordable prices. It's an elegant street from which you can also stop in and visit some of the local cultural attractions (*see Corso Magenta and Sant'Ambrogio*).

Corso Buenos Aires is a long commercial artery (with subway stops Ⓜ1 *Porta Venezia, Lima and Loreto*), that can boast just about everything under the sun. **Corso Genova** (Ⓜ2 *Sant'Ambrogio, tram 2 or 14*) has conserved the look and feel of an Italian street from several decades ago, with all sorts of different stores and a concentration of fashion shops.

Department stores
Near Duomo

La Rinascente B2 – *Via Santa Radegonda 1. www.rinascente.it. See Fashion and Design.*

Excelsior B2– *Galleria del Corso 4.* Ⓜ1/3 *Duomo. www.excelsior milano.com.* Excelsior is a large store-boutique-supermarket for luxury goods that unites fashion, food and design over 7 floors.

Fashion District

Brian&Barry Building B2 – *Piazza San Babila.* Ⓜ1 *San Babila. www. thebrianebarrybuilding.it.* This 6000 sq.m. megastore covers 12 floors. Food (lots of it), recreations, fashion, cosmetics, design and jewelry.

Around the Porta Romana and University

Coin B1 – *Piazza 5 Giornate 1/A. Tram 27. www.coin.it.* This large department store features mainly Italian products. Ristorante Globe (*see Restaurants*). Two other Coin department stores can be found in: *Piazza Cantore 12* (Ⓜ2

Sant'Agostino); and *Corso Vercelli 30–32* (Ⓜ1 *Pagano*).

Brera and Corso Garibaldi
Eataly Milano Smeraldo – *Piazza XXV Aprile 10. www.eataly.it See Markets and Gourmet shops.*

Districts
Near Duomo
Vergelio B2 – *Corso Vittorio Emanuele 10 or Via Unione 2, corner of Via Torino.* Ⓜ1/3 *Duomo. www.vergelio.it.* The best in Italian footwear, including all the major Italian brands. Additional stores in: *Via Vitruvio 3* (Ⓜ1 *Lima*); *Corso Vercelli 2* (Ⓜ1 *Conciliazione*); *Corso Buenos Aires 9* (Ⓜ1 *Porta Venezia*).
Gio Moretti – *Via della Spiga 4. 02 7600 318. www.giomoretti.com.* A boutique of 1300 sqm with women's and men's collections by talented creators.
Marinella Cravatte B2 – *Via Santa Maria alla Porta 5.* Ⓜ1 *Cordusio. www.marinellanapoli.it.* The Milanese location of the country's most famous tie-maker. Founded in Naples in 1914, the company's clients have included Luchino Visconti, J. F. Kennedy and Bil Clinton.

Brera and Corso Garibaldi
ASAP – *Corso Garibaldi 104.* Ⓜ2 *Moscova. www.asaplab.it.* As Sustainable As Possible: a store that focuses on ethical and sustainable consumption, offering clothing and fabrics made with recovered, 100% natural fibers and leather goods tanned with vegetable tannins.
Cavalli e Nastri – *Via Brera 2.* Ⓜ2 *Lanza. www.cavallienastri.com.* A lovely boutique in the heart of Brera that features dresses, shoes, bags and vintage jewelry. It has two other boutiques at *Via Gian Giacomo Mora 3 and 12* (Ⓜ2 Sant'Ambrogio).
Alfonso Garlando – *Via Madonnina 1.* Ⓜ2 *Lanza. www. alfonsogarlando.it.* For over 30 years this shop has been producing footwear in an infinite range of styles. An essential stop for any bride looking for the right shoe.
La vetrina di Beryl – *Via Statuto 4.* Ⓜ2 *Moscova.* Do you collect shoes? Founded by Angelo Beryl and his daughter Barbara, this shop offers bizarre, colorful and original models.
Profumo – *Via Brera 6.* Ⓜ2 *Lanza. www.profumomilano.com.* For 30 years Profumo has offered the most exclusive and refined perfumes and scents designed by the greatest creators of fragrances here in Via Brera.
Spelta – xx. *Via Solferino 1.* Ⓜ2 *Lanza. www.speltamilano.it.* A reference point in Milan for ballet flats: colored, comfortable and fashionable. All handmade. Additional store in *Via Belfiore 7* (Ⓜ1 *Pagano*).

Fashion District
Borsalino B2 – *Galleria Vittorio Emanuele II.* Ⓜ 1/3 *Duomo. www.borsalino.com.* One of the most famous brands in the world, founded in 1857, and known in particular for the felt hat known universally as a "borsalino". Its many styles and models are all made by hand and are distinguished by their materials and the care expended on the details. Another Borsalino store can be found at: *Via Sant'Andrea 5.* Ⓜ1 *San Babila or* Ⓜ3 *Montenapoleone.*

Frette A2 – *Via Montenapoleone 21.* Ⓜ3 *Montenapoleone. www.frette.com.* Founded in 1860, this store offers elegant and and refined household linens.

DoDo B2 – *Corso Matteotti 9.* Ⓜ1 *San Babila. www.dodo.it.* Each gold DoDo animal charm comes accompanied with a special saying that clients use to communicate messages of love, friendship, personal feelings and more.The flagship boutique in Corso Matteotti was designed by archistar Paola Navone. Additional sales points in: *Corso Genova 12 (tram 2 or 14); La Rinascente.*

Mortarotti – B1. *Via Manzoni 14.* Ⓜ3 *Montenapoleone. www. mortarotti.com.* Long-established shop known around the world for its footwear. Two other Mortarotti stores can be found at: *Corso Magenta 29* (Ⓜ1 *Cadorna*); and *Via Belfiore 6* (Ⓜ1 *Pagano*).

Near Corso Venezia

Bianco Latte A/B1 – *Via Turati 30.* Ⓜ3 *Turati. www.biancolatte.it.* Literally "Milk White," this gelateria also features a large store where you can find things for the home, coffee table books, cakes, teas, coffees, marmelades and an assortment of chocolates.

Corso Magenta and Sant'Ambrogio

Bardelli B1 – *Corso Magenta 13.* Ⓜ1/2 *Cadorna. www.mbardelli. com.* Housed in a 19C palazzo, Bardelli has offered elegant men's and women's garments, accessories and footwear for generations.

Pellini B1 – *Corso Magenta 11.* Ⓜ1/2 *Cadorna. www.pellini.it.* Jewels made from resin, crystal, glass, copper, brass and semi-precious stones treated with unmistakable flair. Designer jewelry for three generations. Two other stores at: *Via Manzoni 20 (*Ⓜ3 *Montenapoleone); and Via Morigi 9* (Ⓜ1/2 *Cadorna*).

Sacchi – *Corso Magenta 15/A.* Ⓜ1/2 *Cadorna.* For lovers of luxury gloves, Sacchi has produced exclusively handmade Italian gloves since 1933.

Near Sant'Ambrogio

Kitchen B2 – *Via De' Amicis 45.* Ⓜ2 *Sant'Ambrogio. www.kitchen web.it.* Not far from Corso Genova, this store specializes in all sorts of kitchenware and utensils, and regularly offers cooking classes.

Porta Ticinese and Navigli

Frip B1 – *Corso di Porta Ticinese 16.* Ⓜ2 *Sant'Ambrogio.* The perfect stop for trendy urbanwear, including niche products from as far away as Scandinavia and England. Part of the store is devoted to CDs and vinyl records.

Biffi B1 – *Corso Genova 5.* Ⓜ2 *Sant'Ambrogio. www.biffi.com.* A reference point for fashion-makers and fashion-lovers. The boutique in Corso di Porta Genova has been renovated by Gae Aulenti. Clothes designed by the most famous Italian and foreign names. Corso Genova 6, women and men contemporary fashion and luxury; corso Genova 5, men sportswear.

Marisa Tassy B1 – *Via Molino delle Armi 45. www.marizatassy.it.* Mariza Tassy is a "walk-in wardrobe" to match any woman's desire. An undisputed favorite of the affluent Milanese in search of elegance and good taste.

MARKETS AND GOURMET SHOPS

Even if you're not shopping for anything special, street markets are a perfect opportunity to wander around and enjoy everyday Italian life. Gourmet food shops provide a range of local specialties to sample while you're here, or to tuck in the suitcase and put on the table back home.

🛍 Markets

Almost every neighborhood in Milan has its own street market at least one day a week. Here's a look at some of the most characteristic…

Brera and Corso Garibaldi

Market in Via San Marco – *Via San Marco.* Ⓜ2 *Moscova. Mon and Thu 8.30am–1pm*. This small street market specializes in high quality brand name clothing, collected from unsold merchandise from previous seasons. Prices are competitive, though not cheap.

Near Sant'Ambrogio

Market in Viale Papiniano A2 – *Viale Papiniano.* Ⓜ2 *Sant'Agostino. Tue 8.30am–1pm and Sat 8.30am–5.30pm*. A colorful and somewhat chaotic market where the Milanese come mainly to buy fruit and vegetables. You'll also find clothing and housewares.

Porta Nuova and Isola

🛍 **Market in Via Fauché** A1 – *Via Fauché. Tram 1. Tue 8.30am–1pm and Sat 8.30am–5.30pm*. This market is extremely popular with Milanese women, who flock to this street parallel to Corso Sempione in droves. A sharp eye will help you find famous designer clothing sold for a song. Stalls also sell vintage clothing, scarves and fashion accessories of all kinds. There are even a few food stands.

Porta Ticinese and Navigli

Along the Naviglio Grande, in addition to the famous antiques market (*see below*), every year this neighborhood hosts a special flower fair, the **mostra dei fiori** (Apr) and the art exhibition **Arte sul Naviglio Grande** (May). *For more information, www. navigliogrande.mi.it.*

Mercatone antiquario dei Navigli A/B1 – *Along the Naviglio Grande.* Ⓜ2 *Porta Genova. The last Sunday of every month.* A wonderful place for a walk, even if you've got no room in your suitcase for an 18C chest of drawers.

Fiera di Senigallia A1 – *Around the Porta Genova and neighboring streets.* Ⓜ2 *Porta Genova. Sat 8am–6pm.* This historical flea market, a longstanding tradition in the Navigli neighborhood, is loaded with antiques, artisan handiwork and clothing.

Mercati agricoli e artigianali off map – *Via San Vittore 49.* Ⓜ2 *Sant'Ambrogio e* Ⓜ1 *Conciliazione. www.lacordata.it.* Open every Thu afternoon, this market offers fresh farm products and creative handcrafts. Stalls with cheeses, cold meats, seasonable vegetables and fruit, quality wines and oil, bread, eggs, fabrics, clothes, accessories, jewelry, furnishings, bags, and designer lamps and candles.

Mercato Agricolo dei Navigli off map – *Alzaia Naviglio Grande 116.* Ⓜ2 *Porta Genova. www.mercato-agricolo-navigli.it. Tue, Thu and Sat.* Seasonal products direct from the producer and local specialties.

Gourmet shops

It's hard to walk a hundred meters in Milan without encountering at least one gourmet food shop, traditionally called "gastronomia," but also "salumeria" or "drogheria." These little stores are the perfect place to purchase specialty foods to share at the table with friends. Today many have their own vacuum-sealing machines, so if you want something special to take back home be sure to ask if you can have it put "sotto vuoto."

Duomo and Castello Sforzesco

Galleria del Gusto di Savini B2 – *Galleria Vittorio Emanuele II.* Ⓜ1/3 *Duomo. www.savinimilano.it. See Cafés, pasticcerie and Gelaterie*

Brera and Corso Garibaldi

Antico Pastificio Moscova – *Via della Moscova 27.* Ⓜ2 *Moscova.* Famous Milanese store opened in 1924 that today offers a range of "household" dishes prepared with fresh seasonal ingredients.
Rossi e Grassi – *Via Solferino 12 (on the corner of Via Ancona).* Ⓜ2 *Moscova. www.rg.mi.it.* Considered one of the best in Milan, the range of products on

offer was created more than 40 years ago and is synonymous with high quality ingredients and skillful preparation. There is another store at *Via Ponte Vetero 4. (*Ⓜ1 *Cairoli).*
Centro botanico – *Piazza San Marco 1.* Ⓜ2 *Lanza. See Porta Ticinese and Navigli, p116.*
Strada & Zucca – *Piazza del Carmine 1.* Ⓜ2 *Lanza. www.stradaezucca.it.* Originally a simple salumeria, this small shop on the corner of Via Mercato has become a well-stocked gastronomia, offering a wide range of specialty Italian foods including cheeses, sauces, fresh pasta and more. Gourmet lunches available daily.

Fashion District

Brian&Barry Building B2 – *Piazza San Babila.* Ⓜ1 *San Babila. www.thebrianebarrybuilding.it. See Shopping.*
Rosticceria Leoni B2 – *Corso Venezia, 7/1.* Ⓜ1 *San Babila.* Come here for a real roast chicken, cooked gently on the spit over a fire.

Near Corso Venezia

Linos's Coffee B2 – *Corso Venezia 37.* Ⓜ1 *Palestro. www.linoscoffee.com.* There are 5 blends, available in rotation. Standard packages are 250g and can be sold as beans or ground and vacuum-packed.
Gastronomia de Ponti off map – *Via Plinio 17.* Ⓜ1 *Lima. www.drogheriadeponti.it.* A historic wine shop and grocery store dating from 1934 that offers an interesting choice of labels and specially selected products.

Gastronomia Palazzi off map – *Via Plinio 9.* Ⓜ1 *Lima.* A historic take-away. Pizza slices (wood-oven), chicken on a spit, meatballs and veggie-balls!

Near Corso Magenta

Drogheria Soana B1 – *Corso Magenta 1.* Ⓜ1 *Cairoli.* www.drogheriasoana.net. A traditional store that has remained popular with the Milanese for decades. Note the artistically arranged shop windows, filled with marmelades, bottles of wine, teas, etc.

La Fungheria off map (A1) – *Via Marghera 14.* Ⓜ1 *Wagner.* www.lafungheria.com. Literally "mushroomeria," here you'll find the highest quality Italian mushrooms, as well as truffles, honey, olives, saffron and more. A great place to buy gifts for friends back home. There is another store at *Viale Abruzzi 93.* Ⓜ1 *Loreto.*

Rosticceria Galli off map (A1) – *Corso Vercelli 8.* Ⓜ1 *Pagano.* www.rosticceriagalli.it. What this rosticceria is famous for serving the Milanese for more than 60 years are spit-roasts (chicken, guinea-fowl, pheasant, duck, etc.). Excellent starters too.

Near Via Torino

🍴 **Peck** B2 – *Via Spadari 7/9.* Ⓜ1/3 *Duomo.* www.peck.it. This is the holy temple of Milanese gastronomy. Everything is beautiful, everything is delicious… and everything is expensive. *See also Restaurants.*

Porta Ticinese and Navigli

La Baita del Formaggio A1 – *Via Foppa 5.* Ⓜ2 *Sant'Agostino.* www.labaitadelformaggio.it. A haven for traditional Italian cheeses and foodstuffs that are often impossible to find anywhere else in the city. 300 different kinds of cheeses, salamis and local foods like Mantuan salami, marmelades, honey, fresh pasta, mostarda and more. The store has expanded to offer a culinary happy hour as well.

Centro botanico B1 – *Via Cesare Correnti 10.* Ⓜ1 *Sant'Ambrogio.* www.centrobotanico.it. A small oasis of peace in the city center that offers almost 8000 organic and biodynamic products to support an eco-sustainable lifestyle. Clothing, cosmetics, toys, books, etc. A welcoming Biobar inside offers organic and macrobiotic food.

Porta Nuova and Isola

Baita del Formaggio – *Via Paolo Sarpi 46.* Ⓜ2 *Moscova.* This shop in the heart of Chinatown is bursting with cheeses of all types, including rare Italian varieties. Plus a good choice of cold meats.

Bio c' Bon – *Corso Porta Nuova 52.* Ⓜ2 *Moscova.* Minimalist steel shelves packed with hundreds of organic products from Italy and elsewhere in Europe. There's a bit of everything.

Eataly Milano Smeraldo – *Piazza XXV Aprile 10.* Ⓜ2 *Moscova.* www.eataly.it. Eataly is the "largest market in the world" for top quality food and drink. It contains many small restaurants where you can choose between a perfectly cooked pasta dish, a fried dish cooked before your eyes, fresh mozzarella, etc.

UNUSUAL

Feeling a bit like a trapped tourist? Take a side trip to check out one or more of these unusual destinations, shops that are a living, breathing part of Milan's urban fabric. You won't find other tourists, but you might find something surprising and special to take home with you…

B Movies

Bloodbuster – *Via Panfilo Castaldi 21. 02 29 40 43 04.* Ⓜ1 *Porta Venezia. www. bloodbuster.com.* The shelves in Bloodbuster are chock full of DVDs and VHS tapes from B to Z. You won't find last summer's big blockbuster, but a vast selection of cult films that have helped define the B movie genre: horror (for example Mario Bava); 1970s police flicks, soft porn, trash cinema… As well as books, magazines, movie posters, soundtracks, t-shirts and gadgets.

Comic books

Supergulp – *Ripa di Porta Ticinese 51. 02 83 72 216.* Ⓜ2 *Porta Genova. www.supergulp.net.* A must for comic book fans, Supergulp also sells a wide range of memorabilia connected with comics.

La Borsa del Fumetto – *Via Lecco 16. 02 29 51 38 83.* Ⓜ1 *Porta Venezia. www.borsadelfumetto. com.* One of the oldest and most well-stocked comic book stores in the city. Sells numerous copies in different languages.

Costumes and masks

Buba – *Via Spallanzani 6.* Ⓜ1 *Porta Venezia. 02 29 40 96 34.* Founded in 1974, Buba has become a point of reference for Milan's entertainment industry. The store's shelves are stocked with all sorts of wild costume items, from devil masks to angel wings and everything in between, including hats, shoes, lingerie and more. Well worth a visit even if Halloween is months away!

Home décor

High Tech – *Piazza XXV Aprile 12.* Ⓜ2 *Moscova. www.high-tech milano.com.* Arguably the most popular houseware and housefurnishing store in the city, High Tech is worth a visit just to snoop around. The store develops over countless levels and into dozens of small and large rooms, each filled with designer items for the house. You'll find it tough to walk away empty-handed!

Vintage glasses

Foto Veneta Ottica – *Via Torino 57. 02 80 55 735.* Ⓜ3 *Missori. www. fotovenetaottica.com.* One optician's personal collection of sunglasses has evolved over almost a century into a store stuffed with vintage eyewear. Whether you're looking for John Lennon's famous wire frames or a pair of "butterfly" glasses from the 1950s, this shop is well worth a stop.

SPAS

Treatments at hammams, spas and baths are now common gift ideas, not just pleasant places to relax at lunchtime or hold a business conference. There are a number in Milan and the lake areas. Some hotels reserve spa services exclusively for hotel guests, while others accept outside visitors.

Milan

Hotel Bulgari – *Via Privata Fratelli Gabba 7/b.* Ⓜ3 *Montenapoleone. 02 80 58 05 200. www.bulgari hotels.com.* The spa in this hotel run by the jewelry house is the ultimate in luxury. All wellbeing rituals take place in a lavish interior of mosaics and emerald-glazed panels.

Hammam della Rosa – *Viale Abruzzi 15.* Ⓜ1 *Lima. 02 29 41 16 53. www.hammamdellarosa.com.* A traditional Middle Eastern hammam with a literary café.

QC TermeMilano – *Piazzale Medaglie d'Oro 2 on the corner of Via Filippetti.* Ⓜ3 *Porta Romana. 02 55 19 93 67. www.termemilano. com.* If you like the famous spa in Bormio (196 km northeast of Milan), you will enjoy your experience in this Art Deco building.

SPA Milano Centro – *Corso Matteotti 4-6; co Hotel Boscolo Milano. 02 77 67 96 50. milano. boscolohotels.com/spa-e-benessere/.* A temple of wellbeing, this is the largest spa in the city: 600 sq.m., walls with kaleidoscopic spheres, a waterfall, a sauna, a Turkish bath, and original treatments.

Lake Maggiore

The Lake Maggiore area is famousfor its thermal baths, in particular those near Domodossola, northwest of the lake, in the villages of **Bognanco**, **Crodo** and especially **Premia**, where there is a very modern spa.

Premia Terme – *Cadarese a Premia, 68 km/42.2mi NW from Stresa. 0324 61 72 10. www.premiaterme.com.*

Lake Como

Monticello Spa&Fit – *Via San Michele 16/D, Cortenuova, 41 km NE from Milan. 039 92 30 51. www.monticellospa.it.* Wellbeing center with saunas, a medical spa and thermal baths.

Ti Sana Spa – **1711 Contrada Resort** – *Via Fontana 5, Arlate, 41 km NE from Milan. 039 99 20 979. www.1711.it.* Salt baths, saunas, sensorial showers, hydrotherapy and aromatherapy.

Lake Garda

The **Thermal Baths** at **Sirmione** are state-of-the-art for medical treatments. The thermal water feeds the **Virgilio** (*Piazza Virgilio 1*) and **Catullo** (*Piazza Don Piatti 1*) facilities and the **Aquaria** (*030 9904923; www. termedisirmione.com*) thermal wellness center, which offers relaxation and beauty treatment packages. You'll find the **Parco Termale del Garda** (*045 75 90 988; www.villadeicedri.it*) near **Colà di Lazise**.

CAFÉS, PASTICCERIE AND GELATERIE

Quick and delicious, the city's countless cafés, pastry stores and gelato shops provide perfect sustenance for visitors on the move, from early morning pastries to late evening ice cream. You can sit down at a table for a quick snack, or take your order standing up as many Italians do. Either way the wide variety of foods offered in these locales is sure to set your tastebuds tingling.

Cafés

Italians like to joke that they have more kinds of coffee drinks than they do local dialects. If you're of a mind to move beyond the classic **espresso** and **cappuccino**, here are a few of the more popular coffee drinks you can order. A **marocchino** is essentially a streamlined cappuccino (same foamy milk, cocoa powder and espresso coffee, only less of each), and often comes with a squirt of chocolate or hazelnut sauce. Order a "**caffelatte**" and you'll be served a warm glass of milk with some coffee added, while requesting a "**caffè macchiato**" will provide you with a small glass of espresso and just a touch of foamy warmed milk. Most bars will provide shakers filled with cocoa powder and powdered cinnamon to add to your drink as you see fit. If you'd like a bit of local breakfast, try the omnipresent **brioche**, a simple, flaky pastry that comes either plain or with a range of different marmelade or cream fillings. The most common are apricot, pastry cream and chocolate.

Pasticcerie

Cream puffs, canolis, chocolates, tarts, pies, cakes and more stretch out by the dozens behind curved glass display cases in pastry shops across the city. Here the best advice is none at all: let your taste buds do the exploring. If you visit the city around international holidays like Christmas or Easter, be sure to ask the pastry chef if there are any special seasonal treats. That way you'll discover some of the particular dessert specialties that make an appearance only at certain times of the year, like the **panettone**, a rich, sweet bread filled with candied fruit, nuts or chocolate chips that is available around Christmas.

Gelaterie

For fans of this smooth, sweet and flavorful ice cream it's never too cold for a cupful. You'll find gelateria shops open across the city year-round. There's always a small dish full of colorful plastic spoons on the countertop, and shop clerks will let you try a spoonful of any flavor you'd like before ordering. Cups and cones usually come in three sizes, ranging from two to four different flavors. Keep an eye out for special "artisan" flavors available in many shops, for example basil, caramel and salt, pinolo (pine nut) or parmigiano cheese. Don't be afraid to experiment!

Duomo and Castello Sforzesco

See map p30.

Near Duomo

Panarello B2 – *See Pinacoteca Ambrosiana and Via Torino.*

Taveggia – *See Around the Porta Romana and University.*

Near Piazza della Scala

Café Trussardi B2 – *Piazza della Scala 5.* Ⓜ1/3 *Duomo. www.cafe trussardi.com. See Restaurants.*

Gelateria Grom B2 – *Via Santa Margherita 16.* Ⓜ1/3 *Duomo. www.grom.it.* If you ask a Milanese for the name of the best gelato shop in the city, you will probably be given the name of a historic establishment that he or she has been visiting since childhood, rather than Grom, a successful chain begun in 2003. However, you can be sure that any one of the various Grom branches around the city will serve you a top quality gelato made with the best natural ingredients. Try their fanciful "flavor of the month," often a delightful surprise. Other Grom addresses: *Via Alberto da Giussano 1,* Ⓜ1 *Conciliazione; Corso di Porta Ticinese 51, tram 3; Corso Buenos Aires 13,* Ⓜ1 *Porta Venezia; Corso XXII Marzo 5, tram 27; Piazza Argentina,* Ⓜ1/2 *Loreto. Piazza Gae Aulenti,* Ⓜ 2 *Porta Garibaldi.*

Savini B2 – *Galleria Vittorio Emanuele II.* Ⓜ1/3 *Duomo. www.savinimilano.it* This is an obligatory stop for whoever wants a "luxury" pause in Milan's own drawing-room, the Galleria. Cream puffs, pralines and petits-fours are exhibited like jewels. Don't miss the 500 top quality products downstairs typical of Italian gastronomic traditions.

Near Parco Sempione

Triennale DesignCafé A1 – *Viale Emilio Alemagna 6.* Ⓜ1/2 *Cadorna. www.triennale.org.* This café is often used as a meeting place by lovers of Italian design and international visitors to the Triennale. Choose one of the many different seats donated by leading furniture companies and settle at one of the round tables. Or wander around the mostly white spaces and admire the small temporary art exhibitions, looking out through the large windows onto Parco Sempione. Outside in the park, children can play in one of several playground areas, and if you feel like exploring, you can walk on to one of the other small bars located directly inside the park area, where you can enjoy a cocktail outdoors during the summer months.

Brera and Corso Garibaldi

See map p39.

El beverin B1 – *Via Brera 29.* Ⓜ2 *Lanza. www.elbeverin.it.* A pleasant place to take a coffee and eat fragrant croissants, puff pastries, Sacher torte or petits-fours. Also good for a quick lunch.

10 Corso Como off map (N) – *Corso Como 10.* Ⓜ2 *Garibaldi FS. www.10corsocomo.com.* Much more than a café, 10 Corso Como includes an avant-garde art gallery, bookshop, restaurant, café, 3Rooms Hotel, and a shop filled to the ceiling with exclusive articles ranging from clothes to perfumes. It is a very cosmopolitan space suggestive of New York but presented with the creative design only Milan can produce. You can be sure that, as you sip a drink in the splendid garden café, surrounded by a conservatory of lush perennial plants and seasonal flowers, you are in one of the most fashionable places in Milan.

Bookshop e caffetteria degli Atellani – *Via della Moscova 28.* Ⓜ2 *Moscova. www.atellani.it.* Next to the Mediateca di Santa Teresa, the digital section of the Biblioteca Braidense, there is a cubic glass building unsurprisingly known as The Cube. Inside, a café looks onto a lush garden where you can order Italian wines to sip with a simple dish, sandwich or salad. In the evening the bar-bistro stays open for aperitifs. A small bookshop that specializes in the film world is ideal for cinema lovers.

🍸 **Bar Jamaica** B1 – *Via Brera 32.* Ⓜ2 *Lanza. www.jamaicabar.it.* The Jamaica is one of those bars with a story to tell. Opened in June 1921, between World War II and the 1960s it became a hang-out for an extraordinary generation of artists, writers and photographers, such as Piero Manzoni and Lucio Fontana, many of whose work can be seen in the Museo del Novecento. Although that period is over and, for some, unrepeatable, the Jamaica still exudes the atmosphere of or nostalgia for that cultural vitality. It is certainly an attractive place to have breakfast, and meals are available at all hours.

Radetzky Café off map – *Corso Garibaldi 105.* Ⓜ2 *Moscova. radetzkycafe.com.* A Milan classic in the Mitteleuropa style with a relaxed and informal atmosphere. It serves croissants, cakes, brunch and lunch at all hours, as well as aperitifs.

Fashion district and Corso Venezia

See map p45.

Fashion district

Bastianello off map (B1) – *Via Borgogna 5.* Ⓜ1 *San Babila. www. bastianello.com.* A pasticceria that specializes in fruit-flavoured jellies and sugared almonds. Excellent croissants and ice cream.

Bianco Latte A/B1 – *Via Turati 30.* Ⓜ3 *Turati. www.biancolatte.it. See Shopping.*

Pasticceria Cova B2 – *Via Monte Napoleone 8.* Ⓜ3 *Montenapoleone o* Ⓜ1 *San Babila. www.pasticceriacova.it.* Founded in 1817, Cova has existed in the center of Milan for almost two centuries. It was at one time the center for the patriots of the Risorgimento but today has switched from politics to music, becoming a meeting place for regulars who attend performances at La Scala. The café is great and the patisserie more than refined, offering cakes that look like works of art.

Sant Ambroeus A1– *Corso Matteotti 7. www.santambroeus milano.it.* A vast range of croissants starts the day in the best possible fashion in this historic coffee and cake shop named after the patron saint of Milan (Sant Ambroeus in the Milanese dialect). Pastries, pralines, decorated cakes and traditional Milanese baking recipes perk up the coffee, tea or chocolate break, but here you can also get a quick lunch or aperitif with tramezzini, panini or other snacks.

Near Corso Venezia

Caffè Ambrosiano – *Corso Buenos Aires 20.* Ⓜ1 *Porta Venezia.* An old coffee shop where you can taste one of the best coffee blends in Milan. Vintage atmosphere.

Gelato Giusto – *Via San Gregorio 17. Ⓜ1 Porta Venezia. www.gelato giusto.it.* This small ice creamery was created by Vittoria, who studied at the "Cordon Bleu" French pastry academy in London. She produces a top product with the best raw ingredients, scrupulous respect for their treatment, imagination in their combinations and a passion for quality.

Viel – *Corso Buenos Aires 15. Ⓜ1 Porta Venezia. www.viel-milano.com.* The Viel brothers moved to Milan from the Veneto around 1940, where they wandered the city and schools with small carts selling roasted chestnuts in winter and gelato in the summer. Today a chain of cafés bears their name and this one on Corso Buenos Aires is a favorite with students and famous for its shakes.

Corso Magenta and Sant'Ambrogio

See map p50.

Pasticceria Biffi A1– *Corso Magenta 87. Ⓜ1 Conciliazione. www.biffipasticceria.it.* Standing opposite the beautiful 1905 Casa Laugier built in Art Nouveau style, this patisserie on the corner with Piazzale Baracca is even older, having first opened for business in 1847. Enjoy the cakes and pastries at the tables with a cup of tea or hot chocolate. This is one of the places that proudly produces its own typically Milanese *panettone*.

Café at La Feltrinelli Libri e Musica off map (A1) – *Piazza Piemonte 2. Ⓜ1 Wagner.* At the end of Corso Vercelli, one of Milan's most important shopping streets, you can take a break in the three-story Feltrinelli bookshop, one of the most attractive and luminous in Milan. The café on the ground floor sells coffee, croissants, muffins, panini and soft drinks. The spacious interior and the coming and going of people among the racks of books, CDs and DVDs creates a relaxing cultural atmosphere. And in summer the powerful air-conditioner makes it an excellent refuge from the sultry heat.

Pasticceria Conca – *Via Carducci 11 corner Corso Magenta. Ⓜ1/2 Cadorna.* Here you will find traditional products such as panettone, pan mejno, cream puffs filled with zabaione, cream, pistachio or coffee, and a wide selection of pastries. Also a range of jams and marinated products supplied by approved manufacturers.

Fru Eat Gelateria A1 – *Piazzale Baracca 1. Ⓜ1 Conciliazione.* This bottle-green kiosk in the center of Piazzale Baracca blends in with the trees. It specializes in fruits of all kinds, with excellent shakes made with exotic fruits like mango and papaya. It also has a good choice of ice-creams, whether fruit flavored or chocolate (plain, orange-flavored, with rum or chili) and others.

🍧 **Pasticceria Marchesi** B1 – *Via Santa Maria alla Porta 11/a. Ⓜ1 Cairoli. www.pasticceria marchesi.it.* One of Milan's most famous cake shops, the Marchesi was opened back in 1824 and still retains an atmosphere typical of the early 1900s. Its unaltered appearance, including how the staff are presented, leaves some first-time visitors standing in astonishment. It produces one of

Milan's best panettone and has a wide variety of cakes and sweets of all kinds.

Gelateria Marghera off map (A1) – *Via Marghera 33.* Ⓜ1 *Wagner.* The Marghera is famous for the quality and variety of its gelatos, as the ever-present crowd attests.

Rigoletto – *Via San Siro, corner of Via Sanzio.* Ⓜ1 *Wagner. www. gelateriarigoletto.it.* The flavours at this little ice-cream parlour not far from the Teatro Nazionale are excellent, particularly the fruit-based choices.

Pasticceria San Carlo A1 – *Via Bandello 1.* Ⓜ1 *Conciliazione. www.pasticceriasancarlo.it.* A couple of steps from the Basilica of Santa Maria delle Grazie, the staff in their elegant uniforms serve an excellent home-made gelato at the counter or at the tables outside. In addition to gelato, the San Carlo offers cakes, crepes and other types of sweet.

Shockolat Maggi B1 – *Via Boccaccio 9.* Ⓜ1 *Cadorna. www.shockolat.it.* A contemporary gelato parlor specializing in chocolate flavors: milk chocolate, plain, white, or flavored with orange, rum, cinnamon, ginger, chili and many other possibilities. This is a nice place to refuel with coffee and chocolates before going to see Leonardo's Last Supper in the refectory of the nearby Basilica of Santa Maria delle Grazie.

Sugar – *Via Vincenzo Monti 26.* Ⓜ1/2 *Cadorna.* The right place for breakfast, with excellent cappuccino and croissants, pastries or petits-fours.

Pinacoteca Ambrosiana and Via Torino
See map p55.

Panarello – *Via Speronari 3.* Ⓜ1/3 *Duomo. www.panarello.com.* Despite mostly offering sweets and cakes typical of Genoa, Panarello has earned a reputation for fine Milanese pastries since 1930. It is famous for its tasty tarts, kranz and *biscotti del lagaccio* (aniseed-flavored cookies). There are three Panarello shops around the city: one at *Piazza San Brolo 15*, on the corner of Corso di Porta Romana (A2, *Around the Porta Romana and University*), where the counter is busy with people grabbing a coffee and croissant, and two that also sell gelatos and offer wifi: *Via Tolstoj 1* (off map; A1), *Porta Ticinese and Navigli*), *Piazza S. Francesca Romana 1*, Ⓜ1 *Porta Venezia* (off map; B1), *Fashion Quarter and Corso Venezia*).

Around the University and Porta Romana
See map p61.

Sant Ambroeus A1 – *See Fashion Quarter and Corso Venezia.*

L'Antica Arte del Dolce di Ernst Knam off map (B2) – *Via Anfossi 10. Tram 27. www.eknam.com.* For German chef Ernst Knam, cake-making is an ancient art that allows him to create something new every day. He skillfully experiments with inexhaustible combinations of forms and flavors, using spices, fruits and other foods to produce new types of chocolate, cakes, pralines, biscuits and even a unique product named after himself, the *Knamotto.* Take the trouble to visit this sophisticated shop close to the Rotonda della Besana to taste his creations.

Giovanni Galli – *Corso di Porta Romana 2.* Ⓜ 3 Missori. *www. giovannigalli.com.* Amazing old-style furnishings and delightful marron glacé, pralines and cherry-liqueur chocolates. Other Galli addresses, *Via Victor Hugo 2.* Ⓜ1 *Duomo.*

Pasticceria Paradiso – *Corso di Porta Vigentina 10.* Ⓜ 3 Crocetta. Small historic pastry shop famous for its pear and chocolate cake. Everything else, prepared on the spot, is just as good. Cakes, cream puffs, pralines and savoury pastries. Ice cream in summer.

Sissi off map (B1) – *Piazza Risorgimento 6.* Ⓜ1 San Babila. Looking through the windows you see the pastry cooks at work and satisfied customers who return here each day for their breakfast croissants, or perhaps on Sunday for brunch with savory brioches, sitting at tables in a charming small garden located around back. The *simpatico* bartender will call out "A cappuccino for the young girl," no matter how old the lady in question may be. A popular choice is a tray of Sissi's excellent cookies or cakes.

🍵 **Taveggia** B1 – *Via Visconti di Modrone 2.* Ⓜ1 San Babila. *www.taveggia.it.* The tea room still has the elegant boiseries, chandelier and mirrors it was decorated with in the 1930s when this café-patisserie, which originally opened in 1909, moved to this address and became a favorite with the wealthy circles of Milan. When ordering an espresso or cappuccino at the bar it's difficult not to add one of the tasty pastries on display. The intimate and romantic tea room is ideal for a tête-à-tête.

Gelateria Umberto B1 – *Piazza Cinque Giornate 4. Tram 27.* Some people swear Umberto's is the best gelato shop in Milan and practically everyone recognizes that the creamy flavors are nigh on unbeatable. The ingredients are as fresh and good as can be, which is why the prices are a little higher here than elsewhere, but who cares when you have a scoop of heaven in your hands?

Porta Ticinese and Navigli

See map pp64–65.

La Rinomata Gelateria – *Ripa di Porta Ticinese 1.* Ⓜ2 Porta Genova. Small ice cream shop at the start of the Naviglio in early 20C style. Homemade ice cream made with top quality materials. Delicious flavors, sorbets, shakes and crepes.

Pasticceria Cucchi B1 – *Corso Genova 1.* Ⓜ2 Sant'Agostino. *www.pasticceriacucchi.it.* After wandering around the shops in the busy Corso Genova, take a seat outside this historic coffee and cake shop and watch the people in the large square where seven streets meet. Opened in 1936 but destroyed in a bombing raid in 1943 and rebuilt in the same place, Cucchi has maintained an ambience typical of the 1950s and 60s. It fits the bill for those wanting a quick croissant or cake, or in need of an aperitif and a panino or savory accompaniment.

Pasticceria Gattullo B1 – *Piazzale Porta Lodovica 2.* Ⓜ2 Porta Genova. *www.gattullo.it.* Croissants still warm from the oven and a good cappuccino! And that's just to start, as along the eight-meter counter in red marble

MUST DO

illuminated by large ceiling lights are rows of delicious pastries and cakes, panini, light meals (both hot and cold), plus appetizers and small cakes to accompany your favorite aperitif.

🍦 **RivaReno** B1 – *Viale Col di Lana 8*. Ⓜ2 *Porta Genova. www.rivareno.com*. A gelateria serving delicious and imaginative flavors! The house specialities are real inventions created using unusual combinations and exotic ingredients from around the world: for example, "New York New York," with Canadian maple syrup and caramelized pecan nuts, "Leonardo" with Mediterranean pine nuts, and "Sweet Alabama," creamy chocolate ice-cream with peanut butter. An internet point inside the shop has a rubber keyboard so that dripping gelato can be cleaned off! There are two other RivaReno gelato shops in Milan, at *Via Mercato 20,* Ⓜ2 *Lanza* (*Brera and Corso Garibaldi*) and *Ripa di Porta Ticinese 53*, Ⓜ2 *Porta Genova* (*Navigli*).

Porta Nuova and Isola
See map p70.
Near Corso Sempione
🍦 **Il Massimo del Gelato** A1 – *Via Castelvetro 18. Tram 1*. This gelateria in the Sempione district really has an amazing range of inventive flavors. The English translation of its name is "The best gelato can be!" and who's to say they're wrong? If you can find a better gelato than they make at Il Massimo, then you've found the best gelato shop in Milan. The double-parked cars outside and the line at the door are proof of the place's popularity. It has many original chocolate flavors, but the others too, like pistacchio and

almond, are simply exquisite due to the quality and freshness of the ingredients.

Near Stazione Centrale
La Bottega del Gelato off map (B1) – *Via Pergolesi 3.* Ⓜ2 *Caiazzo. www.labottegadelgelato.it.* Located in a road just off Corso Buenos Aires, this gelato shop is famous for its products made using fruit from the Mediterranean and the tropics, and for its fruits filled with gelato. At Christmas it produces a delicious *panettone* with gelato filling.

Isola neighborhood
CentoGusti B1– *Piazzale Lagosta, angolo via Traù.* Ⓜ3 *Zara. www. centogusti.it*. The name, literally One Hundred Flavors, tells you just what is on offer. From the most common to really extravagant concoctions, like those made with Wasabi, cashew nuts and beer, or Brie and soft fruits! There are even eighteen different flavors of chocolate!

The Lakes
Caffè Broletto – *Piazza del Popolo 24, Arona (L. Maggiore). 0322 46 640.* From one of the loveliest outdoor terraces in Arona you get a view of this traffic-free piazza, a small church and the blue lake. Try one of the fruity cocktails.
Gelateria Cremeria Fantasy – *Via Principessa Margherita 38, Stresa (L. Maggiore). 0323 33 227. Closed Nov–Jan except public hols.* Delicious homemade ice creams in a variety of mouth-watering flavours ideal for cooling off in the heat of summer.

MILAN'S MOVIDA

When offices close down in the evenings, the city's nightlife opens for business. There are bars on almost every corner, open in the evenings with clients lining up for a drink and something to nibble on. If crowded and chaotic is not your style, you can always try a wine bar or wander around one of the city's nightlife neighborhoods to take in the scene…

The Milanese aperitivo

Perhaps more than any other city in Italy, Milan has an active, energetic bar and nightclub scene. The fun starts roughly around six in the evening, when most bars begin offering aperitivi. In Milan the aperitivo, or happy hour, means far more than just drinks. Bars set out dozens of plates filled with different kinds of finger foods, from cold rice and pasta salads to fried vegetables, tiny mozzarella balls, slices of cured meats and much more. The food is free, while drinks can cost anywhere from 4 to 14 euro. These all-you-can-eat happy hour buffets usually substitute dinner.

If loud and crowded is not your style, then look for an enoteca, or wine bar. Here the music is usually lower, and there is more space for clients to simply relax, enjoy their wines and chat the evening away. In these bars waiters often bring plates of food to the table, rather than leaving them out buffet-style. Please note that food delivered to the table sometimes (though not always) comes at an extra charge.

The *movida*

The Spanish word "movida" (literally movement) has been widely adopted by the Milanese to refer to the city's nightlife, including aperitivos, dancing, drinking, attending concerts or theater performances and simply walking around in the evening. The most active nightlife areas in the city are in and around the navigli, in and around Piazza Duomo, in the Brera neighborhood and in and around Porta Ticinese.

Note that although the Milanese enjoying drinking and having a good time, it is unusual to see someone who has clearly had too much to drink. Unlike in other countries where heavy drinking is more openly incorporated into social life, in Milan (and in Italy in general), becoming openly drunk is considered a social faux pas.

Travel global, drink local

While all the city's bars serve standard international cocktails like gin and tonics, mojitos, bloody marys and so forth, there are a few local specialties worth trying.

A Campari Soda is a bitter, spicy and sweet drink with a low alcohol level that was first produced in the late 18C outside Milan. You can order a Campari on its own merits, or enjoy it in one of the classic Milanese aperitivi that feature the drink: the Negroni (gin, vermouth and Campari); the Americano (Campari, sweet vermouth and soda); or the Garibaldi (Campari and orange juice).

Duomo and Castello Sforzesco

See map p30.

Near Duomo

🍸 **Camparino in Galleria** B2 – *Galleria Vittorio Emanuele, corner of Piazza Duomo.* Ⓜ1/3 Duomo. 02 86 46 44 35. www.camparino.it.

Camparino is a symbol of the history of Milan and the ritual of the aperitif in the city. The famous ruby-red bitter was invented by Gaspare Campari, who moved into the Galleria Vittorio Emanuele II as soon as it was opened in 1867. The bar became a meeting place for the well-to-do and was frequented by Giacomo Puccini, Giuseppe Verdi and Thomas Edison. In the 1920s it was decorated in Art Nouveau style with floral decorations. Generations of Milanese have maintained the tradition and meet here at aperitif hour at the bar or tables just a few steps away from the Duomo.

Bar Straf B2 – *Via San Raffaele 3.* Ⓜ1/3 Duomo. 02 80 50 87 15. www.straf.it. The American bar at the Hotel Straf serves aperitifs and cocktails just a few steps from the Duomo, both in the small, very New Yorkish bar-room, where contemporary artistic panels hang on grey cement walls, and on Via San Raffaele, where you can sit on giant cushions that seat 4 or 5 people.

Near Parco Sempione

Bar Bianco A1 – *Inside Parco Sempione, close to the Arena Civica.* Ⓜ2 Lanza. 02 86 99 20 26. www.bar-bianco.com. This bar in the peace of Parco Sempione is especially popular on summer evenings for an aperitif or after-dinner cocktail, seated at the white tables on the patio or on the terrace at the same height as the tree foliage.

Corso Sempione

💡 **A bit of advice** – Starting from the Arco della Pace (A1), this lengthy stretch of Corso Sempione is lined with fashionable bars filled with trendy young Milanese that crowd the pavements from aperitif time to 1–2am. You often have to wait a few minutes to get a table (waiters ask in various tones of voice to those who have finished their drinks either to order another or to make space…). These lively bars boast elegant, designer interiors that create a certain atmosphere, where the customers are often dressed to the nines in the latest fashion: **Jazz Cafè** (*Corso Sempione 8; www.ristorantejazzcafe.com*), where there is also a dance floor; the **Deseo** (*Corso Sempione 2*); and **Living** (*Piazza Sempione 2; livingmilano.com*). There is also a marquetry door that opens onto a corner of pure Bollywood: this is the **Bhangrabar** (*Corso Sempione 1; www.bhangrabar.it*), decorated entirely with Indian furniture, fabrics and cushions. Although the Bhangrabar isn't quite as slick as the other cocktail bars on Corso Sempione, be sure to dress elegantly if you want to feel comfortable in these and other Milanese locales. You'll find that the folks who frequent this trendy street take care to look as fashionable as they can.

Brera and Corso Garibaldi

See map p39.

📍 **A bit of advice** – In **Brera**, the artists' district, you'll find bars, cafés and restaurants with outdoor tables and a fairly Bohemian atmosphere, some more expensive than others but all romantic. **Corso Garibaldi** is very busy at happy hour, when the bars fill with young revelers. **Corso Como** is another popular street for those out on the town, though it doesn't truly come alive until after dinner, when the street's trendy clubs open up for people who feel like dancing. Another type of gathering place close to Corso Como and Corso Garibaldi is the typically British **pub**. There are several welcoming ones where you can have a beer and chat peacefully with your friends.

Brera

Bar Jamaica – *Via Brera 32.* Ⓜ2 *Lanza. 02 87 67 23. www.jamaicabar.it. See Cafés, pasticcerie and gelaterie.*
N'Ombra de Vin – *Via San Marco 2.* Ⓜ2 *Lanza. 02 65 99 650. www. nombradevin.it.* This historic vintner selling top quality Italian and international wines has become a winebar with one of the best selections in Milan. It is set in the refectory of an ancient Augustinian monastery.

Corso Garibaldi

LeRosse – *Corso Garibaldi 79.* Ⓜ2 *Moscova. 02 92 87 04 16. www.lerosse.it. See Restaurants.*
Moscatelli – *Corso Garibaldi 93.* Ⓜ2 *Moscova. 02 65 54 602.* If you want to taste Italian wines with a selection of buffet snacks at aperitif time, this old wine shop is one of the longest established and most authentic.
Radetzky Café – *Corso Garibaldi 105.* Ⓜ2 *Moscova. radetzkycafe. com. See Cafés, pasticcerie and gelaterie.*

Corso Como

Hollywood off map (N) – *Corso Como 15.* Ⓜ2 *Porta Garibaldi. 02 65 98 996. www.discoteca hollywood.it.* The favorite club of fashion models and stylists, Hollywood has managed to retain its 1980s atmosphere.
Loolapaloosa off map (N) – *Corso Como 15.* Ⓜ2 *Porta Garibaldi. 02 65 55 693. www.loolapaloosa.com.* Next door to Hollywood, this bar comes to life at 11pm. The music is very loud and the dance space minimal, unless you want to hop up onto the bar itself and dance with the topless barmen. Famous for meeting people and having fun.
Pitbull Cafè off map (N) – *Corso Como 11.* Ⓜ2 *Porta Garibaldi. 02 29 00 23 43.* A small bar that makes great cocktails and is frequented by a cosmopolitan crowd of fashionable youngsters.

Pubs around Corso Como

Scott Duff – *Via Volta 13.* Ⓜ2 *Moscova. 329 01 42 519. www.scottduff.it.* The unmistakable blue and white flag attracts lovers of Scotland and its pub life. Sitting at large wooden tables surrounded by giant screens broadcasting all the important sports events, you can test beers made by small breweries that the pub's tasters have traced from right across Europe.

MUST DO

Fashion district and Corso Venezia

See map p45.

Fashion district

Bar at the Bulgari Hotel A2 – *Via Fratelli Gabba 7b.* Ⓜ3 *Montenapoleone. 02 80 58 051. www.bulgarihotels.com*. For a hyper-trendy atmosphere in the Brera-Montenapoleone district, this bar is one of Milan's most elegant and exclusive, with a spectacular glass wall that looks out over a small botanical garden. Make sure you try the Bulgari Cocktail. The hotel restaurant menu is available in the bar, served in a more informal manner.

Bar Prima Donna A2 – *Via dell'Orso 7.* Ⓜ1 *Cairoli. 02 87 09 61.* This classy lounge bar in the Milano Scala hotel is great for twosomes: comfortable sofas, diffused lighting, good cocktails… Don't hesitate to ask the waiters to take you to the panoramic terrace at the top of the hotel where there are views across Brera and the rest of Milan.

Near Corso Venezia

35 B1 – *Via Panfilo Castaldi 35.* Ⓜ1 *Porta Venezia. 02 29 53 33 50.* It's like an evening with friends in this small multicultural room. Popular for aperitifs and after dinner drinks, it's easy to find someone to chat with here. If you feel homesick, this is the place for you!

Bar Basso off map (B1) – *Via Plinio 39.* Ⓜ2 *Piola. 02 29 40 05 80. www.barbasso.com*. This is where the "wrong" Negroni cocktail was invented, using champagne instead of gin. Set in a room in 19C-style.

Olga Sapegina/Fotolia.com

Frank B1 – *Via Lecco 1.* Ⓜ1 *Porta Venezia. 02 29 53 25 87. www.frankmilano.it*. This trendy bar has been considered one of Milan's premiere nightlife hotspots for nearly a decade, attracting models, people from the entertainment industry and even the occasional Hollywood movie star. Dress elegantly and prepare to people-watch! Frank's is also a quality bistro, open for breakfast and lunch, serving pastries and small sandwiches in the morning and a broad range of fish dishes, steaks, sandwiches and salads for lunch. Reservations are recommended.

El Paso del Los Toros B1 – *Via Palazzi 7.* Ⓜ1 *Porta Venezia. 02 20 49 870. www.elpasodelostoros.it*. As an Argentine restaurant, you won't be surprised to find beef from the pampas on the menu. But you can also come for happy hour and enjoy the warm, South American atmosphere.

Nottingham Forest off map (B2) – *Viale Piave 1.* Ⓜ1 *Palestro.* *www.nottingham-forest.com*. More than 1,000 experimental cocktails! It seems incredible but when you have the biblically large cocktail list in your hands, you need at least ten minutes to make your choice. The barmen are true alchemists of alcohol and whatever they prepare for you will be a visual spectacle and delicious to boot. The small interior is pleasingly exotic with ethnic furnishings.

Turnè Night Bar off map (B1) – *Via Frisi 3.* Ⓜ1 *Porta Venezia.* *338 12 15 449 or 02 36 50 85 15.* *www.turnenightbar.com*. This young, warm and informal bar is nice for an aperitif with friends. Cocktails and buffet costs only €5. Theme nights: on Thursday "Jazz & Wine," with Italian cheese tastings and jazz; nearly every Sunday there are film showings on the back wall.

Corso Magenta and Sant'Ambrogio

See map p50.

Bar Magenta B1 – *Via Carducci 13.* Ⓜ1/2 *Cadorna. 02 80 53 808*. The Magenta is one of Milan's most famous bars and has been a favorite since 1907. The enormous counter, Art Deco décor and elegant stained glass windows are not easily forgotten. It is suitable for all ages and types: ideal for a beer, aperitif or meal at reasonable prices, and you can sit and work with a laptop during the day.

Around Porta Romana and the University

See map p61.

Refeel off map (B2) – *Viale Sabotino 20.* Ⓜ3 *Porta Romana. 02 58 32 42 27. www.refeel.it*. Live jazz every other Sunday in an American bar furnished with small sofas to give the feeling of a drawing-room. Lively happy hour each evening.

Porta Ticinese and Navigli

See map p64–65.

🕭 **A bit of advice** – This is the epicenter of Milan nightlife. From Corso di Porta Ticinese to the Navigli, the streets are invaded by the city's nightbirds, especially on weekends. An abundance of cocktail bars, restaurants and pubs compete for the attention of a flood of people looking for fun. Many end up drinking their beers and cocktails around the Roman columns in front of the Basilica of San Lorenzo till early morning. There are also bars, restaurants and pubs in the area around Via Tortona and Via Savona, close to Parco Solari.

Brellin Caffè B1 – *Alzaia Naviglio Grande 14.* Ⓜ2 *Porta Genova. 02 58 10 13 51. www.brellin.it*. Despite being a restaurant, the Brellin Caffè in the beautiful Vicolo dei Lavandai also invites people in for nothing more than an aperitif, which you can drink looking onto the Naviglio Grande and enjoying jazz or art evenings in the summer.

Joe Pena's A1 – *Via Savona 17.* Ⓜ2 *Porta Genova. 02 58 11 08 20. www.joepenas.it*. For a Mexican-flavored happy hour and dinner!

MUST DO

La Baita del Formaggio A1 –
See Markets and Gourmet shops.
Le Biciclette B1 – *Via Torti,
corner of Corso Genova.*
Ⓜ2 *Sant'Agostino. 02 58 10 43 25.
www.lebiciclette.com.* Everything
in this "restaurant & art bar" is
inspired by art. Definitely to be
tried, especially at aperitif time.
La Hora Feliz – *Via San Vito 5,
behind the Basilica of San
Lorenzo. Tram 2 or 14.* A little
corner of Cuba in Milan, with a
wide choice of cocktails and a
generous selection of bar snacks.
uca e Andrea off map (A1) –
Alzaia Naviglio Grande 34.
Ⓜ2 *Porta Genova. 02 58 10 11 42.
www.lucaeandreanavigli.it.*
Sip cocktails prepared by
two highly skilled barmen
accompanied by hot, tasty snacks
at one of the most satisfying
happy hours in the Navigli.
Rita A1 – *Via Fumagalli 1.*
Ⓜ2 *Porta Genova. 02 83 72 865.*
Rita is a small and intimate
American bar with excellent
cocktails in a cross-street of Ripa
di Porta Ticinese.
Le Scimmie off map (B1) – *Via
Ascanio Sforza 49.* Ⓜ2 *Romolo.
02 89 40 28 74. www.scimmie.it.*
Live music. *See Entertainment.*
Slice Cafè off map (B1) – *Via
Ascanio Sforza 9.* Ⓜ2 *Romolo.
02 58 10 53 66. www.slicecafe.it.*
One of the cocktail bars
frequented for aperitifs on the
Naviglio Pavese. Good cocktails
and a lively atmosphere.
Woodstock off map (A1) – *Via
Lodovico il Moro 3. Tram 2 or*
Ⓜ2 *Porta Genova. 02 36 56 40 15.
www.woodstockmilano.com.*
Located in front of the Church
of San Cristoforo, this pub has a

choice of more than 600 beers but
also offers cocktails, sliced pizza
and hamburgers. Sports events
shown on giant screens.

Porta Nuova and Isola
See map p70.
⊛ **A bit of advice** – Isola offers live
music, winebars and extravagant
cocktail bars and is a fine
alternative to the more hectic
and trendier districts.

Isola neighborhood
Blue Note – *Via Pietro Borsieri 37.
Tram 7 or* Ⓜ3 *Zara. 02 69 01 68 88.
www.bluenotemilano.com.* Live
music. *See Entertainment.*
Nord Est Caffè – *Via Pietro
Borsieri 35. Tram 7 or* Ⓜ3 *Zara. 02
69 00 19 10. www.nordestcaffe.it.*
Live music. *See Entertainment.*
Frida – *Via Pollaiuolo 3. Tram 7
or* Ⓜ3 *Zara. 02 68 02 60 www.
fridaisola.it.* An extravagant
artistic character gives this bar
an original feel.

Near Chinatown
Byblos Milano – *Via Messina 38.
Tram 12 or 14. 338 80 98 326.
www.byblosmilano.com.* Only
recently opened, this quickly
became one of Milan's trendiest
nightclubs, especially for those
over 25 looking for a stylish and
exclusive ambience.
La Chiesetta – *Via Lomazzo 12.
Tram 4, 12 or 14. 339 79 69 095.
www.lachiesetta.it.* A pub that
serves beer and chupitos in a
small, deconsecrated, late 18C
church.

ALONG THE LAKE

Gorgeous natural scenery, sunsets over the water and sports of all kinds both out on the lake and up along the surrounding mountain slopes. A holiday in this corner of Italy can be as quiet and restful as it can be dynamic and exciting, depending on the way you organize your days.

Lake Maggiore

Lake Maggiore is a veritable paradise for sports enthusiasts, with bike paths, pedestrian routes, hiking, mountain bike paths, horse-riding, golf courses with mindblowing views and every sort of water sport imaginable: sailing, canoeing, kayaking, yachting, waterskiing, scuba-diving, rafting and more. For addresses: *www.illagomaggiore.com*.
Alpyland – *Stresa. 0323 30 295. www.alpyland.com*. This alpine theme park even boasts a rail car bobsled ride. *See also p80*.
Lago Maggiore Adventure Park – *Strada Cavalli 18, Baveno. 0323 91 97 99. www.aquadventurepark.com*. Games and sports in a natural setting on the lakeside: Tibetan bridges, Tyrolean cable slides, ladders, and hanging walkways, an artificial rock climbing wall, a four-station acrojump and a cyclocross circuit (bike hire available).

Lake Como

Here you'll find plenty to do in both summer and winter. You can go sailing, rowing, windsurfing, waterskiing, kite-surfing, canoeing, hang-gliding and paragliding amid unforgettable views, or try your hands and feet at rock climbing, hiking, mountain-biking or horse-riding. There are even seven golf courses to play on. In winter, ski slopes open on mountains around the lake. For addresses: *www.lakecomo.it*.

Lake Garda

The largest lake in Italy, Garda provides a perfect body of water for sailing and windsurfing. Thanks to the area's mild microclimate there are outdoor activities available all year-round: kite-surfing, canyoning, scuba diving, horse trekking, over 1,000 km of mountain bike paths, rock-climbing, free-climbing, paragliding, and various golf clubs and courses. For addresses: *www.visitgarda.com*.
Gardaland – *Via Derna 4, Castelnuovo del Garda. 045 64 49 777. www.gardaland.it*. Kids will love Italy's largest theme park: dizzying roller coasters, adventures on pirate ships and the Temple of Ramses. Near the park you'll find **Gardaland Sea Life Aquarium**, which recreates local freshwater ecosystems as well as that of sharks and other creatures from the Mediterranean, tropical seas and oceans.
Canevaworld – Aquapark and Movieland Park – *Fossalta 58. Lazise sul Garda. 045 69 69 900. www.canevaworld.it*.
Canevaworld includes a large water park, a theme park dedicated to Hollywood films, and two theme restaurants – Medieval Times and the 1950s-style Rock Star Restaurant. There is also a discotheque, Night Festival.

MUST DO

RESTAURANTS

While not quite as awe-inspiring as the _Last Supper_ or the view from atop the Duomo, there can be no denying that excellent food is one thing everyone who visits Italy looks forward to, and Milan won't disappoint. The city provides a rich enough variety – in cuisine, prices and ambiance – that you'll find something for everyone. And out in the lakes region you'll find traditional and local cuisines to make the mouth water.

| _Luxury_ | over 65€ | _Moderate_ | 25€–45€ |
| _Expensive_ | 45€–65€ | _Inexpensive_ | under 25€ |

Dining Options

In the past, names like "**ristorante**" and "**trattoria**" were used to distinguish different kinds of establishments. Ristoranti were generally more elegant and expensive, while trattorie were cheaper and more working class. Today these distinctions are no longer clear cut, and the restaurant's denomination doesn't tell you much about what you can expect to spend after eating there. But there are a few considerations to bear in mind when choosing the kind of restaurant you want to have a meal in. **Enotecas** are a kind of wine bar that usually serve a limited number of hot and cold dishes. Italians generally do not drink wine without eating something too, so you can count on at least a few snacks or simple platters to accompany your drinks. **Pizzerias** specialize in pizzas, but often offer pasta dishes, salads and other options as well. A **locanda** is a restaurant that usually has a few rooms for rent, while the name "**osteria**" is synonymous with trattoria, and generally implies a less expensive dining experience. Note that outside the city these traditions are more often honored than not. For example, in the lake regions you can expect to spend less at a trattoria or osteria than at a ristorante.

Our Selection

We've selected a number of restaurants, trattorias and pizzerias where food is good and prices are right. In Milan, the question "Where shall we eat tonight?" is often a way of saying "What kind of food shall we eat tonight?" so in addition to trattorias serving traditional local cuisine, we've decided to include a number of restaurants specializing in regional food from other parts of Italy. We've also made an effort to evaluate a variety of ethnic restaurants from all over the world. These are often preferred by many Milanese, especially younger people, perhaps because they can already enjoy a perfectly good cotoletta at home! We've made an effort to highlight places near various tourist attractions so that you can combine city exploration with gastronomic discoveries. Our prices reflect the cost of a two-course meal with a carafe of wine. You'll also find a number of sandwich shops (paninoteca) and bars where you can find a good "Italian-style" hamburger, sandwich, piadina or a quick meal, indicating the average price for a simple lunch. Don't forget that you can always have lunch in a café (*see Cafés, pasticcerie and gelaterie*), or substitute a sit-down dinner with one of Milan's popular buffet-style aperitivos (*see Milan's movida*).

Managing Your Menu

Almost everywhere you eat, from the humblest osteria to the most elegant ristorante, you'll find that Italian menus follow more or less the same format. They are divided into four main sections: **antipasti** (appetizers), **primi piatti** (first courses), **secondi piatti** (second courses), **dessert** (desserts). Some menus may also include **contorni** (side dishes), and the first and second courses are sometimes divided into **carne** (meat dishes) and **pesce** (fish dishes). Wines are usually, though not always, offered in a separate menu, along with afterdinner drinks like **amari** (bitters) and **digestivi** (literally, "digestion drinks"), which are herbed liquors.

Business Hours

Like any major metropolis, Milan has many establishments that are open throughout the day and well into the night. But Italians' eating habits remain fairly rigid, and in many places – even those that are open and have staff working and moving around inside – you'll be turned away if you try to sit down and eat outside established hours. **Breakfast** is usually taken in a bar between 8 and 9:30 am, and rarely amounts to much more than a coffee, tea, pastry and fresh fruit. **Lunch** is usually served between 12:30 and 2:30 pm, and **dinner** between 7:30 and 10 pm. Different restaurants close on different days

during the week, though Sunday and Wednesday are the most common closure days. Remember that during August, many establishments close for at least a couple weeks' vacation. On Friday, Saturday and Sunday nights, it is always best to reserve a table when possible.

Light Bites

Milan is a busy, hard-working city, and there are lots of places where you can grab a bite to eat on the fly. In the evenings many Milanese, especially younger men and women, eat a quick meal during **aperitivo hours**, when bars provide free food in exchange for relatively expensive drinks (*see Milan's movida*). Almost all **bars**, **cafés** and **pasticcerie** offer a range of sandwiches and simple lunch dishes. A **tramezzino** is a sandwich made with standard sliced bread, often with the crusts removed. A **piadina** is a typical flatbread from the Emilia-Romagna region. Piadina sandwiches are usually toasted in a hot iron press. Note that while grabbing a bite to eat in a café or pasticceria is almost always less expensive than sitting down at a table in a restaurant, many restaurants offer reduced price **lunch menus** that provide finer fare at competitive prices. In warmer months, **gelaterie** are usually open throughout the day, providing a quick, delicious and refreshing snack option.

Food and Wine

In addition to providing an extraordinary range of regional Italian, international, ethnic and specialty cuisines thanks to the constant flow of immigrants in and out of the city, Milan can also vaunt its own classic culinary traditions. If you want to try something truly local, keep an eye out for these dishes. The **risotto allo zafferano** (saffron risotto) is arguably the most classic Milanese dish, combining strong cheese flavors with delicate and distinctive saffron. Sometimes leftover risotto will also be offered as a crunchy and delicious **riso al salto**. In the winter, many restaurants sell **casoeula**, a mix of boiled pig meat and cabbage that tastes much better than it sounds. Another typical Milanese dish is the **cotoletta alla milanese**, a veal cutlet that has been flattened, breaded and fried, usually served with diced tomatoes and arugula. The **panettone** is a sweet bread usually served around Christmas holidays.

It may seem counterintuitive, since Milan is further from the sea than almost any other Italian location, but the city is famous for fresh fish. Most of the country's fish supply passes through Milan for distribution both in Italy and abroad, and its restaurants reap the benefits.

While Lombardy is not one of Italy's more renowned wine regions, it still produces a number of respectable vintages, including the **Oltrepò Pavese**, **Franciacorta** and **Valtellina**. Grapes have been cultivated in Lombardy for millennia: archaeological finds of *Vitis vinifera silvestris* near Lakes Iseo and Garda dating to the Bronze Age demonstrate that the vine has been present in Lombardy since prehistory.

The province of Milan also has a small wine-making area, which produces the red **San Colombano** around the village of the same name. The winemaking area around **Lake Garda** is well established and its products were appreciated by such figures as Virgil, Strabo, Suetonius and Pliny.

The **Garda DOC zone** is an interregional appellation that comprises the areas around Brescia, Mantova and Verona. It produces white, red, rosé, still, sparkling, dry and sweetish wines from a multitude of different varieties.

Prices and Tips

Prices vary depending on the restaurant and menu, but you should bear in mind that Milan is an expensive city. A pizza and a softdrink will cost you around €15. In a trattoria or simple restaurant you can expect to pay approximately €30 for a good meal, ordering an appetizer, first course and a dessert. Generally speaking, antipasti cost between €6 and €10; primi piatti between €10 and €16; secondi piatti between €12 and €22. A side dish (contorno) is usually served separately.

If you're eating in an upscale restaurant, you should expect to pay at least €40 per person, including wine. Fish restaurants are generally at least €10 more per person. Bread and crackers are billed automatically once you sit down, and will appear on your receipt as "coperto" or "coperti," generally between €2 and €5. Remember that you can always ask a waiter to fill your breadbasket back up at no extra charge. Service is included but you can always leave a tip if you'd like.

Lakeside Cuisines

Lakeside cuisine is renowned for its rich freshwater fish dishes. As an antipasto, many different fish are prepared in **carpioni**, a way of preserving fried or boiled fish in an herbed vinegar dressing. You will often find **anguilla** (eel) on the menu, either marinated, grilled or stuffed and baked in the oven. In and around Lake Iseo many restaurants serve **tinca** (tench), either in risottos or stuffed and baked. The more intrepid visitors may want to experience **lumache** (snails) or **rane** (frogs), traditionally served for people who could not afford to pay for meat, and today considered a gourmet delicacy of the Lombardy region. Moving up the mountainside above the lakes, you'll notice that the cuisine changes, sometimes dramatically. Fish dishes disappear, replaced by game meats and polenta. **Polenta** is popular all over Italy, but especially in this corner of Italy, where cooks serve polenta taragna: corn flour mixed with buckwheat, cooked and dressed with butter and melted cheese.

DUOMO AND CASTELLO SFORZESCO

See map p30.

☺ **A bit of advice** – Always check the prices before sitting down at a table around Piazza Duomo and going towards the Sforzesco Castle via Piazza Cordusio and Piazza Cairoli: many of the bars and restaurants are frequented almost exclusively by tourists and are poor value-for-money. If you wish to spend little, there are fast-food outlets but, if you prefer something special, try the

Castello Sforzesco

M Borgese/hemis.fr

panzerotti at Luini's or have lunch on an old-fashioned tram.
For other eating options in and around Duomo and Castello Sforzesco, *see Cafés, pasticcerie and gelaterie (p115)* and the entries under *Brera and Corso Garibaldi, Fashion Quarter and Corso Venezia, Corso Magenta and Sant'Ambrogio, Pinacoteca Ambrosiana and Via Torino* and *Around the Porta Romana and University*.

Inexpensive

Near Duomo

Luini Panzerotti B2 – *Via Santa Radegonda 16.* Ⓜ1/3 *Duomo. 02 86 46 19 17. www.luini.it. Open 10am–8pm, closed Mon evening and Sun.* A local institution among hungry Milanese that serves *panzerotti* in the shadow of the Duomo – a dough-based snack with speciality fillings from southern Italy.

MUST EAT

Spontini B2 – *Via Santa Radegonda 16.* m1/3 *Duomo. 02 89 09 26 21. Open 11am–1am.* Considered by some to serve the best pizza by the slice in town. Other Spontini addresses: *Corso Buenos Aires 60 (entrance Via Spontini 4) 1,* m1 *Lima; Viale Papiniano 43,* m2 *Sant'Agostino; Via Marghera 3,* m1 *Wagner; Piazza Cinque Giornate, Tram 27.*

Moderate

Near Duomo

Charleston B2 – *Piazza Liberty 8. 02 79 86 31. www.ristorante charleston.it.* Popular with shoppers thanks to its central location.
La Rinascente B2 – *Via Santa Radegonda 1.* m1/3 *Duomo. 02 88 52 471. www.rinascente.it.* The 7th floor of Milan's most famous and chicest store is dedicated to "food and restaurants" of every possible variety: food market, sushi, local artisanal products, wines, sandwiches, cakes, etc. Italian and international cuisine with a view straight onto the cathedral's spires and statues.
Emporio Armani Caffè B1 – *See Fashion Quarter and Corso Venezia.*
Roses off map (B2) – *Piazza Fontana 3.* m1/3 *Duomo.* Impeccable service, imaginative cooking and excellent ingredients are the trump cards at Roses, which also boasts a great decor. Its chic and fluid spaces are ideal for a romantic dinner.

Expensive

Near Duomo

Da Marino – Al Conte Ugolino off map (B2) – *Piazza Cesare Beccaria 6.* m1 *Duomo.* Family-run restaurant that has offered "super classic cuisine" since 1935 based on fresh fish and meat dishes.
Peck B2 – *See Pinacoteca Ambrosiana and Via Torino.*
Vun B2 – *Via Silvio Pellico 3.* m1/3 *Duomo. www.ristorante-vun.it.* Magnificent, austere and minimalist: the Vun is run by a young Neapolitan cook who specializes in his local cuisine but also offers a phenomenal choice of the best of the rest of the boot.

Piazza della Scala

Café Trussardi / Ristorante Trussardi alla Scala B2 (*luxury*) – *Piazza della Scala 5.* m1/3 *Duomo. Closed Sun. 02 80 68 82 95. www.cafetrussardi.com.*
The famous Italian fashion company has transformed the ground floor of this 19th-century palazzo into a single space housing a concept store and an elegant and trendy café with tropical plants inside and out in a vertical garden created by French botanical designer Patrick Blanc. It is outdoors in particular, with large windows looking onto Piazzetta Filodrammatici close to the artists' entrance to the Teatro alla Scala, that visitors can relax with one of the excellent Italian or international wines from the cellar, or with an innovative cocktail concocted by the barmen, with a limited but superb selection of meat and fish dishes, sandwiches, hamburgers, a cheese plate with walnut bread, a delicate dessert or the dish of the day.
On the first floor, the **Trussardi alla Scala** restaurant is one of the most elegant and well-established in Milan.

Near Castello Sforzesco

ATMosfera B2 – *Piazza Cairoli.* Ⓜ1 *Cairoli. 02 48 607 607 (Italian free-phone). www.atm-mi.it ("Restaurant tram" in the section "Other services"). atmosfera@atm.it.* This restaurant travels through the streets of the center in two historic tram carriages! For dinner it leaves at 8pm from the square in front of the Sforzesco Castle. Fixed menu at €65euros which you have to book at least 15 days in advance. .

Rovello 18 B2 – *Via Tivoli 12.* Ⓜ1 *Cairoli. 02 72 09 37 09. Closed Sat lunchtime and Sun.* One of the three most reliable trattorias in the center, where high-quality meat and fish dishes are on offer. The style is nostalgic with lots of dark wood but with brightly colored paintings on the walls.

Luxury

Don Carlos B1 – *See Fashion Quarter and Corso Venezia.*

BRERA AND CORSO GARIBALDI *See map p39.*

🕭 **A bit of advice** – Sitting at an outside table with views of small squares among the narrow streets of the artists' district of old Brera is certainly an enjoyable experience, but it is for just that reason that the prices are above average. For lower prices, Corso Garibaldi and its surrounding streets has plenty of bars often packed with Milanese at aperitif time, plus restaurants and pizzerias.

Inexpensive

Ham Holy Burger – *Via Palermo 15.* Ⓜ2 *Moscova. 02 87 55 10. www.hamholyburger.com.* Here the humble hamburger is worthy of the adjective "gourmet" used to describe them on the menu – which is not your average printed list but an iPad! The waiter hands it to you at your table with the smile of someone aware of being technologically ahead of the field. The hamburgers are in fact delicious, served with meat from Piemonte and excellent cheeses and vegetables. The only disappointment is that they are pretty small and of course much more expensive than their fastfood rivals, though well worth trying at least once.

Obikà Mozzarella Bar – *Via Mercato 28 (corner of Via Fiori Chiari).* Ⓜ2 *Lanza. 02 86 45 05 68. www.obika.it.* There's nothing Japanese about this name: obikà is Neapolitan for "here you are." Surrounded by a designer interior in glass and metal, here you can be initiated into the different varieties of buffalo mozzarella. Aperitifs with small mozzarella balls and titbits from 6.30pm. Also on the top floor of La Rinascente store in Piazza del Duomo.

Pizzeria Sibilla – *Via Mercato 28.* Ⓜ2 *Lanza. 02 39 66 35 61.* Small pizzeria with few tables and a very simple decor, where you can enjoy one of the best Neapolitan pizzas in the city.

Moderate

LeRosse – *Corso Garibaldi 79.* Ⓜ2 *Moscova. 02 92 87 04 16. www.lerosse.it.* "The Reds" ("Le Rosse") referred to in the name are on view inside, polished like sculptures. These are cold meat slicing machines. Cured or cooked ham, mortadella, salame, bresaola, speck and the local *culatello di zibello* melt in the mouth with excellent cheeses and other Italian specialities, accompanied of course by a glass of good wine and often the sound of John Coltrane or Miles Davis in the background. What could be nicer?

Serendib – *Via Pontida 2.* Ⓜ2 *Moscova. 02 65 92 139. www. serendib.it. Closed lunchtime.* Serendib, the ancient name for Sri Lanka, means "make happy." It's a tough challenge but this restaurant succeeds! Faithful to its origins, the menu offers Sri Lankan and Indian dishes. Don't miss the exotic Happy Hour (5–8.30pm) with a wide choice of Asian beers and wines from around the world.

Expensive

La Torre di Pisa – *Via Fiori Chiari 21.* Ⓜ2 *Lanza. 02 80 44 83. www.trattoriatorredipisa.it.* Historic, warm and family atmosphere trattoria in Brera that offers Tuscan cuisine with only the best ingredients: top notch extra virgin olive oils, freshly made pasta, and meats chosen with care.

Timé – *Via San Marco 5.* Ⓜ2 *Moscova. 02 29 06 10 51. www.ristorantetime.it. Closed Sat lunchtime and Sun.* There just had to be a restaurant in the artists' district with imaginatively decorated walls and furnishings, portraits and pictures. The exuberance of the interior immediately puts you in a good mood, the service is conscientious and the menu offers creative dishes using Italian ingredients. A cheaper menu is offered at lunchtime.

Luxury

Antica Trattoria della Pesa off map (N) – *Viale Pasubio 10.* Ⓜ2 *Moscova. 02 65 55 741. www. anticatrattoriadellapesa.com. Closed Sun.* This trattoria founded in 1880 trades on its past. The wood-lined walls and majolica stoves take you back in time, perhaps to the 1930s, when the future Vietnamese leader Ho Chi Minh lived above the trattoria, as is indicated by a plaque on the wall outside. It is not surprising that the trattoria is frequented by Milanese wishing to revisit the past or by Asian diplomats. The cooking is typically Lombard with the speciality being *ossobuco* served with *risotto alla Milanese.*

FASHION DISTRICT AND CORSO VENEZIA
See map p45.

🔅 **A bit of advice** – Set close to the showrooms of the great fashion designers, the restaurants in the fashion district of the city go for the luxury market with refined interiors and exclusive cuisine. Continuing towards Corso Venezia and the area of the public gardens, Milan's multiethnic character is reflected in the presence of restaurants from all round the world.

Inexpensive

Near Corso Venezia

Panino Giusto off map (B1) – *Via Malpighi 3.* Ⓜ1 *Porta Venezia. 02 29 40 92 97. www.paninogiusto.it.* Here the panini offer a selection of fillings, like seasoned cured ham, bresaola from Valtellina, chicken, turkey, salmon, cheeses and vegetables. There is also a range of salads and plates of cold cuts, cheeses, meat or fish with vegetable side dishes. Other outlets in the Panino Giusto chain, open all day from noon till 1am, can be found close to the Duomo at *Via Borgogna 5,* Ⓜ1 *San Babila* (B2), at *Corso Garibaldi 125,* Ⓜ2 *Moscova* (*Brera and Corso Garibaldi*), at *Corso di Porta Ticinese 1, tram 3* (B1, *Porta Ticinese and Navigli*), and elsewhere in the city.

La Piccola Ischia off map (B1) – *Via Morgagni 1.* Ⓜ1 *Porta Venezia. 02 20 47 613. www.piccolaischia.it. Closed Sat and Sun lunchtime, Wed*. This pizzeria is thought by many to be the best interpreter in Milan of the Neapolitan pizza, made using a wood-burning oven.

Shangri-La off map (B1) – *Via Lazzaretto 8.* Ⓜ1 *Porta Venezia. 02 29 51 08 37. www.ristorantecineseshangrila.com*. The lighting and warmly colored walls create an elegant and, if the restaurant is not full, intimate Asian atmosphere. Chinese and Thai cooking.

Moderate

Fashion district

Bottiglieria da Pino B2 – *Via Cerva 14.* Ⓜ1 *San Babila. 02 76 00 05 32. Closed Sun, first week Jan, Aug and last week Dec*. A down-to-earth trattoria with home cooking and decent prices. Lunch only.

Emporio Armani Caffè A2 – *Via Croce Rossa 2.* Ⓜ3 *Montenapoleone. 02 72 31 86 80. www.armaniristorante. com*. The café of the Armani megastore is open for breakfast, lunch, aperitifs and dinner. Luxury without flamboyance and good Italian cooking.

Near Corso Venezia

Da Ilia B1 – *Via Lecco 1.* Ⓜ1 *Porta Venezia. 02 29 52 18 95. www.ristorante-ilia.it. Closed Fri lunchtime*. A good restaurant with traditional cooking, from pastas and risottos to the classic *cotoletta alla Milanese* and tasty Dishes of the Day, generally meat-based. The interiors are simple with large illustrations on the walls; the outdoor section in summer is more attractive.

Da Giannino – L'Angolo d'Abruzzo off map (B1) – *Via Pilo 20.* Ⓜ1 *Porta Venezia. 02 29 40 65 26. www.dagianninolangolodabruzzo.it. Closed Mon*. What a pleasure it is to discover the cuisine of Abruzzo in Central Italy, even more so in sizeable portions. Spaghetti, tortellini and tagliatelle in different sauces, lamb and veal, smoked cheese… The tables are rather narrow but they recreate the simplicity and atmosphere of family-run trattorias: this one has been owned by the same family for generations.

Vietnamonamour off map (B1) – *Via Pestalozza 7.* Ⓜ2 *Piola. 02 70 63 46 14. www.vietnamonamour. com. Closed Mon lunchtime and Sun*. This restaurant would certainly have pleased the writer Marguerite Duras, who would have enjoyed the atmosphere of her homeland, Vietnam. The cuisine is very delicate and the dishes give off delightful aromas. Favorite ingredients are ginger, dill, cinnamon and turmeric for marinating meat and fish, and coconut milk, curry powder, and orange or honey sauces. There is no better place to fall in love with Vietnamese food and dream of a trip to the Far East.

Expensive

Near Corso Venezia

Al Girarrosto da Cesarina B1 – *Corso Venezia 31.* Ⓜ1 *San Babila. 02 76 00 048. www.algirarrosto.com. Closed Sat and Sun lunchtime.* Nothing has been altered in this "vintage" restaurant that offers excellent Lombard cuisine. From *risotto all'ossobuco* to *costoletta alla milanese* and stuffed courgette flowers.

Lucca off map (B1) – *Via Panfilo Castaldi 33.* Ⓜ1 *Porta Venezia. 02 29 52 66 68. www.ristorante lucca.it. Closed Sat lunchtime and Sun.* Sitting in diffused light surrounded by views of the Tuscan landscape reminiscent of medieval frescoes, you are assailed by the desire to order a *bistecca alla fiorentina.* Also good are the pastas and the desserts, accompanied by a good wine. In the bistro room connected to the restaurant, pencils are provided on the tables so you can draw on your serviette! The best are hung on the walls.

I Malavoglia B1 – *Via Lecco 4.* Ⓜ1 *Porta Venezia. 02 29 53 13 87. www.ristorante-imalavoglia.com. Closed Mon lunchtime and Sun.* Like the novel by Giovanni Verga from which it takes its name, *I Malavoglia* (1881), the restaurant is "set" in Sicily with the seafood and fish entrées, pastas and main courses that make the island's cooking famous.

Joia – off map (B1) – *Via Panfilo Castaldi 33.* Ⓜ1 *Porta Venezia. 02 29 52 21 24. www.joia.it.* Simple, plain rooms and vegetarian

cuisine presented with an oriental flavor. An "extraordinary lunch" in a dedicated space offers a small selection of specialties to accompany a fixed dish. In the evening, in the dining room with visible kitchen, a few less ambitious but always interesting dishes at restricted prices.

Timé A1 – *See Brera and Corso Garibaldi.*

Luxury

Fashion district

Paper Moon B2– *Via Bagutta 1. 02 76 02 22 97.* Ⓜ3 *Montenapoleone. www.papermoonmilano.com.* A traditional, elegant choice in Milan's fashion district.

Don Carlos A2 – *Via Manzoni 29, Grand Hotel et de Milan.* Ⓜ3 *Montenapoleone. 02 72 31 46 40. www.ristorantedoncarlos.it. Closed lunchtime. Don Carlos* as in the name of the opera written in 1867 by Giuseppe Verdi, who was a long-time guest in the suite in the Grand Hotel et de Milan. Boiseries, red wall lamps, period photographs, paintings and sketches from the museum of the Teatro alla Scala create a romantic, elegant and timeless interior. The menu focuses on Lombard and Piemonte specialities with a creative touch.

Near Corso Venezia

La Risacca Blu off map (B1) – *Viale Tunisia (angolo Via Tadino 13).* Ⓜ1 *Porta Venezia. 02 20 48 09 64. larisaccablu.it. Closed Tue lunchtime and Mon.* One of the best fish restaurants in Milan, where lovers of seafood are spoilt for choice, but with prices to match.

CORSO MAGENTA AND SANT'AMBROGIO

See map p50.

👁 **A bit of advice** – This area of the city, with its avenues and elegant town-houses, is one of the most attractive to walk around and relax in at a restaurant table. In Via Vincenzo Monti, a lovely street shaded by trees, there are numerous restaurants and bars, most of which specialize in lunchtime menus.

Inexpensive

Kota Radja A1 – *Piazzale Baracca 6.* Ⓜ1 *Conciliazione. 02 46 88 50. www.kotaradja.it.* Kota Radja was one of the first Chinese restaurants to open in Milan, long before the recent proliferation. The interior features dark colors, pictures, ornaments, vases and colored and gilded statues in a successful mix of kitsch and elegance to create a relaxing and serene atmosphere in which to enjoy Chinese but also Japanese cooking to the sound of Far Eastern music.

Pizzeria Biagio B1 – *Via Vincenzo Monti 28.* Ⓜ1 *Cadorna. 02 49 87 166.* "Biagio's" is the answer to the question "where do the locals go to eat a pizza hereabouts?" Of course the pizzas are of excellent quality but the place is just as pleasing for its simple, informal and unpretentious interior, good for spending time with friends, and with outdoor tables on the quiet, tree-lined Via Vincenzo Monti.

BoccascenaCafé B1 – *Corso Magenta 24.* Ⓜ1 *Cadorna. 392 92 43 823. Open lunchtime, and evenings when theater performances are given, closed Sat and Sun.* In the courtyard of Palazzo Litta, around an ancient drinking-trough for horses transformed into a fountain presided by a statue of Poseidon, the BoccascenaCafé offes a fast, low-cost lunch, with a choice of first and second course dishes, vegetables, panini and piadine.

De Santis B1 – *Corso Magenta 24. 02 72 09 51 24.* Ⓜ1 *Cadorna. www. paninidesantis.it.* This tiny eatery with few seats prepares superb panini made on the spot, using crusty bread and exceptionally tasty fillings. Ideal for a quick bite. Other De Santis addresses: *La Rinascente,* Ⓜ1/3 *Duomo.*

Stelline Caffè B1 – *Corso Magenta 61.* Ⓜ1 *Cadorna or Cordusio. 02 97 68 70 38. www.stellinecaffe.it. Closed Sat evening and Sun.* After admiring the majestic magnolia in the courtyard and entering Palazzo delle Stelline, you discover this tiny bar and an unexpected flower and tree garden that many people passing down Corso Magenta outside are totally unaware of. Seated either at an outside table facing the garden or inside the bar, you have a choice of panini, piadine and salads, to follow with a dessert, which you can enjoy in the serenity of this bar protected from the hurly-burly of the street.

Expensive

La Brisa B1 – *Via Brisa 15.* Ⓜ1 *Cadorna or Cordusio. 02 86 45 05 21. Closed Sun lunchtime and Sat.* La Brisa stands opposite a Roman archaeological site. The inventive local cooking it offers is well worth investigating. In summer an open-air service is given on a veranda that looks onto a garden.

Pane e Acqua A2 – *Via Bandello 14.* Ⓜ1 *Conciliazione. 02 48 19 86 22. www.paneacqua.com. Closed Mon lunchtime and Sun*. If you are looking for something unusual, here's a place that won't disappoint. A partnership with an art gallery means that the furniture and decorations in this small bistro-restaurant change regularly. The cooking, however, remains delightfully contemporary and creative.

PINACOTECA AMBROSIANA AND VIA TORINO

See map p55.

⊙ **A bit of advice** – It's impossible not to visit Peck's at least once: you only have to walk in to see that its fame as a temple of Milanese gastronomy is amply deserved. The products are all of top quality, which makes it ideal for choosing gifts of the very best and genuine Italian food. Continuing down Via Torino, you find bars and eateries for quick bites, but this area close to Duomo is always packed, by shoppers in particular. To find a restaurant in a less frantic zone, turn off towards Corso di Porta Romana (*see Around the Porta Romana and University*). If you continue along Via Torino, you are heading for the Navigli (*see Porta Ticinese and Navigli*).

Moderate

La Fettunta – *Via Santa Marta 19/A.* Ⓜ1/3 *Duomo. 02 80 56 630. Closed Sun*. Just a hop, skip and a jump from the Pinacoteca Ambrosiana, this is a small Tuscan restaurant where the meal begins with a characteristic slice of *fettunta*, a slice of toasted bread rubbed with garlic, soaked with olive oil and topped with tomatoes and salt. This is followed by a choice of Tuscan specialities, meat in particular, like *dadolata di manzo*.

La Vecchia Latteria – *Via dell'Unione 6.* Ⓜ1 *Duomo. 02 48 44 01. Closed Sun*. Good vegetarian food and shared tables at this busy lunch place in central Milan.

Trattoria Milanese – *Via Santa Marta 11.* Ⓜ1 *Cordusio. 02 86 45 19 91*. An agreeable restaurant serving traditional Milanese cuisine. Tasty starters (the best Russian Salad, apart from your grandmother's), risotto alla milanese all'onda (and also a fine risotto al salto), wonderful main dishes (traditional roasts, so not really for a business dinner), excellent wine list (especially the reds), at a not inflated price. Book and ask for the main dining-room.

Expensive

Cantina della Vetra – *Via Pio IV 3 angolo Piazza Vetra. Tram 3. 02 89 40 38 43. www.cantinadellavetra.it. Closed lunchtime except Sat and Sun*. A large veranda with a view onto the Basilica of San Lorenzo is the place to try typical and special Italian dishes. The cheerful setting is also romantic, particularly in the evening when you can dine by candlelight.

🍴 **Peck** B2 – *Via Spadari 7/9.* Ⓜ1/3 *Duomo. 02 80 23 161. www.peck.it. Closed Mon morning and Sun*. Walking around Milan's most elegant grocery shop is a pleasure to the eyes: the best foods and drink from across Italy and around the world are laid out in perfect and immensely inviting order – cold cuts, cheeses, sauces, oils, vinegars… On the upper floor you will find coffees, teas and chocolate, and you can eat first and second course meals made, of course, using Peck's excellent products. There is also a wine shop on the ground floor where each day a selection of labels are available for tasting.

Just around the corner, at 3 Via Cesare Cantù, the **Peck Italian Bar** (*7.30am–8.30pm; 02 86 93 017*) sells dishes and panini made using products from the Peck shop in an ultra-contemporary setting where businessmen go to cut a fine figure.

Luxury

Cracco – *Via Victor Hugo 4. Ⓜ1/3 Duomo. 02 87 67 74. www.ristorantecracco.it. Lunchtime Tue–Fri 12.30am– 2.30pm; dinner Mon–Sat 7.30– 11pm.* Modern, stripped down and rationalist: that's the decor but it also describes the cuisine, with touches of creativity and experimentation added in equal parts.

AROUND PORTA ROMANA AND THE UNIVERSITY

See map p61.

🙂 **A bit of advice** – The area around the Università Statale is dotted with bars and panini shops frequented by students. There are also a few restaurants and trattorias in and around Corso di Porta Romana that are more satisfying, with traditional regional cooking, like the Roman restaurant Giulio Pane e Ojo, and

the Calabrese cooking at Dongiò, where the portions are large and prices not high. They are so popular, however, that it is best to book, especially in the evening.

Inexpensive

Bar della Crocetta A2 – *Corso di Porta Romana 67. Ⓜ3 Crocetta. 02 54 50 228.* One of the most famous bars in Milan for its expensive, extremely good, and fortunately very large panini. Open every day from 10.30 am to 1am.

Moderate

Giulio Pane e Ojo off map (A2) – *Via Muratori 10. Ⓜ3 Porta Romana. 02 54 56 189. www. giuliopaneojo.com. Closed Sun, by reservation only in the evenings.* The cooking is typically Roman, with pasta dishes like *spaghetti cacio e pepe* or *bucatini all'amatriciana* (with a sauce of oil, cured pig jowls, onion, tomato and pecorino cheese) and main courses like *abbacchio* (young lamb) roasted or with artichokes. The lunch menu is simpler and cheaper and in the evening you really must book because the place, run by young people, has become quite famous. It is informal and fun, with yellow walls, good lighting and rustic characteristics.

La Cantina di Manuela off map (B2) – *Via Carlo Poerio 3. Ⓜ1 Porta Venezia. 02 76 31 88 92. www. lacantinadimanuela.it.* You eat surrounded by wine bottles in a young and dynamic environment. Boards at the counter indicate which wines are available for tasting by the glass, otherwise you simply choose a bottle from the shelves. Elaborate accompanying dishes use products typical of different Italian regions. At lunchtime the place is popular with professional people who often have one of the many salads. These are replaced in the more relaxed evening atmosphere by list of entrées.

Dongiò off map (A2) – *Via Corio 3.* Ⓜ*3 Porta Romana. 02 55 11 372. Closed Sat lunchtime and Sun. Booking advised.* A simple and very busy family-run restaurant, of which few are left these days. Homemade cooking typical of Calabria with fresh pastas, *'nduja* (a spicy cold meat) and of course the very tasty Calabrese chillis.

Globe B1 – *Piazza 5 Giornate 1. 8th floor in the COIN building. Tram 27. 02 55 18 19 69. www. globeinmilano.it.* If shopping in the large COIN store stimulates your appetite, go up to the top floor where a modern open space with panoramic terrace will amaze you with its wide-ranging cuisine: national, regional and with fish specialities. Brunch and lounge bar every day except Monday, till 2pm.

Ba – Ba Reeba B1 – *Via Corridoni 1.* Ⓜ*1 San Babila. 02 76 02 26 84. www.babareeba.it. Closed Sat lunchtime and Sun.* One of the most fashionable restaurants for Milanese wanting to spend an evening in the euphoric atmosphere of their Spanish "cousins." A glance through the door at the visually dazzling red and yellow interior will give you the idea. A typical paella (like the *valenciana*) is enough to lay waste to your hunger but you might prefer to start with tapas and follow

with a meat or fish dish, though these are somewhat expensive.

Trattoria Del Nuovo Macello off map – *Via Cesare Lombroso 20. 02 59 90 21 22. www.trattoriadel nuovomacello.it.* It was baptized in 1927, when the new "slaughterhouse" (macello) opened opposite it, thirty years after the grandfather of one of the present partners had taken control of the place, having recognized its potential from the fact that the threshold was so worn! And he was right! The dishes are from a past age but the treatment absolutely contemporary.

Expensive

Giacomo Bistrot off map (B1) – *Via Pasquale Sottocorno 6.* Ⓜ*1 San Babila. 02 76 02 33 13. www.giacomoristorante.com.* The ambiance of this refined bistro is suggestive of New York or Paris, with its red velvet wall seats, fawn-colored books on the shelves and subdued lighting. It offers non-stop food from midday to midnight.

Masuelli San Marco – *Viale Umbria 80.* Ⓜ*3 Lodi. 02 55 18 41 38. www. masuelli-trattoria.com. Closed Mon lunchtime, Sun, 3 weeks Aug and 25 Dec–6 Jan. Booking advised.* This historic family-run restaurant dates from 1921. Seasonal local dishes vary by the day of the week.

PORTA TICINESE AND NAVIGLI

See map pp64–65.

🙂 **A bit of advice** – The zone between Corso di Porta Ticinese and the streets parallel to the Navigli is the busiest in Milan in the evening. Wine bars, pubs,

The Navigli

P. Jacques/hemis.fr

aperitif bars and clubs attract
thousands of people, especially
at the weekends when the streets
literally heave with youngsters.
So, if you are looking for a
restaurant, be sure to book first.
The prices are generally above
average, particularly those facing
onto the Navigli. Via Savona and
Via Tortona, where restaurants
and drinking places can be found,
are also very lively. As these areas
are less frequented during the
day, some restaurants offer a
simpler and cheaper menu at
lunchtime. A number of bars and
trattorias can be found around
the Parco Solari.

Inexpensive

C'era una volta una Piada
A1 – *Viale Coni Zugna 37.*
Ⓜ2 *Sant'Agostino. 345 90 04 683.*
www.ceraunavoltaunapiada.it.
Closed Sun lunchtime. For a quick
lunch-break, here you can have
a classic piadina – focaccia filled
with your choice of cold meat with
cheese, vegetables and sauces.
Premiata Pizzeria – *Via De Amicis
22. 02 89 40 06 48. www.premiata-*

pizzeria.it. Great pizzas and
attractive surroundings at this
busy place in the Navigli district.

Moderate

Be Bop – *Viale Col di Lana 4. 02 83
76 972. www.beboppristorante.com.*
Restaurant and pizzeria with
gluten-free and soya options.
Langosteria 10 A1 – *Via Savona 10.*
Ⓜ2 *Porta Genova. 02 58 11 16 49.*
ww.langosteria10.it. An eclectic
marine decor for this restaurant
offering seafood and
Mediterranean specialities.
Relaxed atmosphere. For a quick
lunch, also fish-based, you can
visit its younger brother, the
Langosteria Bistrot (*Via privata
Bobbio 2, corner via Conizugna*).
Sant'Eustorgio – *Piazza
Sant'Eustorgio 6. 02 58 10 13 96.
www.sant-eustorgio.it.* Traditional
and pleasant with a menu of
Italian classics.
Trattoria Madonnina off map (B1)
– *Via Gentilino 6. 02 89 40 90 89.
Open Mon–Sat lunchtime and
Thu–Sat evenings. Closed Sun.* A
characteristic, informal trattoria
with checked tablecloths.

Expensive

Al Pont de Ferr off map (A1) – *Ripa di Porta Ticinese 55.* Ⓜ2 *Porta Genova. 02 89 40 62 77. www.pontdeferr.it.*
Situated in front of the old iron bridge (*pont de ferr* in Milanese dialect) alongside the Naviglio Grande, this restaurant is simple and rustic inside but the cuisine is very refined. It offers a cheaper menu at lunchtime.

Al Porto A1– *Piazzale Generale Cantore.* Ⓜ2 *Sant'Agostino or Porta Genova. www.alportomilano.it.* In the 19C the building was the Porta Genova Customs House. Today it is a classic seafood restaurant very popular due to the quality of its fish, whether cooked or raw.

Cantina della Vetra B1 – *See Pinacoteca Ambrosiana and Via Torino.*

Carlo e Camilla in Segheria off map (A1) – *Via Giuseppe Meda 24. 02 83 73 963. www.carloecamillain segheria.it. www.peck.it. Closed Sun.* This Carlo Cracco gastro-bistrot has been opened in a former sawmill. It offers prepared meals with top quality ingredients but at decidedly low prices to make the finest cooking available to a wider public. Enjoy – at a long table.

202 The Grill A1 – *Via Cesare da Sesto 1.* Ⓜ2 *Sant'Agostino. 02 87 23 64 15. www.202milano.com* A welcoming restaurant all in white, furnished with taste in American style. The kitchen's open to public view. A wide choice of excellent hamburgers and fine desserts.

La Scaletta A1 – *Piazzale della Stazione di Porta Genova 3.* Ⓜ2 *Porta Genova. 02 43 98 63 16. www.lascalettamilano.it. Closed Sat lunchtime and Sun.* Three brothers, one the chef and the other two working in the dining-room, demonstrate their good taste in the plain but relaxing decor enlivened by contemporary paintings on the wall, and in the dishes on the menu, which reinterpret traditional Lombard and Italian dishes, sometimes in a surprising manner. The garden too is very pleasant in summer.

Wicky's – *Via San Calocero 3.* Ⓜ2. *Sant'Ambrogio. www.wicuisine.it. Closed Mon lunchtime and Sun.* Wicky's offers almost fusion cooking inspired by Ayurvedic precepts. It uses Mediterranean products with "intrusions" of oriental flavors and Japanese techniques learned by the chef-owner, naturally, in the Land of the Rising Sun.

Luxury

Tano Passami l'Olio off map (A1) – *Via Villoresi 16.* Ⓜ2 *Porta Genova. 02 83 94 139. www.tanopassami lolio.it. Closed lunchtime and Sun.* Subdued lighting, a romantic atmosphere and creative meat and fish dishes ennobled by extra-virgin olive oil supplied from a dispenser. The dishes on offer include delicious *spaghetti alla chitarra* with botargo in a sauce of Grana Padano cheese, honey and champagne.

PORTA NUOVA AND ISOLA

See map p70.
🕙 **A bit of advice** – A number of good restaurants and other eateries can be found in the streets that run off Corso Sempione, in particular Via Procaccini and Via Castelvetro, one of which

is Bon Wei, the best Chinese restaurant in Milan, and La Rosa dei Venti for fish-lovers. Other Chinese restaurants but with very cheap prices are of course scattered along Via Sarpi in Milan's Chinatown. Isola, the district that lies between Porta Garibaldi and Centrale railway stations, is busy in the evenings and has pleasant restaurants, clubs and wine bars, especially along Via Borsieri (the home of the Blue Note jazz club, where you can also eat).

Inexpensive

Casati 19 B1 – *Via Casati 19.* Ⓜ1 *Porta Venezia. 02 29 40 29 94. www.ristorantepizzeriacasati19.it. Closed Mon*. A simple pizzeria-cum-restaurant where you can eat a good pizza in an intimate atmosphere created by attractive table lamps.

Moderate

Bon Wei A1 – *Via Castelvetro 16/18. Tram 1. 02 34 13 08. www.bon-wei.it. Closed Mon.* The cooking in this restaurant with dark, modern rooms flooded with natural light from the large windows is prevalently Cantonese (though Peking duck is on the menu). The ingredients are as fresh as can be and the presentation very studied. Perhaps the best gourmet Chinese restaurant in the city, certainly the most elegant ethnic eating place.

Kanji B1 – *Via Filzi 10.* Ⓜ2 *Centrale FS. 333 58 01 985. www.kanjimilano.com.* "All you can eat" every evening, a formula that tempts many Milanese to try this Japanese restaurant. And they are not disappointed. The sushi are very good, the decor plain but attractive.

Osteria Opera Prima B1 – *Via Paolo Lomazzo 29. Tram 1 or 19. 02 31 63 00. www.osteriaoperaprima.it.* Simple and fragant Mediterranean cooking (the mix of fried squid, scampi, prawns and zucchini is great) in a lovely restaurant that has a special children's play area open in the evenings.

Expensive

La Rosa dei Venti A1 – *Via Piero della Francesca 34. Tram 1. 02 34 73 38. www.ristorantelarosadei venti.it. Closed Mon*. This small restaurant has well-spaced tables and a kitchen leading to the diners. It is ideal for fish-lovers, starting with the La Rosa dei Venti entrée, consisting in five different types of fish. The dishes are imaginative and good value-for-money.

SAN SIRO

Expensive

Fiorenza – *Piazzale dello Sport 20.* Ⓜ1 *Lotto. 02 33 20 06 59. www.ristorantefiorenza.com. Closed Mon*. This family-run restaurant in a small Art Nouveau building opposite the race course has an elegant interior typical of the early 20th century. It offers an inviting menu of fish and meat dishes and has a charming garden.

FIERA MILANO RHO-PERO

⊘ **A bit of advice** – There are 88 break areas in the new Rho-Pero convention complex, 8 of which are self-service and 2 prestigious restaurants with table service: MIB and Sadler. Break areas are located both inside the pavilions and, more often, along the central walkway (Corso Italia and Ponte dei Mari) of the exhibition complex.

Moderate

La Barca – *Via Ratti 54, Rho. 02-9305534. www.trattoriala barca.it.* The name gives a hint of its cuisine: seafood specialties that vary according to what's available on the day, and with a small digression into the cooking traditions of Puglia. This family-run restaurant has a modern decor.

Expensive

D'O – *Via Magenta 18 in San Pietro all'Olmo, hamlet of Cornaredo, 11 km southwest of the Fiera. 02 93 62 209. www. cucinapop.do. Closed Sun and Mon*. It is worth the trouble to travel a few kilometers to try the cooking of chef Davide Oldani, what he refers to as "pop cuisine." Though taking its cue from traditional recipes, every dish will surprise you with its utterly original combinations of ingredients and flavors. The menu changes often as the restaurant's philosophy is to use exclusively products in season. The reduced price lunchtime menu is very popular and, given the place's success, you have to book if you want to find a table.

Luxury

Unico – *Viale Achille Papa 30, Palazzo World Join Center (top floor). 02 39 26 10 25. www.* *unicorestaurant.it. Close Sat lunchtime*. The view from the twentieth floor of the World Join Center takes your breath away. But then so too do the clever combinations of the food!

LAKE MAGGIORE

Inexpensive

Café delle Rose – *Via Ruga 36, Verbania Pallanza. 0323 55 81 01. Closed Sun.* Atmospheric surroundings, good music and a reasonably priced bistrot menu. **Italia** – *Via Ugo Ara 58, Isola dei Pescatori (L. Maggiore). 0323 30 456. www.ristoranteitalia-isola pescatori.it.* A simple trattoria and bar with a wisteria-canopied terrace over the lake. The restaurant boat will ferry you to or from Stresa. Lake fish.

Moderate

Dei Cigni – *Vicolo dell'Arco, corner of Viale delle Magnolie, Verbania (Pallanza). 0323 55 88 42. Closed Tue-Thu lunchtime*. A few square tables, the atmosphere of old Pallanza, and a romantic panoramic terrace overlooking the lake: an excellent place to enjoy a dish of lake or sea fish, perhaps as part of the fixed price menu formula, or one of the meat-based alternatives. **Osteria del Castello** – *Piazza Castello 9, Verbania (Intra). 0323 51 65 79. www.osteria castello.com. Closed Sun*. It has been a custom to meet up here for a glass of wine after a day's work, perhaps as a fisherman on the lake, for a century. The simple rustic furnishings, with dark walnut seats and benches and wall shelves crowded with wine bottles, are a direct reference to that early time. The cooking too is very unpretentious, with regional preparations of pasta and perch that can be eaten beneath a pergola in summer.

Expensive

Amélie – *Via I Maggio 17, Baveno (L. Maggiore). 0323 92 44 96 or 339 87 52 621 (mobile). www.ristoranteamelie.it. Lunch Tue–Sat reservation 24 hours before.* Few tables, smart interior and excellent cuisine.

Piemontese – *Via Mazzini 25, Stresa. 0323 30 235. www. ristorantepiemontese.com. Closed Mon.* Right in the center of the town but only a couple of steps from the lakeside, the Piemontese is one of the most romantic restaurants in Stresa. It offers regional dishes from Piemonte like risotto or braised beef with Barolo to start with, a variety of fish and meat dishes to follow, and delightful desserts to finish. In summer you can eat outside beneath a pergola.

Luxury

Il Sole di Ranco – *Piazza Venezia 5, Ranco, 4 km N from Angera. 0331 97 65 07. www.ilsolediranco.it. Closed Tue except in high season.* Another restaurant where you can eat beneath a pergola in summer with a fine view of the sparkling lake. The menu sparkles, with dishes made from local ingredients blended alchemically in a mix of tradition and modernity that produces golden results. The interior is elegant and the winter garden a delight.

LAKE ORTA

Moderate

Ai Due Santi – *Piazza Motta 18, Orta San Giulio. 0322 90 19 2. www. aiduesanti.com.* This restaurant is in a delightful location on the picturesque small square that faces the embarkation point for San Giulio island. It serves seasonal, Mediterranean cuisine in its two typical, stone-walled dining rooms.

Luxury

Teatro magico – *Via Gippini 11, Orta San Giulio. 0322 91 19 77. www.hotelsanrocco.it.* Situated in one of the most romantic and charming spots on the lake, this elegant restaurant offers beautiful views of the picturesque San Giulio island. Enjoy creative cuisine in a charming, relaxing atmosphere on the lakeside terrace in summer.

Villa Crespi – *Via Fava 18, Orta San Giulio. 0322 91 19 02. www. villacrespi.it. Closed Tue lunchtime and Mon.* Your attention is caught by the profusion of stuccowork and decorations in this 19th-century Moorish lakeside villa, but it is soon returned to the table by the creative cooking of the young Neapolitan chef, with its colors and flavors that merge the gastronomic traditions of South and North Italy, Piemonte in particular.

LAKE COMO

Moderate

Al Porticciolo 84 – *Via Valsecchi 5/7, 0341 49 81 03. www.porticciolo84.it. Closed Mon and The.* Excellent, carefully prepared seafood in tasty dishes served in a small, elegant but rustic setting, with a fireplace and two large aquariums. Located on the Valsassina road.

Osteria L'Angolo del Silenzio – *Viale Lecco 25, Como. 031 33 72 157. www.osterialangolodel silenzio-como.com. Closed Mon*. A simple restaurant with a pleasant courtyard garden offering generous dishes from the local area, especially Lombardy, accompanied by wines from across all Italy.

Osteria il Pozzo – *Piazza Garibaldi, Menaggio. 0344 32 333. Closed Wed*. Enjoyable trattoria that offers sizeable, tasty meals typical of Friuli. Good value-for-money.

Expensive

Gatto Nero – *Via Monte Santo 69, Rovenna, hamlet of Cernobbio. 031 51 20 42. www.ristorante gattonero.com. Closed Mon–Tue lunchtime*. Many customers are attracted by the summer terrace with its extraordinary view over the lake and surrounding mountains, but also by the elegant and somewhat mysterious dining-rooms rendered romantic by candlelight. Traditional fish dishes.

Luxury

Mistral – *Via Roma 1, Bellagio. 031 95 64 35. www.ristorante-mistral.com. Closed Mon–Fri lunchtime in Summer*. Located on the lake promontory in the famous town of Bellagio, the chef's "molecular" cuisine offers innovative dishes alongside traditional recipes. You have to travel far and wide to find such inventive combinations as Sicilian red prawns with guacamole ice cream, coconut cream and cuttlefish ink waffles.

LAKE LUGANO

Moderate

Bottegone del Vino – *Via Magatti 3, Lugano, Switzerland. 091 92 27 689. Closed Sun*. In the cheerful, welcoming atmosphere of this characteristic wine bar, you can enjoy regional dishes, cheeses and cold meats and choose from more than 200 wine labels.

Grotto Antico – *Via Cantonale 10, Bioggio. 5 km/2mi NW from Lugano*. Rustic and yet exclusive group of buildings dating back to 1800. Surrounded by greenery it offers service in the summer on the terrace. Traditional cuisine and seasonal dishes.

Grotto dell'Ortiga – *Strada Regina 35, Manno. 0041 91 60 51 613. www.ortiga.ch*. Rustic building with summer service under a light and airy pergola. Enjoy the good cuisine with dishes from the tradition of the Italian "poor" from various regions.

LAKE GARDA

Inexpensive

Aurora – *Via Ciucani 1, Soiano del Lago (L. di Garda). 10km/6.2mi N of Desenzano on the S 572. 0365 67 41 01. Closed Wed.* Good food at decent prices – a rarity for a restaurant specialising in fish dishes. A good choice.

Moderate

Gardesana – *Piazza Calderini 5, Torri del Benaco (L. Garda). 045 72 25 411. www.gardesana.eu.* This elegant hotel with restaurant and terrace caffè has a lovely

Lake Garda

P. Jacques/hemis.fr

location beside the tower and overlooking the port.

Osteria dell'Orologio – *Via Butturini 26, Salò. 0365 29 01 58. www.osteriadellorologiosalo. com.* A quick pause for a glass of wine and snacks or a proper lunch with grilled meat and other local delicacies? In this young, informal trattoria in the center of the town, the choice is yours.

Expensive

Pace – *Piazza Porto Valentino 5, Sirmione. 030 99 05 877. www.pacesirmione.it.* In this quiet spot on Sirmione peninsula, you can sit on the veranda with the lake at your feet or, during the summer months, beneath a pergola covered with ivy and dog-rose. The freshwater fish soup is one of the best dishes in this lakeside hotel restaurant.

Luxury

Vecchia Malcesine – *Via Pisort 6, Malcesine. 0457 40 04 69. www.vecchiamalcesine.com.*

Closed Wed. A couple of paces and through the garden and you find yourself in this colorful restaurant with a panoramic lake view where the chef offers his imaginative interpretation of the local recipes and lakefish dishes.

LAKE ISEO

Inexpensive

Il volto – *Via Mirolte 33, Iseo. 030 98 14 62.* Set in the gorgeous town center, this long-established restaurant offers mostly local dishes. An inn-type setting with a long wine list.

Osteria Ai Nidrì – *Via Colombera 2, Iseo. 030 98 08 60.* Created from the renovation of a 15C farmhouse, this refined restaurant retains a rustic touch and offers a menu dedicated to the local cuisine.

Moderate

Il Paiolo – *Piazza Mazzini 9, Iseo. 030 98 21 074. Closed Tue.* If you like the substantial and genuine tastes of cold cuts, homemade pasta, meats and lake fish, try Il Paiolo in the historic center of Iseo.

Uva Rara – *Via Foina 42, Monticelli Brusati . 8.5 km/5.2mi from Iseo. 030 68 52 643. www. hostariauvarara.it.* An ancient farmhouse dating back to the 15th century; the characteristic vaulting of the ceilings is in stone; furnishings are in excellent taste and professional management guarantees full enjoyment of some fine local recipes.

MUST EAT

HOTELS

Visited year-round by tourists and businesspeople, Milan offers many different kinds of accomdation. Room prices range from average to expensive, and can vary significantly depending on location and quality. Beware that prices are at a premium during trade fairs, conferences and important events, while they tend to be lower during the off-season. Hotel prices in the small towns around the lakes are not excessive, whether you're staying in a family-run guesthouse or an elegant palazzo. Rooms with a view of the lake generally cost more.

Luxury	**over 260€**	*Moderate*	**100€–180€**
Expensive	**180–260€**	*Inexpensive*	**under 100€**

Our Selection

Our price categories are for a double room in high season, when prices are at their highest. Bear in mind that off-season specials are often available on websites. Offers of this kind may well reduce a hotel indicated here as "Expensive" to the "Moderate" category. The symbol ☕ indicates that breakfast is included in the price. In any case, you are strongly advised to inquire beforehand and check the rates that apply to your stay. In the summer, visitors are advised to verify that lodgings have air-conditioning (especially for basic or inexpensive premises).

☺ **A bit of advice** – The **Michelin Guide Italia** is updated every year and includes a very wide selection of hotels and restaurants.

Milan's Hotel Tax

In September 2012 Milan initiated a tourist tax for hotel rooms. The fee is per person, not per room. Fixed rates range from €1 to €5 for each night of stay in accordance with the type, class and number of stars of the accommodation facility. During July, August and from 15 December to 10 January all rates are reduced by 50% to help sustain off-season tourism. Under-18s, the disabled and their assistants are all exempt from the tax.

Tips for Visitors

Book as far in advance as possible to ensure the best rooms at the lowest prices. Internet is now the main way hotels offer discounts and promotions: you can often find very good prices on hotel websites as well as on sites dedicated to hotel reservations.

Before booking a flight to Milan, check the calendar of events because room prices rise notably during international events, in particular during the most important trade fairs held at the Rho-Pero convention complex and the two Fashion Weeks (*see p100*), as well as during the Italian Grand Prix, held in nearby Monza (19km/11.8mi NE of Milan). Unless you are interested in these events, try to visit Milan at another time. If you come during one of these periods, bear in mind that it will be almost impossible to find a hotel room at the last minute within 20 km of the city center. When choosing where to stay in the city, take into consideration the proximity of metro stations and tram and bus stops. Hotels outside the city center offer decidedly lower prices. Often it is worth the trouble to travel 15-20 minutes on public transportation (like most Milanese workers do) to save on accommodation costs, as long as you're willing to forego spending the night next to the Duomo or in the Fashion District.

High and Low Season

Conventions, trade fairs and big international events have the most influence over Milan's high and low tourist seasons. During the months when few events are taking place and the weather is either too hot (July-August) or too cold (January), room prices are lower. Summer is high season around the lakes, when tourists and many Milanese spend their holidays by the water. The prices are therefore higher from June to August, and lower in the spring and autumn.

Hotels in Milan

All the leading hotel chains have at least one hotel in Milan, often in the center or in a strategic position close to well-connected railway stations. Other hotels, known in Italian as *alberghi*, are family-run and attempt to maintain their individuality. The number of stars the hotel displays is very indicative but by no means a guarantee. Two stars denotes a simple, unpretentious facility, in the best of cases with satisfactory or even very good levels of comfort and cleanliness. Three stars means the hotel claims it fully satisfies its customers' requirements, offering all comforts and services, mostly with free wifi. Four and five star hotels add proportional degrees of comfort and attention to their guests' individual needs.

Nonetheless, hotels do not always fully meet their clients' expectations and the commonest criticism leveled at Milanese hotels is that they do not deserve the two/three/four or five stars on display. Our selection aims to identify those hotels that offer excellent value-for-money. But it also seems useful to include certain exclusive hotels with exorbitant prices, designed by famous designers or stylists, that offer the very best in terms of Italian style and aesthetics.

Hotels in the lake regions

There is a lot of choice around the lakes of northern Italy, ranging from small, family-run guesthouses that serve breakfast included, to large hotels in either modern buildings or magnificently renovated historical palazzi, with plenty of windows that look out over the lakes and surrounding mountains. Often these hotels have their own restaurant and offer both half-board and full-board formulas.

Then there are luxury resorts with their own swimming pools, tennis courts, wellness centers and top quality restaurants.

Most of these hotels offer discounted prices and promotions via the internet. Make sure you book as early as possible if you want to find a room in high season, especially more spacious accomodations with a view of the lake. Room prices and offers can be especially interesting in spring and autumn, particularly if you consider that the weather is usally mild and pleasant. Some hotels close between November and February.

Bed and Breakfasts

Sometimes indistinguishable from a hotel, a B&B may be the hosts' home – an apartment, house or villa with rooms to rent (usually between two and four). Normally a B&B offers a cosier atmosphere than a hotel. The experience is often delightful and reasonably priced. Credit cards might not be accepted. Enquire about curfews before booking, however.

For an overview of B&Bs in Milan and the lake areas, contact **Bed & Breakfast Italia** (*06 68 78 618, www.bbitalia.it*) or try the following websites: www.caffelletto.it; www.bedandbreakfast.it and www.interhome.com.

Youth Hostel

It's very difficult to find low-cost accommodation in Milan. One of the few is **Ostello Piero Rotta** (*Viale Salmoiraghi 1;* Ⓜ1 *QT8; 02 39 26 70 95; www.hostelmilan.org*). It belongs to Hostelling International and is only open to youth hostel members (for information, www.hihostels.com). The hostel is situated close to the QT8 metro station and roughly a 20-minute subway ride from the Duomo. It has rooms with 2, 3 and 4 beds with a private bathroom; the cheapest rooms have 6 beds and you have to share the bathroom on the ground floor. Prices include breakfast and free wifi. In Italy, youth hostels are run by the **Associazione Italiana Alberghi per la Gioventù** (**AIG**, *06 48 71 152; www.aighostels.it*).

Campsites

There are plenty of well-equipped campsites around the lakes. Book early, especially for the summer months. For information, contact **Confederazione Italiana Campeggiatori** (*055 88 23 91, www.federcampeggio.it*). You can also try the following websites: www.campeggio.com, www.camping.it and www.campingitalia.it.

DUOMO AND CASTELLO SFORZESCO

See map p30.

Moderate

Near Castello Sforzesco
Hotel Lancaster off map (A1) – *Via Abbondio Sangiorgio 16. Tram 1 or* Ⓜ1/2 *Cadorna. 02 34 47 05. www.hotellancaster.it. 30 rooms.* In a calm residential district close to the Arco della Pace and entrance to Parco Sempione, this 19th-century building in Art Nouveau style has welcoming, simply decorated rooms at competitive prices. It is ideally situated if you want to start your day with a walk or run in Milan's largest park.

Expensive

Near Duomo
Albergo Rio B2 – *Via Mazzini 8.* Ⓜ1/3 *Duomo. 02 87 41 14. www.albergorio.it. 39 rooms.* 🖃. The Rio has simple rooms with somewhat dated furniture but they are functional and the prices proportionate (good value off-season) considering how close it is to the Duomo. The quietest rooms are those that look onto the courtyard or are on the top floors. Breakfast of coffee and croissants included.

Near Castello Sforzesco
Antica Locanda dei Mercanti B2 – *Via San Tomaso 6.* Ⓜ1 *Cairoli.*

**02 80 54 080. www.locanda.it.
21 rooms**. With its reception on the
first floor and external similarity
to the rest of the street, this 18th-
century palazzo is not immediately
apparent as a hotel. However, on
entering it feels like you are coming
home rather than walking into an
impersonal hotel. The rooms are
welcoming and well-lit and four
even have a private terrace. Ideal
for a romantic stay.

Luxury

Near Duomo
The Gray B2 – *Via San Raffaele 6.*
Ⓜ1/3 *Duomo. 02 72 08 951. www.
hotelthegray.com. 26 rooms*. Each
room is unique, even down to the
tiny details! Modern equipment
is everywhere (wifi, LCD TV, etc.)
and the bathrooms have large
hydromassage baths. The hotel
is "gray" in name only, in reality it
exudes class, creativity and style
like few others in the city.
Hotel Gran Duca di York B2 –
*See Pinacoteca Ambrosiana and
Via Torino.*

BRERA AND CORSO
GARIBALDI *See map p39.*

Expensive

Maison Moschino – *Viale Monte
Grappa 12.* Ⓜ2 *Porta Garibaldi FS.
02 29 00 98 58. 65 rooms*. This
elegant Neoclassical palazzo was
once a railway station on a line
between Milan and Monza. Today
the famous Italian fashion house
has redesigned the interior on the
basis of sixteen design concepts
linked to fables! With names like
"Life is a Bed of Roses," "Sleeping
in a Ballgown" and "Alice's Room,"

the rooms are modern, luminous
and seem to come straight out of a
children's book.

Luxury

Antica Locanda Solferino – *Via
Castelfidardo 2.* Ⓜ2 *Moscova.
02 65 70 129. www.anticalocanda
solferino.it. 13 rooms*. A warm
atmosphere and furnishings from
the early 20th century in a high-class
residence that offers an interesting
alternative to the standard hotel.
Breakfast served in the room,
hydromassage baths, wifi.
Hotel Cavour – *Via Fatebenefratelli
21.* Ⓜ3 *Turati. 02 62 00 01. www.
hotelcavour.it. 113 rooms*.
Understated elegance. Run by a
Milan family of hoteliers.

FASHION QUARTER
AND CORSO VENEZIA
See map p45.

Moderate

Near Corso Venezia
Hotel Sempione off map (B1) –
Via Finocchiaro Aprile 11.
Ⓜ3 *Repubblica. 02 65 70 323.
www.hotelsempione.it. 49 rooms*.
🛏. This family-run hotel has rooms
in simple, pale but cheering colors,
all with LCD televisions. Buffet
breakfast included, wifi.

Expensive

Near Corso Venezia
NH Machiavelli off map (B1) –
Via Lazzaretto 5. Ⓜ3 *Repubblica.
02 63 11 41. www.nh-hotels.it.
106 rooms*. 🛏. Plain but
welcoming rooms with wooden
floors, open common spaces for
all guests. An excellent breakfast,

a lounge bar in the garden, restaurant, free wifi on the ground floor.

Hotel Sanpi off map (B1) – *Via Lazzaro Palazzi 18.* Ⓜ1 *Porta Venezia. 02 29 51 33 41. www.hotel sanpimilano.it. 79 rooms.* ⌷. The hotel is small but has lovely spaces, like the internal courtyard where breakfast is served. Elegant rooms with wooden floors, the most comfortable (and newest) of which are on floor B1. Free satellite and pay TV, minibars, wifi.

Luxury

Fashion Quarter

Armani Hotel Milano A2 – *Via Manzoni 31.* Ⓜ3 *Montenapoleone. 02 88 83 88 88. milan.armani hotels.com. 95 rooms.* Giorgio Armani personally chose the furnishings and decor of this hotel, which has no rival in terms of aesthetic elegance. The different types of room and suites to choose from will meet the most exacting taste, and will particularly suit men with discriminating style.

Bulgari Hotel A2 – *Via privata Fratelli Gabba 7/b.* Ⓜ3 *Montenapoleone. 02 80 58 051. www.bulgarihotels.com. 69 rooms.* The famous jewelry maison has produced a tribute to luxury, with heartening colors and luxurious materials in the rooms, and a superb spa in which the green glass hammam is reminiscent of an emerald. The exclusive restaurant looks onto an unexpected and delightful garden where meals are served throughout the summer season, including Sunday brunch.

Four Seasons B2 – *Via Gesù 6/8.* Ⓜ3 *Montenapoleone. 02 77 088.*

www.fourseasons.com/milan. 169 rooms. The hotel has succeeded in perfectly harmonising the architectural details of the original building (a 15th-century monastery) with elegant contemporary design. The rooms, which used to be the monks' cells, are now fitted with the best of modern fittings and equipment. Creative cooking in the exclusive Il Teatro restaurant.

CORSO MAGENTA AND SANT'AMBROGIO
See map p50.

Moderate

Hotel Ariosto A1 – *Via Lodovico Ariosto 22.* Ⓜ1 *Conciliazione. 02 48 17 844. www.hotelariosto.com. 48 rooms.* Relax in the attractive red rooms in this Art Nouveau palazzo close to Leonardo's painting The Last Supper. The elegant internal courtyard has its own garden.

Hotel Metrò off map (A1) – *Corso Vercelli 61.* Ⓜ1 *Wagner. 02 49 87 897. www.hotelmetro.it. 40 rooms.* ⌷. The day starts well in this family-run hotel in one of Milan's most famous shopping streets with a large and excellent breakfast served in the room in the panoramic roof garden. Elegant rooms with satellite TV and minibar.

Expensive

Antica Locanda Leonardo A1 – *Corso Magenta 78.* Ⓜ1 *Conciliazione. 02 48 01 41 97. www.anticalocandaleonardo.com. 16 rooms.* ⌷. Facing onto an internal courtyard, the rooms are furnished in different styles, from ancient to classic to modern, with evident attention paid to the details. The hotel combines a family welcome with a sophisticated ambience close to Santa Maria delle Grazie and *The Last Supper*, a quiet zone in the evening.

Ariston Hotel B2 – *Largo Carrobio 2.* M1 *Duomo, then tram 3. 02 72 00 05 56. www. aristonhotel.com. 52 rooms.* A tower built in the 1950s is the setting for this hotel redesigned in accordance with the principles of bio-architecture (i.e. architecture that respects life and the environment), an approach that is apparent in the entrance hall and minimalist designer rooms. It is located strategically between the area of the Basilica of Sant'Ambrogio and the district of Corso di Porta Ticinese and the Navigli, which can be explored on the bikes made available free of charge by the hotel.

PINACOTECA AMBROSIANA AND VIA TORINO   See map p55.

Moderate

Hotel Zurigo off map (S) – *See Around the Porta Romana and University.*

Expensive

Ariston Hotel – *See Corso Magenta and Sant'Ambrogio.*
Albergo Rio – *See Duomo and Castello Sforzesco.*

Luxury

Hotel Gran Duca di York B2 – *Via Moneta 1/a.* M1/3 *Duomo. 02 87 48 63. www.ducadiyork.com. 33*

rooms. ⌐. This is an 18th-century palazzo close to the Pinacoteca Ambrosiana with modern rooms furnished with classical elegance.

AROUND PORTA ROMANA AND THE UNIVERSITY   See map p61.

Moderate

Hotel Zurigo off map (A2) – *Corso Italia 11/a.* M3 *Missori. 02 72 02 22 60. www.hotelzurigo.com. 42 rooms.* ⌐. A modern hotel in a period building with carefully chosen furnishings, lighting, and alternation of warm and cool colors. The rooms are rather small but well equipped, comfortable and with wooden flooring. Bicycles available free of charge and a large breakfast is included in the price.

Expensive

Albergo Rio A1 – *See Duomo and Castello Sforzesco.*
Hotel Dei Cavalieri – *Piazza Missori 1. 02 88 571. www.hotel deicavalieri.com. 177 rooms. On lively piazza.* Contemporary décor, pleasant atmosphere. Restaurant with panoramic terrace.

PORTA TICINESE AND NAVIGLI   See map pp64–65.

Moderate

Hotel Des Etrangers off map (A1) – *Via Sirte 9. Autobus 50. 02 48 95 53 25. www.hoteldesetrangers.it. 94 rooms.* ⌐. Set in a quiet area though close to the lively Navigli district, this hotel offers comfortable, well-kept rooms with wifi and satellite TV. Underground parking available.

Hotel Regina – *Via Correnti 13. 02 58 10 69 13. www.hotelregina.it. 43 rooms.* Grand, elegant hotel with a glass-covered courtyard lobby.

Expensive

Ariston Hotel off map (B1) – *See Corso Magenta and Sant'Ambrogio.*
Nhow Milano off map (A1) – *Via Tortona 35.* Ⓜ2 *Porta Genova. 02 48 98 861. www.nhow-hotels.com. 246 rooms.* ☕. In the heart of the Milan designer district, the Nhow Milano reflects a zone in rapid change. The colors, glass ceilings, lighting effects and creative decor make it more than a simple place to stay. Wifi, minibar.

PORTA NUOVA AND ISOLA
See map p70.

Moderate

Near Stazione Centrale
Hotel Albert B1 – *Via Tonale 2, angolo Via Sammartini.* Ⓜ2 *Centrale FS. 02 66 98 54 46. www.alberthotel.it. 62 rooms.* ☕. Two late 19th-century buildings connected by an internal courtyard with simple but comfortable rooms. Large and good quality breakfast.
Hotel Charly B1 – *Via Settala 76.* Ⓜ2 *Caiazzo. 02 20 47 190. www. hotelcharly.com. 20 rooms.* ☕. This very pleasant and peaceful hotel occupies two small Art Nouveau villas. The well-lit and well-equipped rooms look onto a quiet street or the hotel garden where breakfast is served.

Hotel Salerno B1 – *Via Vitruvio 18.* Ⓜ1 *Lima. 02 20 46 870. www. albergosalerno.it. 19 rooms.* ☕. A hotel on two floors with sizeable, well-kept rooms.

Expensive

Near Stazione Garibaldi
Maison Moschino – *See Brera and Corso Garibaldi.*

Near Stazione Centrale
Hotel Colombia B1 – *Via Lepetit 15.* Ⓜ2 *Centrale FS. 02 66 92 532. hotelcolombia milano.com. 48 rooms.* A recently renovated hotel with comfortable rooms in minimalist style. An elegant feature is the internal garden where you can enjoy a drink by candlelight.

OUTSIDE THE CITY CENTER

Northwest

◎ **A bit of advice** – If you are looking for comfortable accommodation from which to visit the **Rho-Pero convention complex**, consider the many Italian and international hotel chains that, in addition to running large hotels in the center of Milan, have expanded into the business market surrounding the city's trade fair center. These are the websites of the largest chains that have a hotel close to the fair complex:
ADI Hotels (*www.adihotels.com*), **Atahotels** (*www.atahotels.it*), **Best Western** (*www.bestwestern.it*), **Holiday Inn** (*www.holidayinn.com*), **Marriot Hotels & Resorts** (*www. marriott.com*), **NH Hotels** (*www.

nh-hotels.it), **Una Hotels & Resorts** (www.unahotels.it).

Moderate

B&B Tara Verde – *Via Delleani 22.* Ⓜ*1 Buonarroti (dir. Rho Fiera Milano) or De Angeli (dir. Bisceglie). 02 36 53 49 59. www.taraverde.it. 3 rooms.* ☕. Curtains and fabrics from India and the Middle East bring life to this Art Nouveau villa in a quiet private road in an elegant, busy district. The three rooms each have a dominant color: green, lilac and dark red. A large breakfast is served in the peaceful oasis of the garden.

Hotel Mirage – *Viale Certosa 104/106. Tram 14. 02 39 21 04 71. www.hotelmirage-milano.com. 86 rooms.* ☕. For people arriving at the fair complex by road, the Hotel Mirage is located advantageously close to the main motorways. Its clientele are mainly businesspeople, the rooms are in classic style, some with wooden flooring.

The Hub – *Via Privata Polonia. S Certosa. A4/A8, Viale Certosa exit. 02 78 62 70 00. www.thehub hotel.com. 162 rooms.* ☕. The rooms are divided into Classic, Superior and Deluxe categories and are similar to a small apartment with parquet flooring and contemporary designer furniture. They are fully equipped, including free wifi. During fairs and conventions there is a free shuttle from the hotel to Rho-Pero convention complex (4 km) and the Fiera Milano City conference center (5 km). Special services are offered to children and women, and there is a panoramic swimming pool, hammam and gym on the top floor.

Inexpensive

Hotel Delizia – *Via Archimede 86. Tram 27. 02 74 05 44. www.hotel delizia.com. 14 rooms.* In a small, recently renovated building, this hotel offers clean and very quiet rooms with new though inexpensive furniture. Wifi and satellite TV are provided. It is easily reached from Linate airport on the 73 bus and is just a few stops from Piazza Duomo on tram number 27.

Hotel San Francisco – *Viale Lombardia 55.* Ⓜ*1/2 Loreto. 02 23 60 302 / 61 309. www.hotel- sanfrancisco.it. 30 rooms.* Simple, comfortable, brightly colored rooms, some of which look onto a garden where breakfast is served in summer. Free wifi. The nearby metro station of Loreto (lines 1 and 2) gives rapid access to the city center.

Expensive

Vietnamonamour – *Via Pestalozza 7.* Ⓜ*2 Piola. 02 70 63 46 14. www.vietnamonamour.com. 4 rooms.* ☕. This charming b&b in a villa built in 1903 is typified by its love for Vietnam, as seen in its sign, furniture and hushed atmosphere. Breakfast served in the garden. Intimate and pleasant, the restaurant offers delicious Vietnamese dishes (*see Restaurants*).

Luxury

Nu Hotel – *Via Feltre 19/b.* Ⓜ*2 Udine. 02 97 15 451. www. nu-hotel.com. 38 rooms.* ☕. The natural light that floods the interiors from the large windows and the harmony of the design,

MUST STAY

inspired by Japanese minimalism, are relaxing to the mind and eye, with pale wood, pure colors and lines, and hanging beds. The atmospheric lounge bar and restaurant on the roof garden are also powerful attractions. Free wifi and private parking.

Southwest

Expensive

Hotel La Spezia – *Via Spezia 25.* Ⓜ*2 Romolo. 02 84 80 06 60. www. hotellaspeziamilano.it. 76 rooms.* ☞. Close to the Navigli and not far from the city by-pass on the west side, Hotel La Spezia has very modern, light-filled rooms decorated with photos of the Milan of the past. Buffet breakfast in the panoramic roof garden and wifi are included in the price.

Southeast

Moderate

Mec Hotel – *Via Tito Livio 4. Tram 16 or* Ⓜ*3 Lodi TIBB FS. 02 54 56 715. www.mechotel.it. 40 rooms.* ☞. Classic, plain rooms with minibar and wifi. A buffet breakfast is available on payment.

LAKE MAGGIORE

Inexpensive

Hotel Aquadolce – *Via Cietti 1, Verbania (Pallanza). 0323 50 54 18. www.hotelaquadolce.it. 13 rooms.* ☞. This welcoming, well-kept hotel has all modern comforts without sacrificing the warmth of a traditional atmosphere. The day begins with a buffet breakfast in

the glass room. The landing-stage, like the historic center, is just a couple of steps away.

Hotel Il Chiostro – *Via Fratelli Cervi 14, Verbania (Intra). 0323 40 40 77. www.chiostrovb.it. 100 rooms.* ☞. Housed in a converted 17C convent this hotel retains a monastic calm with a frescoed reading room, charming cloisters and simple rooms.

Moderate

Hotel La Fontana – *Strada Statale del Sempione 1, Stresa. 0323 32 707. www.lafontanahotel.com. 19 rooms.* ☞. Set in a 1940s villa, this hotel has rooms with lake views and a retro décor. Reasonable prices.

Hotel Rigoli – *Via Piave 48, Baveno. 0323 92 47 56. www. hotelrigoli.com. 34 rooms.* ☞. The rooms are spacious and the public areas are sunny and pleasant. There's a lakeside terrace garden with lovely views over the Isole Borromee. The restaurant offers half-board.

Luxury

Grand Hotel Majestic – *Via Vittorio Veneto 32, Verbania. 0323 50 97 11. www.grandhotelmajestic.it. 80 rooms.* Set in a 19C *palazzo* on the shore of Lake Maggiore, the Majestic boasts a private beach, wellness center, garden with lake view, luxurious rooms and a restaurant that serves gourmet dishes. The terrace of the Grand Hotel Majestic has its own bar and offers views of the surrounding mountains and Borromee Islands. The ferries that cross the lake can be boarded at nearby Pallanza.

LAKE ORTA

Moderate

Hotel Garni La Contrada dei Monti – *Via Contrada dei Monti 10, Orta San Giulio. 0322 90 51 14. www.lacontradadeimonti.it. 17 rooms.* ☎. A charming hotel in a beautifully restored 18th-c. palazzo; great attention to detail in the rooms.

Expensive

Hotel San Rocco – *Via Gippini 11, Orta San Giulio. 0322 91 19 77. www.hotelsanrocco.it. 80 rooms.* ☎. The hotel is set in a renovated 16C monastery on the lake shore. It has a swimming pool and offers a superb view over the island of San Giulio. The elegantly furnished rooms nearly all have a lake view. The hotel is located close to Switzerland and the prealpine valleys, and its refined, Michelin-starred restaurant offers regional and international dishes.

LAKE COMO

Moderate

Hotel Silvio – *Via Carcano 10/12, Bellagio. 031 95 03 22. www.bellagiosilvio.com. 20 rooms.* ☎. Family-run since 1919, this charming place has a stunning location and an excellent restaurant with a lovely summer terrace. Fish from the lake, caught by the owner himself, feature on the menu.
Locanda Del Notaio – *Piano Delle Noci 22. Pellio Inferiore, 10 km north of Argegno. 031 84 27 016. www.lalocandadelnotaio.com 17 rooms.* ☎. Located between

lakes Lugano and Como, the inn is surrounded by a huge garden and offers elegant rooms in rustic style. Lugano can be reached by car in about 30 minutes.
Locanda Sant'Anna – *Via per Schignano 152, Argegno, 20 km north of Como in the direction of Menaggio. 031 82 17 38. www.locandasantanna.net. 9 rooms.* ☎. At the entrance to the village, just beside the Sanctuary of Sant'Anna, this tranquil hotel will delight lovers of peace with its large garden fronting onto the lake. Well-equipped rooms and the possibility of half-board.

Expensive

Hotel Il Perlo Panorama – *Via Valassina 180, Bellagio, 2.5 km from the center, on the Como road (shuttle service). 031 95 02 29. www.hotelilperlobellagio.it. 17 rooms.* ☎. One of the loveliest views imaginable! The hotel stands above the point that separates the two arms of the lake. Great rooms with a balcony or charming fully-equipped studios.

Luxury

Grand Hotel Tremezzo – *Via Regina 8, Tremezzo. 0344 42 491. www.grandhoteltremezzo.com. 98 rooms.* ☎. For a princely stay, this 1910 palazzo in Art Deco style offers all the comforts. Pastel-colored rooms with good quality furniture, views onto the lake or park, three swimming pools (either facing the lake or indoor), wellness center with open-air hydromassage bath, and a tennis court. Excellent lake cooking in the **La Terrazza** restaurant.

LAKE LUGANO

Inexpensive

Hotel Rondanino – *Via Rondanino 1, Lanzo D'Intelvi. 031 83 98 58 / 30 09. www. rondanino.it. 14 rooms.* 🛏.
In this former 19th-c. farm in a pinewood, relaxation is the watchword. Horse-riding available at discounted prices at the nearby Il Bivacco stables. The restaurant offers local cuisine.

LAKE GARDA

Inexpensive

Agriturismo Il Bagnolo – *Bagnolo di Serniga, Salò. 0365 20 290. www.ilbagnolo.it. 9 rooms.* 🛏.
This farm guesthouse has a wonderful setting and serves excellent food, made with their own produce.

Moderate

Hotel Cangrande – *Corso Cangrande 16, Lazise, 5km/3mi S of Bardolino on the N 249. 045 64 70 410. www.cangrandehotel.it. 17 rooms.* 🛏. A charming hotel with simple, attractive rooms, including one incorporated into the medieval stone walls.
Hotel Desirée – *Via San Pietro 2, Sirmione. 030 99 05 244. www. hotel-desiree.it. 18 rooms.* 🛏.
An unpretentious hotel in a quiet location not far from the beach and the thermal baths. Standard rooms all have balconies.
Hotel Miravalle – *Via Monte Oro 9, Riva del Garda. 0464 55 23 35. www.hotelvillamiravalle.com. 28 rooms.* 🛏. A central location,

lovely garden and swimming pool plus simple yet stylish rooms and free wifi.
Hotel Palazzina – *Via Libertà 10, Gargnano. 0365 71 118. www. hotelpalazzina.it. 25 rooms.* 🛏.
There's a relaxed atmosphere at this hotel, which boasts two large panoramic terraces and an open-air swimming pool.
Hotel Pace – *Piazza Porto Valentino 5, Sirmione. 030 99 05 877. www.pacesirmione.it. 22 rooms.* 🛏. This early 20th-c. hotel has hosted such famous guests as James Joyce and Ezra Pound. It stands in the historic center facing the lake. Well-equipped rooms with a comfortable sitting area. Private garden with deckchairs and a landing-stage. Half- or full-board available at the hotel restaurant (*see Restaurants*).

LAKE ISEO

Moderate

Antica Casa Fenaroli – *Via San Pietro 22. 349 002 71 16 (mobile). www.anticacasafenaroli.com. 3 rooms.* 🛏. A historic 16C building carefully restored to offer an atmosphere of times past where you can enjoy your stay in an exclusive and welcoming setting.
Hotel Rivalago – *Via Cadorna 7, Sulzano, 6 km/3.7mi NE of Iseo. 030 98 50 11. www.rivalago.com*.
Hotel Rivalago offers spectacular views onto Lake Iseo and Monte Isola. The rooms are spacious and comfortable, wifi is available and there is a garden with a swimming pool. Buffet breakfast on the terrace and the lake ferries moor just two minutes away on foot.

MILAN

INDEX

THE LAKES

INDEX

INDEX

List of Maps

INDEX

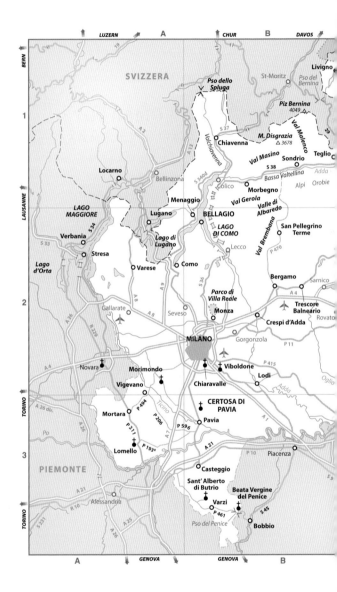

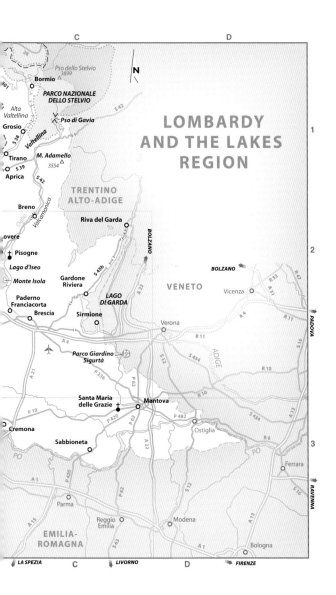

LOMBARDY
AND THE LAKES
REGION

NOTES